THE
INCARNATE
WORD

University of Illinois Press   Urbana Chicago London

THE
INCARNATE

Cary Nelson

WORD
Literature
as verbal space

Acknowledgments

William Carlos Williams: "The Flower," "The Lesson," and lines from "Labrador," "The Mind Hesitant," "Seafarer," and "May 1st Tomorrow" from *Collected Later Poems*. Copyright 1948 and 1950 by William Carlos Williams. Reprinted by permission of New Directions Publishing Corporation and MacGibbon & Kee Ltd.

Archibald MacLeish: "Where the Hayfields Were" from *Collected Poems 1917–1952*. Copyright 1962 by Archibald MacLeish. Reprinted by permission of Houghton Mifflin Company.

Paul Klee: "Calix Abdominis," "Heavily Fructified," and "Figure" from *The Thinking Eye*, ed. Jürg Spiller, reproduced by permission of Wittenborn and Company; "Leaning," permission S.P.A.D.E.M. 1972 by French Reproduction Rights, Inc.

Henry Moore: "Helmet Head No. 5." Reproduced by permission of the artist.

Anonymous: "Christ." From *Illuminierte Handschriften aus der Slowakei*, by Alžběta Güntherová and Ján Mišianik. Prague: Artia.

Carsten Svennson: Untitled. From *Erotic Art 2*, compiled by Drs. Phyllis and Eberhard Kronhausen. Copyright 1970 by Tantra, Inc. Reproduced by permission of Grove Press, Inc.

Anonymous: "Creating an Imaginary Space." From *The Theatre of the Bauhaus*, ed. Walter Gropius. Reproduced by permission of Wesleyan University Press, publisher.

William Blake: Plates from *Jerusalem*, collection of Mr. and Mrs. Paul Mellon; "God Blessing the Seventh Day," private collection in England; "The Ancient of Days," collection of Sir Geoffrey Keynes; "The Stygian Lake, with the Ireful Sinners Fighting," National Gallery of Victoria, Melbourne; "The Trinity," reproduced by permission of the Trustees of the British Museum.

Salvador Dali: "Raphaelesque Head Exploding." Collection of Siobhán Stead-Ellis.

Hans Bellmer: "Woman on a Sofa." Reproduced by permission of London Arts Gallery.

Avinash Chandra: Untitled drawing. Reproduced by permission of the artist.

© 1973 by The Board of Trustees of the University of Illinois
Manufactured in the United States of America
Library of Congress Catalog Card No. 79-188131

ISBN 0-252-00191-5

For Paula

Preface

The Incarnate Word has gone through several extensive revisions, and at every stage generous and energetic readers have assisted. William Rueckert and Robert Folkenflik of the University of Rochester each read early drafts of most of the chapters, and amplified my sense of the book's cohering structure. Oliver Grosz of the University of Southern California read the chapter on *Pearl*, and Ripley Hotch of the University of Illinois read the chapter on Swift; each offered detailed suggestions that helped those essays toward what clarity they may possess. Laurence Jacobs of the University of Illinois provided incisive comments on the critical issues central to each chapter. Edward Brandabur of the University of Illinois read the manuscript carefully, and without his assistance and encouragement the book might well be yet in my study.

I also thank Michael Harper of Brown University, and Carol Kyle, Daniel Majdiak, Alan Purves, Michael Shapiro, Jack Stillinger, John Stokes, and Brian Wilkie of the University of Illinois for their assistance and enthusiasm, and Eva Benton of the University of Illinois Library for her unflagging persistence in securing the books I required. An earlier version of the chapter on Williams was published in the *Journal of Modern Literature* (1971).

I am grateful to the Graduate Research Board of the University of Illinois for supporting this study with a summer faculty fellowship, and to the Research Committee of the Department of English for subsidizing the cost of typing and Xeroxing.

Contents

THE
INCARNATE
WORD

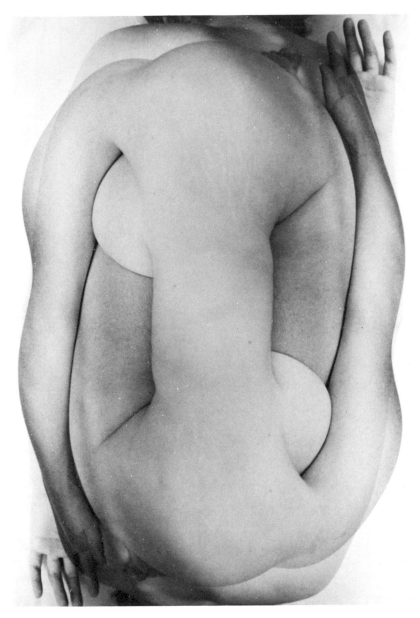

1. Cary Nelson, "Nude from Altair 4."

ONE

Introduction

1
Literature and criticism

> They can barely stand by themselves;
> many, swollen to the point of bursting,
> overflow with inner space
> into days which enclose
> an ever vaster fullness,
> until the entire summer becomes a chamber,
> a chamber within a dream.
>
> Rainer Maria Rilke, in Bachelard,
> *Poetic Imagination*, 92

The Incarnate Word explores the nature of verbal space in a succession of texts. While I consider space inherent to literary form, I also use the term as a critical and perceptual tool. Pure spatiality is a condition toward which literature aspires, but which it never achieves. The desire to overcome time competes with the temporal succession of words. Some critics argue that our understanding of metaphors in the first stanza of a poem must exclude relationships that occur later. But our first reading experience cannot be recovered, and it is colored by associations that the words acquired before the poem was written. When we reread a poem, its metaphors interact across the linear sequence of words—each line occurs in the context of the entire poem. Often, however, we willingly and deliciously suspend our knowledge of what is to come; we revel in a mixture of anticipation and submission that is actually assisted by our familiarity with the entire text. That part of the

3

temporal structure which is genuine and eternal retains its drama no matter how many times we read a work. Yet literature also generates a sense of accomplished form that sets all its temporal events outside time. Our perception of form depends on associations accumulated at a deeper level where a work of literature becomes a space encircled by the self. I have tried, out of need, to devise a criticism that treats both the total space of a work and its ongoing structure. The resulting book is theoretical and committed to criticism as a form of literature. The language is metaphorically dense; it mediates between creative writing and exclusively rational discourse.

I view verbal form as an author's projection of a self-protective and self-generative space that transcends or escapes historical time. The writer's need to create is gradually transferred to the reader, both sharing a desire to enact the work. Thus an author's "vision" exists for us as a text that generates a self-sufficient world when we read it. Each chapter inhabits and possesses one idiosyncratic world; as a critic, I enter the space of a work and discover the way it energizes my mind. Each essay is a perceptual dialectic in which author and critic move toward simultaneity. Verbal space is the locus of an interaction between the reader and the text.

Although I am concerned with the experience of literature, my approach is not simply impressionistic. I see literature as a unique process in which the self of the reader is transformed by an external verbal structure. Yet the reader never passively submits to the radical inwardness of an author's vision. Reading is both ecstatic and painful, for we are both hunter and hunted. Although the book records these interactions, as we move toward temporary repose in a particular work, the chapters do not completely correspond to the reading situation. Each time a reader performs an act of literature, the results are different. The essays synthesize repeated readings; they relate the common texture of several encounters, and should provide an entrance into the works considered.

Set beside one another, the chapters form a field of possibilities;

the works are a series of alternative spaces which can be entered and energized by the imagination. Conceived spatially, the book is a revolving wheel with each chapter at the end of a spoke and the reader at the hub. Although the essays are arranged historically, the image of the wheel also suggests a recurring archetype of perception, in which each spoke rises in its turn—the same yet different. The book is structured to serve as a dialogue with history. Each chapter finds its metaphors in the particular work, but the book as a whole repeats expectations of confrontation and eventual submission.

Identification with verbal space never absolutely frees us from historical contexts, but it may temporarily free us from the impulse toward historical assimilation. Disguising the influence of external pressure, literature gives the illusion that its formal boundaries are achieved purely through internal fruition. Reading has power because it offers not an imaginary world entirely available to rational explication, but a universe which, however ambiguous, is wholly present to the mind. The reader enjoys for a time the sense that his own life is a form moving toward completion. A vision is the experience of ontological closure. We are reborn to a universe in which we both live and die.

Like the landscape of dreams, the verbal events of literature are dispersed in the body of the reader. He becomes an actor who stages a universe in the theater of his flesh. A book's finite language could be endlessly elaborated, but a vision frees us from the need or desire to say the words. Language becomes revelation by resonating toward inclusive silence. Only our temporary repose in this expanse satisfies the impulse toward closure. It is finally the silence of the human body celebrating a plenitude of words.

Perceived as an external structure, verbal space becomes an emblem for the physical structure we inevitably carry with us. Language fills the space inhabited by human consciousness—the human body. The body which ripens and decays is the space where temporal events are truly simultaneous. In reading, the self projects and encircles its privacy in a new and startling form. In this movement toward vision, associative density increases to the point where word becomes flesh.

These chapters are a wheel of alternative postures, of fleshly spaces. Visionary space is the child born of our cohabitation with the language on the page. When we shape our bodies to the rhythm of literature, the self truly becomes both cave and landscape. The privacy of verbal space is a playfulness of empty and full. In a recurring dream of words, we evacuate a space in our bodies which we hesitantly encircle and fill. Reading draws us from different times toward the same space—the body. It is then—in the archetype of revelation, which is always our sudden awakening to the upsurge of the body—that the self becomes a vehicle for a universe become organic. To read is to fold the world into the body's house.

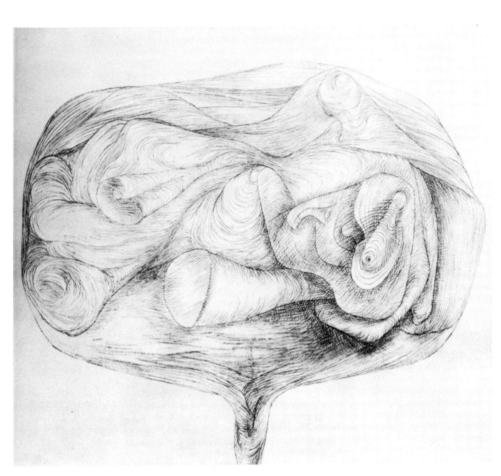

2. Paul Klee, "Calix Abdominis" (Belly Bud). Spatio-plastic interpenetration.

2

Reading Borges: the metaphysics of form

It is what the dead close on, finally; I imagine them
Shutting their mouths on it, like a Communion tablet.
                              Sylvia Plath, *Ariel*, 11

Picasso declares that "the only way to see the *Guernica* is to feel oneself into its center."[1] In the context of a landscape so massive and manifestly agonized, Picasso's words challenge our ability to endure the painting's form. But Borges's delicate fictions, pared to a minimum of language yet resonant with a world of discourse, do not seem to contain enough room for us at all. If anything, the stories of *Ficciones* or the still more economical parables of *El Hacedor* tempt us to consume them, to place them at our center instead of placing ourselves imaginatively at their center. Borges is too gentle to take us over by massive assault; he will not allow himself the space of a novel to win our allegiance. Rather he pretends to unfold his brief stories for our inspection in absolute and meticulous detail. Like the dreamer in "The Circular Ruins," he appears to create the body of his story with "minute integrity" and unobtrusively insert it as a humble object into our universe.

The most graceful of illusionists, Borges coaxes us to suspend our disbelief and then insinuates his stories into our center; as we read, they gradually efface the world of our experience with the repercussions of a fiction. Like Hladik in "The Secret Miracle," Borges fills a single moment with a lifetime of illusions; each brief tale masks an entire universe. His fables are literally not large enough for us to wander in forever; they become complete worlds for us

---

1. Quoted by Victor J. Papanek, "A Bridge in Time," *Verbi-Voco-Visual Explorations*, ed. Marshall McLuhan (New York, 1967), p. 5.

only because we want them to. And we want them to because
Borges carefully stimulates that desire.

Borges succeeds because he can depend upon our complicity.
His stories are—uncannily—temptations, and their forbidden fruit
is eternally regrown. Each time we read "The House of Asterion,"
we reexperience and even relish the sensation that Asterion is
human, despite our knowledge that he will once again become the
Minotaur. Within his house, unnervingly symmetrical and bloody,
there are no contradictions. Its open doors, "whose number are
infinite," all look inward. We can inhabit and share Asterion's
self-perceptions: "What will my redeemer be like?, I ask myself.
Will he be a bull or a man? Will he perhaps be a bull with the
face of a man? Or will he be like me?" (140).[2] This innocently
arrogant, half-animal intelligence becomes a metaphor for the
self; the intrusion of Theseus not only transforms our ongoing
experience but also confronts us suddenly with our own image.
Borges preserves our relationship with Asterion, paradoxically, by
ending it: in the final lines of the story, we must take his strange
animal otherness into ourselves. The revelation does not destroy
our sympathy but sets it apart, perfects it. Our experience of the
story thus becomes an object for infinite contemplation. In its
mere two pages, we are at once both hunter and hunted.

Borges's work is a pure example of self-conscious literature,
where books are written about writing books, where the reader is
made aware that a work creates itself before his eyes. But Borges
also makes us uncomfortably conscious that we participate in the
creative act. The most obvious examples of this doubleness—intrusions of the author's name, direct addresses to the reader—are
supplemented by Borges's famous plagiarisms and pretended plagiarisms, the mixture of true and false documentation. As his
readers soon learn, the footnotes by the "Editor" were written by
Borges himself. These intrusions, in their diverting playfulness,

2. Jorge Luis Borges, *Labyrinths*, ed. Donald A. Yates and James E. Irby (New
York, 1964). Quotations are documented internally.

deceptively distract us from the more profound and dangerous ambivalence of the written word. Thus, for all their surface brilliance, Borges's stories also deal with the darker metaphysics of confrontation and submission to aesthetic form.

Borges tempts us into "The Library of Babel" by offering a single metaphor for the universe: "The universe (which others call the Library) is composed of an indefinite and perhaps infinite number of hexagonal galleries, with vast air shafts between, surrounded by very low railings" (51). Thus revealing in the first sentence what promises to be the whole point of the story, Borges with deceptive frankness invites us to share the perspective of the omniscient narrator. Surely, we assume, there is no danger in toying with this notion of the universe as a library, yet even as we submit to the metaphor, we can expect an inevitable reversal to undermine our point of view.

The Library embodies perfect order extended to infinite volume. Its hexagonal galleries are numberless, the shafts between them bottomless. "Once I am dead," writes the narrator, "there will be no lack of pious hands to throw me over the railing; my grave will be the fathomless air; my body will sink endlessly and decay and dissolve in the wind generated by the fall, which is infinite" (52). Borges adapts the famous definition of God to make his library both banal and invisible by its very omnipresence: "*The Library is a sphere whose exact center is any one of its hexagons and whose circumference is inaccessible*" (52). In its infinite order, the Library is potentially knowable yet can never be wholly known. Faced with this intolerable paradox and lacking the key to its simple geometry, the librarians become violent and arbitrary mystics. Set against a background of sudden and terrifying mechanical recurrence, our human failings make the Library a world of absolute uncertainty. The hexagonal galleries are inhabited by most ungeometrical madmen: "These pilgrims disputed in the narrow corridors, proffered dark curses, strangled each other on the divine stairways, flung the deceptive books into the air shafts, met their death cast down in a similar fashion by the inhabitants of remote regions" (55). We seem to explore the Library most profoundly through our sense of touch, as though lost in a nightmare of blindness. Its pathways are identical and thus untraceable. We suspect that the Library at its inaccessible extremities is animate and even capable of self-duplication. Its mindless regularity tricks us into permitting unspeakable dimensions to fill our minds; then the metaphor is subjected to a controlled disintegration that leaves the reader its only possessor. The story spirals drunkenly inward and is saved from chaotic dissolution only by a reduction so deft and unforeseen that it traps us unaware. The last paragraph leaves us desperately lost in the initial metaphor—filled with the paradoxes and dark ambiguities of this spatial universe. But the story does not end here, for a final footnote collapses the airy distances of the Library into a single volume of infinite density:

> Letizia Álvarez de Toledo has observed that this vast Library is useless: rigorously speaking, *a single volume* would be sufficient, a volume of ordinary format, printed in nine or ten point type, containing an infinite number of infinitely thin leaves. (In the early seventeenth century, Cavalieri said that all solid bodies are the superimposition of an infinite number of planes.) The handling of this silky vade mecum would not be convenient: each apparent page would unfold into other analogous ones; the inconceivable middle page would have no reverse. (58)

This final claustrophobic image consummates our reading experience. No longer wandering in the vast labyrinths of the Library, for a moment we hold the immensity of the universe trembling in our minds. The initially external and objective narrative was a delusion, for the story succeeds quite apart from our detached interest in the Library as a metaphor. It is we, not the universe, who succumb to the book we hold in our hands. The self of the reader collapses into the space of a single volume.

Borges organizes many of his stories around such spatially self-enclosed metaphors. In the course of a few pages they undergo substantial metamorphosis, and he specializes in the final lightning stroke, which absorbs the whole series of permutations in a single image and transforms them. "The Circular Ruins" describes an old magician who meticulously dreams a son into existence. Ignorant of his origin, the boy is sent to a nearby temple to perform rituals for the Fire God. The old magician hears with pride of his magical feats—only a phantom, the boy is impervious to fire—yet fears the boy will seek to understand his extraordinary powers and discover his true nature, and "to be the projection of another man's dream, what a feeling of humiliation, of vertigo!" (50). The magician's brooding is interrupted when the ruins he inhabits catch fire: "In a birdless dawn the magician saw the concentric blaze close round the walls. . . . He walked into the shreds of flame. But they did not bite into his flesh, they caressed him and engulfed him without heat or combustion. With relief, with humiliation, with terror, he understood that he too was a mere appearance, dreamt by another" (50). With this revelation, the linear narrative doubles back on itself in an image of dreamers within dreamers—an infinite chambered nautilus whose identical segments are all contained within one another. We wonder whether Borges himself has dreamed his readers, for our physical substantiality is only as secure as our rigid self-image. With the final image we understand the ecstatic self-dispersal foreshadowed at the beginning of the story, when the magician disembarks unseen in "the unanimous night."

The dreamer realizes his illusory nature only after he has successfully created another in his dreams, and the revelation is inseparable from his submission to the self-absolving fire. Indeed, creativity in Borges is an act of self-assertion that often negates the self. Tzinacán, the imprisoned Aztec priest in "The God's Script," deciphers the random spots on a jaguar and learns the secret key to the world's mysteries, an incantation which would empower him to escape his prison or reshape the world. But the vision that revealed the incantation also revealed a labyrinth of illusion and eliminated for him all interest in himself: "I know I shall never say those words, because I no longer remember Tzinacán. . . . This is why I do not pronounce the formula, why, lying here in the darkness, I let the days obliterate me" (173).

This peculiar combination of absolute power and passivity is like the indifference of a God who becomes an agnostic in the universe he himself created. Like the stories themselves, the power terrifies and attracts. We approach them with "the sensation of uneasy magic" that the narrator of "Funes the Memorious" feels when he learns that Funes, the enigmatic boy whose perception of time is exact and uncanny, has been hopelessly paralyzed. Like Hladik in "The Secret Miracle," Funes becomes an artist of memory in the stillness of his body: "Funes remembered not only every leaf of every tree of every wood, but also every one of the times he had perceived or imagined it" (65). Able to absorb time for his infinite contemplation, he learns to abstract the formal geometry of what to us are formless perceptual events—"the changing fire and its innumerable ashes . . . the many faces of a dead man throughout a long wake" (64). Like art, Funes can make space dense by filling it with time. Though he lies motionless, his intense perceptions accumulate at an intolerable velocity: "the least important of his memories was more minute and more vivid than our perception of physical pleasure or physical torment" (66). "I alone," he tells the narrator, "have more memories than all mankind has probably had since the world has been the world" (64). Like Tzinacán's professed indifference to his imprisonment, Funes's power is defined and confirmed by paralysis. Like the innocent mask offered by the stories, paralysis embodies the ambiguity of terrifying and unknown forces held in check. Funes—"the solitary and lucid spectator of a multiform, instantaneous and almost intolerably precise world" (65)—threatens to devour a world which has no power to stop him. The narrator comes to realize Funes's demonic potential: "I thought that each of my words (that each of my movements) would persist in his implacable memory; I was benumbed by the fear of multiplying useless gestures" (66). The fear is of becoming as absolute and immortal as a work of art—a fear of being possessed and devoured, as though Funes could absorb his gestures (or his image) faster than he could create them. As Funes's motionless body, swarming with images, drifts toward a terrible homogeneity of pure energy, he dies "of congestion of the lungs"—the last line of the story. "All solid bodies are the superimposition of an infinite number of planes," reads the footnote to "The Library of Babel," but we can comprehend such absolute density only in a book whose language is our breathing. "Congestion of the lungs" is the final density of words. At the point of death, Funes is a fearful Medusa's head who almost turns the reader's body to stone. He seems older than the pyramids and as secretly demonic.

As Freud knew, our response to the Medusa's head mingles fear with desire. In a dream of words, we flee from a monster who is motionless, yet our fear of being overtaken increases as we run. "Funes the Memorious" unveils the narrator's secret need to be known, finally to be annihilated in the mind of a perceiver. Our willingness to cooperate again and again with Borges's deceptions is evidence enough that they give us something we need and want. In fictional terms, at the level where all Borges's stories are parables of writing and reading, we recognize our desire to succumb to the demonic self-sufficiency of form. If literature usurps the ritualistic functions of religion, these tiny eucharistic stories offer us the ritual of repeated death: "who knows whether tonight we shall not see it in the labyrinths of our dreams and not even know it tomorrow" (239).

Borges himself suggests that a writer's creations may finally reveal only the lineaments of his own face, that all perception mirrors the self.[3] But for writer and reader, his tales satisfy the need to experience a self wholly other: "Diodorus Siculus relates the story of a broken and scattered god. . . . Men have lost a face, an irrecoverable face, and all long to be that pilgrim. . . . Perhaps some

3. "Through the years, a man peoples a space with images of provinces, kingdoms, mountains, bays, ships, islands, fishes, rooms, tools, stars, horses, and people. Shortly before his death, he discovers that the patient labyrinth of lines traces the image of his own face." Borges, in Richard Burgin, *Conversations with Jorge Luis Borges* (New York, 1969), p. 157.

feature of that crucified countenance lurks in every mirror; perhaps the face died, was obliterated, so that God could be all of us" (238-39). In his brief parable "Borges and I," Borges wins our affection by describing his delicate estrangement from his public self, from the famous writer who postures and pretends. The charming portrait of his gentle feud with "Borges" keeps the conflict manageable until the final sentence: "I do not know which of us has written this page." The parable of "Borges and I" is paradoxically a demonic fusion that dissolves our security utterly—for we can never know which of *us* has read the page: "it is a tiger which destroys me, but I am the tiger; it is a fire which consumes me, but I am the fire. The world, unfortunately, is real; I, unfortunately, am Borges" (234).

In its self-enclosed otherness, verbal form is a mirror which reveals our image: "In our dreams (writes Coleridge) images represent the sensations we think they cause; we do not feel horror because we are threatened by a sphinx; we dream of a sphinx in order to explain the horror we feel" (240). After this preface to the parable "Ragnarök," the narrator recounts a dream in which the gods of Olympus return after long absence to be greeted by human applause and celebration. But the rejoicing is cut short when one of the gods erupts in a harsh, victorious gargle.

> From that moment, things changed.
>
>   It all began with the suspicion (perhaps exaggerated) that the Gods did not know how to talk. Centuries of fell and fugitive life had atrophied the human element in them. . . . Very low foreheads, yellow teeth, stringy mulatto or Chinese mustaches and thick bestial lips showed the degeneracy of the Olympian lineage. . . . Suddenly we sensed that they were playing their last card, that they were cunning, ignorant and cruel like old beasts of prey and that, if we let ourselves be overcome by fear or pity, they would finally destroy us.
>
>   We took out our heavy revolvers (all of a sudden there were revolvers in the dream) and joyfully killed the Gods. (241)

We create the gods of Olympus in our own image and attempt

to project them into a dimension outside time. But left utterly to themselves, the gods degenerate from the humanity which formed them. At last we must kill them because we cannot bear what they reveal to us of ourselves.

In a sense, all Borges's stories reveal the perceiver who lives, like the narrator of "The Immortal," in a labyrinth of his own devising —arbitrary, mad, devious. In another story, a visiting Arabian king wanders in humiliation through an intricate labyrinth designed for the king of Babylon. Escaping with God's help at last, he retaliates by conquering Babylon and carrying its captured king home to die of thirst and hunger in another labyrinth, a labyrinth without walls or stairways, the heart of the Arabian desert.[4] Lönn-rot in "Death and the Compass" asks to be deceived by the most minimal labyrinth he can devise—a straight line; as he realizes in the end, the solution to the puzzle of aesthetic form, the key to the metaphysics of reading, is the image of his own death.

But to possess fully the absolution of ourselves would require a form with no external surfaces, a form that undoes the world. Borges therefore continually rewrites his final story, and his work yearns to be a hall of mirrors effacing the central image beyond recovery, "a dream dreamt by no one" (248). Like Borges's Shakespeare, who disguises himself as king, clown, and lover to mask a cold and faceless emptiness in himself, we continually rediscover our own desolation. After the experience of form, the return to our own inconclusive lives is almost intolerable. It is a fate shared equally by writer and reader, in the unspeakable intimacy of words. Empty and full, Borges's fictions pursue the ravishing otherness of complete self-revelation—the unachievable archetype of form.

4. "The Two Kings and Their Two Labyrinths," *The Aleph and Other Stories,* ed. and trans. Norman Thomas di Giovanni (New York, 1970).

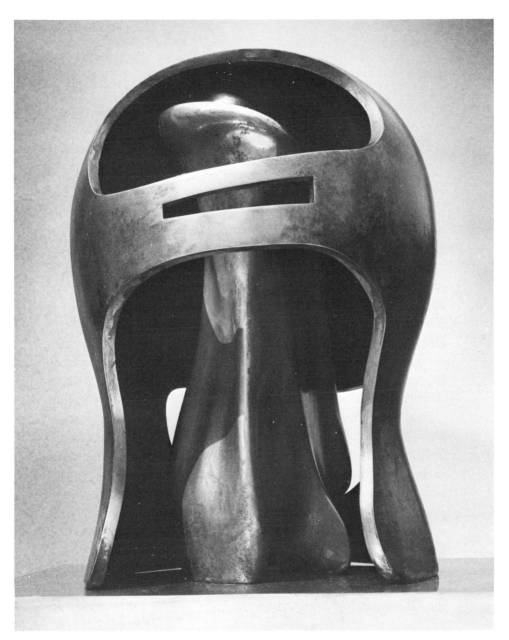

3. Henry Moore, "Helmet Head No. 5."

3
The protagonist's body:
Death Kit as a model
of enclosed space

in our heads
bodies collapse
and grow again

Sam Cornish, *Generations*, 67

Susan Sontag once remarked that she would like to understand her need to write in the third person.[5] Her novels are dedicated to such primary acts of self-projection; their language creates a consciousness that contains the world. Wholly idiosyncratic, *Death Kit* creates a space of radical consciousness in which all value is relative; the novel hovers at the point where it would no longer need to be read. This unique and self-sufficient vision is contained in a totally private verbal space. In *Death Kit* this privacy is realized in the body of the central character.

Death Kit progresses toward an inclusive and enclosing metaphor. Death, defined at the end of the book as "being completely inside one's own head" (310–11),[6] is achieved by including every preceding object of perception. All the characters and their interactions, even the physical landscape, become features of the protagonist's verbal situation. The novel comes to fruition as a consciousness encircled by its own metaphors. Diddy, the commonplace protagonist who dreams at the center of *Death Kit*, begins and ends in a tunnel. When the novel comes full circle, the tunnel is continuous and complete, a shell without exit: "Abruptly though unclearly, Diddy understands the reason why, despite all

5. A reading given at New York University, Fall 1966.
6. Susan Sontag, *Death Kit* (New York, 1967). Quotations are documented internally.

his hard thorough scanning of the dark tunnel ground as he marches back and forth, he's been unable to find the pink and white Glory of the Sea. It's because he's already inside it (now). The discarded shell, no longer small, is as vast and capacious as the tunnel. Tunnel and shell can substitute for each other, so Diddy can wander in either as he sees fit" (104).

The immense interior distance of tunnel and shell is created by the novel's enclosure in its metaphors. Distinguished by textures alternatively opaque and diffuse, these metaphors fill the landscape of the novel; they provide the controlling obsessions of Diddy's consciousness. *Death Kit* denies us any sense of historical or social context; it celebrates and fulfills a wholly absorbed ontology, "the unachievable goal being, eventually, to leave no empty space at all. Let the vacuum be filled. The house properly ordered. A plenum of death" (309).

As we enter Diddy's swollen universe, the trembling familiar hive of his mind, our passage is marked by an ambiguous murder. The death of a workman in the tunnel, publicly described as an accident, becomes the novel's unifying obsession. With a growing sense of self-possession, Diddy toys with theatrical public declarations of guilt, yet in fact he is absorbed only by the private symbolism of declaration. The murder energizes a black sun in his head; its dark internal light fills every object he encounters. The murder precipitates Diddy's experience of the world as a single density.

Until his consciousness is freed to assert its coextension with the universe, Diddy is imprisoned in a body at perpetual war with the world. It is not a body he can endure or even acknowledge as his own. He dreams instead of a body assaulted by no abrasive surfaces, a viscous body which absorbs everything it touches. Now, with the black sun burning in his head, Diddy meets Hester, a blind girl who is as remarkably "opaque to him as he's invisible to her" (32). "The faces of the blind," he muses, "are not in dialogue with other faces as faces. Only with other faces as flesh" (89). At first "unnerved by the blind girl's infinite enclosure in herself" (87), Diddy manages their sightless encounter and discovers his body can be

housed happily in hers. Their movement together is easy and pre-
conscious; they are idle, "Becalmed. Like a pair of moist happy
ducks" (238). In Hester's blind presence, Diddy finds that objects
soften and blend with his own movements. Yet her body does not
altogether yield to his frictionless universe. Her continual and
sometimes antagonistic presence is a "huge flat stone . . . lying on
his chest" (256).

But gradually Diddy discovers that his perceptions can perfectly
shape Hester to suit his needs. She is actually a spectrum of dolls he
can choose from. The hard, unyielding, "opaque side of Hester"
(279), the persistently intrusive object-doll, may be discarded by
the side of the tracks in his private tunnel. Now Diddy dances
freely in the environment softened by her blindness; now he fully
possesses the murdered workman. Celebrating his freedom in a
space that enfolds the world, Diddy murders Incardona again and
with additional detail. The original workman and the palpable
Hester-doll both retained some impenetrable secret identity of
their own; they stimulated Diddy but left him confined to a space
that seemed afterward even more constricted. Now he dwells exclusively in the huge world of his own head. The resurrected
workman, the liberated Hester—familiar and personalized figures
—are Diddy's playmates in a magic world of infinite duplication.

"Diddy," at *Death Kit*'s end, "has perceived the inventory of
the world" (312). The world of his life is a sequence of rooms
among which his attention wanders. In this dense space, time is
only an accumulation of deaths; each cluster of objects is painlessly
put to sleep in the privacy of his body. At any moment the particulars of his world-inventory float in the amber of his thoughts
like forms stillborn.

The novel, the zone of space Diddy explores, achieves its own
stillness and death. The novel is the process by which Diddy accumulates his comfortable death. His still body is the accomplished
form of the book. The events of *Death Kit* are finally released
from their narrative context; they drift aimlessly in the dense,
familiar liquid of Diddy's sleep. "Diddy has made his final chart;

drawn up his last map" (312). His once threatening labyrinth is now peacefully fused and simultaneous; admitting no externality, his tautological body dreams in an infant universe ripe with death: "Diddy, naked, with his seamless sense of well-being. The narrow toes of his highly arched feet grip the dirty stone flooring as he walks. His testicles, drooping in the warm air, fall pleasantly against the inside of his thighs. His arms swing freely at his sides. His shoulders are relaxed, not tensed; his head held erect. And the entire surface of his skin seems coated with an effulgent smoothness, as if rinsed in sleep" (292).

Centering

The point sets itself in motion and an essential structure grows, based on figuration.
> Paul Klee, *The Thinking Eye*, 21

The shape of the body awake, the shape of the resurrected body, is . . . not a straight line but a circle.
> Norman O. Brown, *Love's Body*, 137

Centering . . . is to feel the whole in every part. When you center clay on the potter's wheel, you take a lump of clay, and by moving it upwards into a cone and outwards into a plane, you create a condition of balance between the outside and the inside, so that when you touch the clay at a single point the whole mass is affected. Centering has nothing to do with a center as a place. It has to do with bringing the totality of the clay into an unwobbling pivot, the equilibrium distributed throughout in an even grain. The substance of the clay has to be brought to a condition of stillness at the same time that it is spinning, it has to be worked so that there is no difference in quality between the surface and the interior, a balance between the inner consistency and influences from without. So that when we stick our fingers into it to open it up into a vessel, the inside will be as firm and malleable as the outside, and will be able to create a space which will be a container.
> M. C. Richards

Centering, swallowing, emptying—all the eyes look inward.
> (C.N.)

Centering—"a supremely rooted plant still able to swivel."
Malcolm de Chazal, *Plastic Sense*, 36

Time is a circle which is endlessly revolving. The descending arc is the past and the rising arc is the future.
Jean-Luc Godard, *Alphaville*, 37

In this closed, endless movement, the need for counter-movement disappears. . . .
Paul Klee, *The Thinking Eye*, 397

the clusters of figures and the landscapes glide like visions in a dream; they seem to obey the laws of a magical space where things gravitate freely towards each other, where buildings seem to float on a fluid surface.
Mario Praz, "Hieronymus Bosch," 61

4. Anonymous, "Christ." Illuminated manuscript, c. A.D. 1341.

TWO   *Pearl:* the circle
as figural space

Heaven is exactly in the middle of the chest of the man
who has faith.

Salvador Dali, in Gérard, ed., *Dali*

For hit is wemleʒ, clene, and clere,
And endeleʒ rounde, and blyþe of mode,
And commune to alle þat ryʒtwys were.
Lo, euen inmyddeʒ my breste hit stode.

[For it is spotless, pure, and clear,
And round without end and blythe of mode,
And shared by all who were righteous.
Lo, exactly in the center of my breast it stood.]

Pearl (737-40) [1]

In the history of geometric symbolism, no form has been more
universally valued than the circle. From the point and the linear
figure to the wheel and the sphere, the circle moves by rotation,
diffusion, and enclosure. If we wish both to abstract and to protect our intimacy, the circle offers the ideal and immutable environment. Within its pure enclosure we may discover our natural
situation or create a new situation for ourselves. [2] The sense of fulfillment in *Pearl* derives, in part, from the poem's continuous

1. E. V. Gordon, ed., *Pearl* (London, 1966). Quotations are documented internally from this edition by line. Modernized translations, adapted from Gordon's
notes and glossary and from translations by Sister Mary Vincent Hillman and
others, have been provided.

2. Cf. Georges Poulet, *The Metamorphoses of the Circle*, trans. Carley Dawson
and Elliot Coleman (Baltimore, 1966), pp. vii-xxvii.

anticipation of a completed circular form—a form finally both circular and spherical, designed by the poet to protect and nurture the seed of his innocence.

Pearl criticism commonly describes the frame of the poem as circular, but does not pursue the observation. Louis Blenkner points to the deliberate artistry in the poem's "cyclical nature . . . ending with an echo of the opening line, and the very symmetry of the governing plan." Robert Garrett likens the poem's form to a huge pearl. With greater awareness of aesthetic form, Ormerod Greenwood calls the poem "a wreath woven of words."[3] In the most literal sense of its circularity, *Pearl* is like a rite de passage in which the narrator ventures into a dream world and returns. As a linear narrative, its structure resembles that of *Sir Gawain and the Green Knight*. Yet Gawain's circular journey away from and back to Arthur's court required no crafted and formal circular construction. Nor must the circular structure of a dream vision be minutely controlled, for *Piers Plowman* is loosely digressive and associative.

But *Pearl*'s intricately articulated language and detailed linkage between stanzas show conscious decision in every line: the poet offers us more than a narrative circle whose verbal structure is a mere decorative frame. The circular structure of *Pearl* is integral to our most vital experience of the poem and its vision. Far from being a transparent vessel for thematic content, it is for both poet and reader the continuous context of the poem's creation. The interaction between narrative and aesthetic form is total; thus when the poet uses traditional Christian symbolism to further the story, his imagery is never merely thematic but is woven formally and intricately into the poem's metaphorical progression. Form and content in *Pearl* are not simply parallel or complementary—they are the same.[4]

3. Louis Blenkner, "The Theological Structure of *Pearl*," *The Middle English "Pearl*," ed. John Conley (Notre Dame, Ind., 1970), p. 221; Robert Max Garrett, *The Pearl: An Interpretation* (Seattle, 1918), p. 35; Ormerod Greenwood, intro., *Sir Gawain and the Green Knight* (n.p., 1956), p. 9.

4. Cf. Wendell Stacy Johnson, "The Imagery and Diction of *The Pearl*," *Middle*

For poet and reader, the delicate reverberations of alliterative language and the symmetrical patterning of image and metaphor create a verbal space that is entirely self-enclosed. John Crawford observes that "the poet has written a poem in the way that more spatially oriented men might build a cathedral."[5] But the Pearl-poet *was* aware that literary forms have spatial implications, for he constructed his poem with precise attention to its three-dimensional density. *Pearl*'s circumference encircles a space made resonant with words; as we explore the poem's outer frame, the language leads us into its third dimension.

The narrator's circular journey through the dream world accompanies the largest and most obvious features of the poem's circular construction, the echo words that link the stanzas in a continuous chain and the lines of the last stanza that echo the first. Christ's words in the parable of the vineyard thus double as an epigram for the outer structure of *Pearl:*

> "Þus schal I," quod Kryste, "hit skyfte:
> Þe laste schal be þe fyrst þat strykeȝ,
> And þe fyrst þe laste, be he neuer so swyft"
> ["Thus," said Christ, "shall I arrange it:
> The last shall be the first who comes,
> And the first the last, be he never so swift"]
>
> (569–71)

These words occur near the middle of the poem and amplify Christ's directions for distributing the day's wages: "Bygyn at þe laste þat standeȝ lowe, / Tyl to þe fyrste þat þou atteny" [Begin with the last who stands least, / Until you reach the first] (547–48). The first shall be last and the last first; the beginning is the end and the end is the beginning. When we reread the poem, Christ's words in the middle transport us simultaneously to the

---

English "Pearl," ed. Conley. Johnson explores the meaning of the poem through its form, focusing on repeated images of natural renewal, water, blood, and light; his outline of the overall image-scheme amplifies the treatment of this imagery below.

5. John F. Crawford, intro., *The Pearl* (San Francisco, 1967), p. 116.

beginning and to the end. The final stanza of *Pearl* completes a circle which returns the reader to the beginning of the story.

To the circular structure of the narrator's journey, the poet adds the theme of cyclic renewal in nature, birth revealed in death. In the first stanza we learn that the narrator's pearl was lost in a garden, falling "Þurʒ gresse to grounde" (10). With its brilliance "so clad in clot" [so clad in clay] (22), the pearl is described as a seed that will not be lost in vain (34). At first the narrator's only comfort is the fine flowers and herbs that will grow from the grave the lost pearl seeds, but his traditional observation—"For vch gresse mot grow of grayneʒ dede" [For all new grass has to grow from dead grains] (31)—is to resonate prophetically through the poem. These images are echoed in later images of human death. Pearl tells the dreamer that "Þy corse in clot mot calder keue" [Your body in clay must colder sink] (320), that "oure corses in clotteʒ clynge" [our bodies waste away in clods] (857). The narrator describes his living body in similar words: "I am bot mol" [I am but dust] (382); "I am bot mokke and mul among" [I am but mingled with muck and mold] (905).

In the endless cycle of nature, life grows and dies and new life grows. All flesh is grass. The narrator's reference to Mary as "Fenyx of Arraby" (430) suggests the conventional notion that the Church, too, must celebrate life in death throughout history. But as the maiden tells him, this understanding of earthly mutability is flawed. The eternal reality of the Church subsumes its earthly changes, just as the pearl lost in the garden retains a true and greater beauty. To mourn its physical loss is to mourn needlessly: "For þat þou lesteʒ watʒ bot a rose / Þat flowred and fayled as kynde hyt gef" [For what you lost was but a rose / Which flowered and failed most naturally] (269–70). Like the pearl, the body must die and "oure flesch be layd to rote" (958) to find its true life. Imagery of natural renewal is thus transformed by the reality of death and resurrection. When Pearl reminds the dreamer that the Lord "lelly hyʒte your lyf to rayse, / Þaʒ fortune dyd your flesch to dyʒe" [faithfully promised your life to raise, / Though fortune caused your flesh to die] (305–6), the themes converge in her image of the human body as a seed to be reborn. In Christ's parable of the vineyard, the metaphor of the full harvest amplifies the imagery of dying germination, invoking also the harvest season in which the poem takes place. Pearl and seed are paralleled by ripe grapes harvested at the point of perfect fullness; those who follow Christ, who labor in his vineyard, are themselves harvested at the moment of spiritual ripeness—"þay arn boȝt fro þe vrþe aloynte / As newe fryt to God ful due" [they are bought from the earth afar / As new fruit ripened for God] (893–94).

The dreamer sees only appearances; he fails to perceive eternal reality incarnate in the cycles of nature: the seed of germinating death is the seed of deathless germination, and the cycles of heaven are eternally and continuously fruitful. For an instant in his final vision, the dreamer beholds the trees along the river that flows from the throne of God—trees at every moment dying into life, endlessly seeding and bearing fruit, beginning and ending in a cycle that is infinite and indivisible:

> Aboute þat water arn tres ful schym,
> Þat twelue fryteȝ of lyf con bere ful sone;
> Twelue syþeȝ on ȝer þay beren ful frym,
> And renowleȝ nwe in vche a mone.

> [All around that river are shining trees,
> Which quickly bear twelve fruits of life;
> Twelve times a year they yield in full strength,
> And renew afresh at every moon.]

> (1077–80)

Cyclic renewal in nature is fulfilled by this glimpse of eternal fruitfulness in heaven, where each instant is an infinite circle of continuous generation.

The narrator's return to his earthly garden completes his circular journey and prefigures the completed circle of human history. In a stanza near the middle of *Pearl,* the poet summarizes this history as a series of three events:

Inoȝe is knawen þat mankyn grete
Fyrste watȝ wroȝt to blysse parfyt;
Oure forme fader hit con forfete
Þurȝ an apple þat he vpon con byte.
Al wer we dampned for þat mete
To dyȝe in doel out of delyt
And syþen wende to helle hete,
Þerinne to won wythoute respyt.
Bot þeron com a bote astyt.
Ryche blod ran on rode so roghe,
And wynne water þen at þat plyt:
Þe grace of God wex gret innoghe.

[It is known well enough that noble mankind
Was first fashioned for perfect bliss;
Our first father forfeited it
Through an apple that he bit upon.
For that food we were all condemned
To die in sorrow, away from bliss,
And then to go to the heat of hell,
To dwell there without respite.
But a remedy came for that at once.
Precious blood flowed on the cruel cross,
And blessed water; then at that plight,
The grace of God grew great enough.]

(637–48)

The poem links this history to three states of human existence: life in the Garden of Eden—the Fall and the intervening years in the secular garden of troubled attempts to perceive truth and submit to grace—Christ's sacrifice, and, through grace, eternal life in the garden of the New Jerusalem. The dream vision in *Pearl* takes place in the middle garden of flawed human consciousness. Locating his vision here, the poet can extend his metaphor to the beginning and the end of time, for the fallen earthly garden also prefigures our redemption. The poet invests the jeweler's garden with the promise of transformation. The narrator's journey and the poem's circular structure become figures for man's return to a state of grace and a new Eden, for the restoration of innocence that completes the circle of human history: at the apocalypse, time curves back upon itself and links the end with the beginning in a perfect circle.[6]

Thus we enter the boundless sphere of God's presence, the kingdom which the dreamer can glimpse but cannot yet enter. The lost pearl, repeatedly linked to the kingdom of heaven, offers the poem its supreme circular image: a perfect sphere—circularity made dense, or a circle filled. The pearl, we are told, is "so rounde, so reken in vche araye, / So smal, so smoþe her sydeȝ were" [so round, so perfect in every array, / So fine, so smooth its surfaces were] (5–6). Here as elsewhere in the poem, roundness is a figure for the apocalypse, the kingdom of heaven made manifest. Both the pearl and the sphere of heaven are "endeleȝ rounde," round without end. The roundness of the pearl recurs in its image as a seed, in the ripe grapes of the vineyard parable, and in the stones that the dreamer perceives as pearls. The brightest of all earthly spheres, the sun and moon, prefigure the luminous totality of the kingdom of heaven.

The poem also offers a more specific theological source for roundness as prefiguration. As the middle of the poem tells us, Adam forfeited heavenly bliss "Þurȝ an apple þat he vpon con byte" (640). His sin was the bite that spotted the perfect fruit, or

---

6. Completion of the circle brings an end to historical time. In one allegorical reading of *Pearl*, the jeweler's garden identifies Eden as both man's world before the Fall and the place to which he will return at the end of time. Marie Padgett Hamilton, "The Meaning of the Middle English *Pearl*," *Sir Gawain and Pearl: Critical Essays*, ed. Robert J. Blanch (Bloomington, Ind., 1966). Hamilton cites the legend that Adam is buried on Calvary as another version of the notion that past and future will fuse in the fullness of time; similarly, the cross is identified with both the forbidden tree and the tree of life in the Garden of Eden. Christian eschatological thinking is treated in Karl Löwith, *Meaning in History* (Chicago, 1949), and by several authors included in *Man and Time* (New York, 1957), vol. 3 of Joseph Campbell, ed., *Papers from the Eranos Yearbooks*. The papers by Gilles Quispel and Henri-Charles Puech are perhaps most relevant in the present context. Eschatology in mystical and visionary writings is traced by Hugo Rahner, *Greek Myths and Christian Mystery* (London, 1963). Mystical sources relevant to *Pearl* are cited by Hamilton, "Meaning of the Middle English *Pearl*," and Blenkner, "Theological Structure of *Pearl*."

flawed its sphere. Thus he flawed the human sphere as well: "Al wer we dampned for þat mete" (641); when we lost Eden, we lost both innocence and immortality. The poem's use of "spot" as both "flaw" and "place" elaborates the image of our violated earthly sphere: before man was banished from it, Eden was his whole world; endless and indivisible, it *was* the human sphere. But when Adam spotted the apple, Eden itself became not simply flawed but, literally, a spot—merely a location, a bounded space. Until grace is restored, we remain estranged from the round world of our former bliss. Unlike the flawless and spotless pearl, the apple and the round world are both spotted and flawed.

But Christ's sacrifice has freely given us God's blessing. Though Adam forfeited the perfect roundness and transcendent spotlessness of eternity by violating the roundness of the apple, God will restore the earthly sphere to its former roundness:

> Now is þer noȝt in þe worlde rounde
> Bytwene vus and blysse bot þat he wythdroȝ,
> And þat is restored in sely stounde;
> And þe grace of God is gret innogh.
>
> [Now there is nothing in the round world
> Between us and bliss, but what he withdrew,
> And that is restored in a blessed hour,
> And the grace of God is great enough.]
>
> (657–60)

No longer estranged by our flaws, our human presence will once again fill the whole of our earthly sphere.[7] Like the pearl, it will be "wythouten spot."

The flawed sphere and the bitten apple, the lost pearl and the round world from which we are estranged, prefigure collectively the perfect roundness of heavenly bliss. As images densely woven into the poem, they also prefigure the roundness of its completed verbal structure. The entire outer frame of the poem participates in

7. Rahner, *Greek Myths and Christian Mystery*, p. 56, quotes a fifth-century passage from Maximus of Turin: "'Wonderful is this mystery of the cross, for by this sign the whole round world is saved.'"

this verbal drama of prefiguration. Though *Pearl* forms a circle, the famous missing line (472) serves to flaw its perfect structure. Crawford recognizes that the missing line may be deliberate, and speculates that the poet "may have avoided formal perfection for fear of excessive vanity offending God."[8] As it stands, though, the poem lacks one line to equal 1212, the number of apocalypse and of the twelve tiers of the New Jerusalem; thus its form embodies not the sphere of heaven but the violated sphere of human existence, the flawed circumference of human understanding. How many readers, listing the number of lines as 1212, have wanted to perfect its form? *Pearl's* partial roundness, aching for completion, is the emblem of a flawed circle. It is an appropriate vehicle for our fallen perception—for the poet's expression of his vision and our experience of it.

The pearl that the jeweler lost in the garden, the perfect sphere of God's presence, and the pearl revealed in the dreamer's vision of heaven are perfect circles, but the poem is not. The poem has the form of a pearl deliberately flawed, a bitten apple, a broken circle, a world that sorely needs the grace of God. In the end of time God will restore the missing line and complete the poem's circle. The poem conceived in the jeweler's garden is the seed, or pearl, which ripens to link the beginning and the end of time. It is a seed already planted in the garden of human history—the seed of our ripening death.

Within its circular frame, *Pearl* resonates with metaphors of light, liquid, endlessly flowing movement, and the perfect roundness of the pearl itself. Though the poet draws on traditional medieval symbols, the poem accumulates internal associations that are even more potent. The space of *Pearl* encircles its metaphors and finally creates a sphere which is at once earthly and divine.

Images of liquid movement—flooding, pouring, drowning, gushing, flowing, cleansing—contribute crucial energy to this structural

8. Crawford, *The Pearl*, p. 118.

resonance. For as the middle of the poem tells us, man's history is a history of water and blood:

> Innoghe þer wax out of þat welle,
> Blod and water of brode wounde.
> Þe blod vus boʒt fro bale of helle
> And delyuered vus of þe deth secounde;
> Þe water is baptem, þe soþe to telle,
> Þat folʒed þe glayue so grymly grounde,
> Þat wascheʒ away þe gylteʒ felle
> Þat Adam wyth inne deth vus drounde.
> Now is þer noʒt in þe worlde rounde
> Bytwene vus and blysse bot þat he wythdroʒ,
> And þat is restored in sely stounde;
> And þe grace of God is gret innogh.

> [Enough there flowed out of that fountain,
> Blood and water from broad wounds.
> The blood bought us from the bale of hell,
> And delivered us from the second death;
> The water is baptism, truth to tell,
> That followed the lance so cruelly ground,
> Which washes away the deadly sins
> Which Adam drowned us with in death.
> Now there is nothing in the round world
> Between us and bliss, but what he withdrew,
> And that is restored in a blessed hour,
> And the grace of God is great enough.]
>
> (649–60)

Willful and reckless acts led to both the Fall and the Crucifixion. Yet the bite that wounded the apple and the lance that wounded Christ are also linked to the liquid floods that followed. Adam's sins drowned the human race in mortality, but Christ's blood, incarnate in the waters of baptism, cleanses the drowning waters of our guilt. Thus, when the dreamer's disappointment leads him to speak recklessly (325–36), his apology explains that his "herte watʒ al wyth mysse remorde, / As wallande water gotʒ out of welle" [heart was all disturbed with loss, / As welling water goes out of a fountain (or well)] (364–65). Christ's blood on the cross also flows from a fountain or well (649–50). The metaphor links the narrator's remorse with Christ's sacrifice and, through the poem's associations, verbally transforms his reckless speech into an occasion for grace. Earlier Christ tells the angry vineyard laborers that the reward of bliss will flow equally over them all, for God is generous with his grace: "He laueȝ hys gyfteȝ as water of dyche, / Oþer goteȝ of golf þat neuer charde" [He pours out his gifts like water from a dike, / Or like streams from a gulf that ceaselessly flows] (607–8).

The two historical acts of reckless violation (the Fall and the Crucifixion) are treated in the eleventh section, whose refrain line is "þe grace of God is gret innoghe": human violence is thus the occasion for God's bountiful forgiveness. Water and blood in *Pearl* move toward grace and ecstasy. The movement culminates in the final moments of the dreamer's vision, when grace proves great enough to overcome all human sin. Christ's gentleness and his agony, his forgiveness and his gushing blood, are subsumed in an outpouring of his bliss:[9]

> Bot a wounde ful wyde and weete con wyse
> Anende hys hert, þurȝ hyde torente.
> Of his quyte syde his blod outsprent.
> Alas, þoȝt I, who did þat spyt?
> Ani breste for bale aȝt haf forbrent
> Er he þerto hade had delyt.
>
> The Lombe delyt non lyste to wene.
> Þaȝ he were hurt and wounde hade,
> In his sembelaunt watȝ neuer sene,
> So wern his glenteȝ gloryous glade.
>
> [But a wound full wide and wet ran

9. Cf. Rahner, *Greek Myths and Christian Mystery*, p. 69: "The water of life gushes forth at the foot of the tree of life, and life was only given to that water through God's atoning death upon the cross"; Rahner also quotes, p. 54, from the apocryphal Acts of Andrew: " 'O Cross, that art planted in the earth but bearest fruit in heaven.' "

Close to his heart, cruelly torn through his skin.
From his white side his blood gushed out.
Alas, I thought, who did that wrong?
Any breast ought to have burned up in sorrow
Before it took delight in that.

The Lamb's delight no one could doubt.
Though he was hurt and had a wound,
In his countenance it never showed,
His glances were so gloriously glad.]

(1135-44)

The waters of baptism incarnate this bliss on earth, and in a process that demonstrates "the reciprocal attraction existing between nature and grace,"[10] all water comes to express God's love. As the dreamer follows the earthly river, his senses are unusually responsive to the beauty around him. Then, prepared by the maiden, he transcends his flawed understanding of the river as a physical boundary: momentarily freed from his senses at last, he sees the true nature of the river as a source of salvation, an endless outpouring of grace (1055–62). For the dreamer, God's grace briefly mediates the two rivers of the poem, and the adorned and decorated natural river is revealed in its eschatological form as the luminous river of the New Jerusalem.

Water is thereby linked to light.[11] The river the dreamer discovers is radiant, and the forest around it is bright with shimmering light and glistening trees (80):

In þe founce þer stonden stoneȝ stepe,
As glente þurȝ glas þat glowed and glyȝt

Þat alle þe loȝe lemed of lyȝt,
So dere watȝ hit adubbement.

10. Ibid., p. 98.
11. Ibid., p. 82, illustrates the traditional connection with an example from ninth-century church symbolism: "The cross is also a bringer of light, and when men seek to express this mystery in explicit liturgical form, they do so by lowering a burning candle into the baptismal font as a sign that, by the power of the cross, the water is a source of the *lux perpetua*, the everlasting life of light. . . . What we witness here is a symbol of Christ crucified giving water the illuminating power of the Spirit."

> [In the riverbed stood glistening stones,
> Which glowed and gleamed like light through glass
>
> So that all the water gleamed with light,
> So precious was its adornment.]
>
> (113–14, 119–20)

The stones in the riverbed sparkle like precious gems; crystal cliffs and jewel-like rocks illuminate the landscape. Their "glemande glory" [gleaming glory] (70) is unbelievable and surpasses the brightest light the dreamer has ever experienced—in comparison, "Þe sunnebeme3 bot blo and blynde" [The sun's beams are but dark and dim] (83). This extraordinary radiance increases (the refrain line is "more and more") until the dreamer beholds the maiden across the shining river surrounded by rising rays of light.

Yet the perfect radiance of the New Jerusalem surpasses even this. For the dreamer, the maiden shining in the forest "stonge myn hert ful stray atount" [threw my heart into astounded confusion] (179); hooded in his own darkness, he "stod as hende as hawk in halle" [stood as quiet as a hawk in hall] (184). But the light of heaven is a sight "No fleschly hert ne my3t endeure" [No fleshly heart could ever endure] (1082); transfixed, he "stod as stylle as dased quayle" [stood as still as dazed quail] (1085). Invoking the same metaphors, the dreamer's final vision encompasses and transcends all his earlier descriptions of the natural paradise. "Golde as glasse" (1025), the streets gleam with light, the buildings are adorned with precious gems, and the whole city shines with rays brighter than the sun. God himself is a flowing river of light: "A reuer of Þe trone Þer ran outry3te / Watz bry3ter Þen boÞe Þe sunne and mone" [From the throne straight forth there ran a river / Brighter than both the sun and moon] (1055–56).

The metaphors of light and water are linked to the theme of endlessness and continuous renewal. Like the dreamer's forest stream "Þat dry3ly hale3" (125), the luminous heavenly river, whose banks bear trees that endlessly renew themselves, also flows unceasingly. The dreamer has learned that the Lord's generosity is timeless and infinite ("Þer is no date of hys godnesse," 493), that heavenly bliss is unceasing (729), that peace "schal laste wythouten reles" (956), and that Jerusalem's already infinite "glory and blysse schal euer encres" (959). His brief vision of the heavenly city allows him to experience all this, for each unique moment of his vision encompasses infinite time and space:[12]

> blysned þe borȝ al bryȝt.
> Þurȝ woȝe and won my lokyng ȝede,
> For sotyle cler noȝt lette no lyȝt.
>
> [the city shone all bright.
> Through wall and dwelling my vision went,
> For clear and transparent, nothing stopped the light.]
>
> (1048–50)

From the dreamer's first view of this heavenly city, where each gate is set with a "parfyt perle þat neuer fateȝ" (1038), the pearl enters his vision in various forms. The association of pearls with liquid, light, and eternity borrows power from the lapidary tradition where pearls were said to be engendered by the dew of heaven,[13] i.e., by God's grace. Because it grows in the sea like the seed of an oyster's womb, the pearl is an image of nature generating a perfect sphere. Two forms fuse in its space: the abstract circle and the rich earthly sphere restored in its flawlessness.

The pearl is also linked to the sphere of heaven, for both are "wemleȝ, clene, and clere . . . and blyþe of mode" [spotless, pure, and clear . . . and blythe of mode] (737–38); both are "endeleȝ rounde" (738), round without beginning or end. Eternal flowing

---

12. Cf. G. Van der Leeuw, "Primordial Time and Final Time," *Man and Time*, p. 328, who cites the conception that each moment in time is "perfectly round."

13. "Margarita is chef of al stons þat ben wyȝt and preciose, as Ised seyþ. And it haþe þe name margarity for it is founde in shellis which ben cokelis or in mosclys and in schellfyssh of þe see; þis bredyng is schellfyssh, and it is genderd of þe dewe of heuen, which dewe þe schell fissh receyueþ in certen tymes of þe ȝer, of þe which dew margarites comen. Some ben cleped vnyons. . . . And þey ben best wyȝt, cler and rownde. . . ." Joan Evans, *English Medieval Lapidaries* (London, 1933), pp. 107–8, quotes here the fifteenth-century *Peterborough Lapidary*, which copies earlier sources.

roundness fulfills the poem's figural circularity and finds its perfect form in the "clene cloystor" (969), the pure and bright enclosure of the heavenly city. The New Jerusalem, with its "glymme pure," is a translucent sphere; infinitely extended, it can yet be instantaneously apprehended. Like the pearl, the Lamb is "wythouten spotte3," his flock is "wythouten flake" and "wythouten mote," and their city is a "mote wythouten moote." Like "spot" of the poem's opening stanzas, "mote" doubles as "flaw" and "place" —the heavenly city is both without blemish and without mortal corporeality or mere location; it is both flawless and boundless. The dreamer's vision of flowing light diffusing in an endless sphere (or pearl) suggests Boethius's famous description of eternity as the perfect and simultaneous possession of a limitless existence.

As a symbol with a rich history of associations in patristic exegesis and lapidary writings, the pearl is less an index to the poem's meaning than its ritual source of energy. Pearls in the poem are variously decorous, luminous, flowing, formal, static, and personal. Linked to imagery and plot, they animate all the space within the poem's circumference. As the poet's central image, the pearl is also the visionary point where other images converge—a bright sphere of radiance around which the circular frame of *Pearl* revolves. Opening and closing the poem, linked to earth and to heaven, the pearl is an appropriate figure for the transcendence of fallen earthly perception. It begins as a round and perfect gem; it becomes a seed, a form of decorative description, and a maiden whose face is like polished ivory (178). Her name is Pearl, and her flawlessness embodies the roundness of heavenly bliss. Her mode of dress, circularly set with pearls ("Wyth precios perle3 al vmbepy3te," 204), is like the language of the poem; her crown of pearl is the poem's structure in miniature. Addressing the maiden as a pearl adorned in pearls, the dreamer also describes the poem.

The pearl participates as both enclosure and enclosed in the poem's associative structure, and gives internal and particularized force to its verbal space. Pearls enclose Pearl, the maiden who in turn encloses a perfect pearl (221–22). The dreamer envisions his pearl set at last in a heavenly "garlande gay," while he, in his earthly enclosure, dwells in a "doel-doungoun" [prison of sorrow] (1186–87). But the maiden gives other images to earthly enclosures, calling the jeweler's garden "a forser" [treasure chest] containing the lost pearl; the dreamer should prize "þe kyste þat hyt con close" [the chest that encloses it] (271), for its coffer is "þis gardyn gracios gaye" (259–60). The kingdom of heaven, likened to the pearl of price, is an enclosed point of infinite perfection (740), but for the Lord's company it is also Christ's chamber (904), a "mynster mete" [fitting cathedral] (1063). When the narrator is given the Eucharist at the end of the poem, he takes Christ's body symbolically into his own; after death he will find life in Christ, as a limb of his body (456–60), enclosed in the heavenly sphere of God's presence.

The lost pearl, the heavenly pearl, and the pearls at the gates of the New Jerusalem and in the procession of virgins are perfect spheres; their illumination is diffused throughout their circumference. The recurrent source of luminous radiance, the pearl itself has no center of brilliance: the pure light of eternity is everywhere equal. Nor can the poem be divided at its true center, for its central line is indeterminate.[14] As the fifty-first and numerically central stanza tells us, the kingdom of God is also indivisible:

> "Of more and lasse in Godeȝ ryche,"
> Þat gentyl sayde, "lys no joparde,
> For þer is vch mon payed inlyche,
> Wheþer lyttel oþer much be hys rewarde;
> For þe gentyl Cheuentayn is no chyche,
> Queþer-so-euer he dele nesch oþer harde:
> He laueȝ hys gyfteȝ as water of dyche,
> Oþer goteȝ of golf þat neuer charde.

14. The two points that represent the poem's outer form by invoking the beginning and the end of time (ll. 570–71 and 637–48) occur near but not *in* the center of the poem.

Hys fraunchyse is large þat euer dard
To Hym þat matȝ in synne rescoghe;
No blysse betȝ fro hem reparde,
For þe grace of God is gret inoghe."

["Of more and less in the kingdom of God,"
That gentle one said, "lies no uncertainty,
For there each one is paid alike,
Whether little or much be his reward.
For that gentle ruler is no miser,
Whether he deals mild or harsh:
He pours out his gifts like water from a dike,
Or like streams from a gulf that ceaselessly flows.
Great is his heritage who always paid reverence
To him who rescues sinners;
No bliss is withheld from him,
For the grace of God is great enough."]

(601–12)

This occurs in the dreamer's dialogue with the maiden, as he struggles to overcome his flawed human understanding. She offers him "grace," the echo word here, and the final promise that "þe grace of God is gret inoghe." For the dreamer and the poem, this central stanza is a fountain of grace that will never run dry; as we move through the poem's space toward its center, grace generously diffuses through its circular form and simultaneously moves us out toward its circumference. Without grace, the whole human sphere is fallen; with it, there is nothing in the round world between man and bliss. Nor is there any barrier between poet (or reader) and the blissful realization of the poem's form.

As Pearl tells the dreamer, we move at last within the completed and eternal circle of God's will:

For þoȝ þou daunce as any do,
Braundysch and bray þy braþeȝ breme,
When þou no fyrre may, to ne fro,
Þou moste abyde þat he schal deme.

> [For you can prance like a stricken doe,
> Struggle and bray in your wild anguish,
> When you can move no farther, to or fro,
> You must endure what he ordains.]
>
> (345-48)

From the beginning to the end of time, all human action is encompassed by the sphere of God's presence. This apocalyptic circle is the true form of all that we do and all that we are—it consummates our history and redeems us from it. In its flawed and earthly incarnation, the circle is the form the poet chooses for the figural structure of his poem.

In his brilliant essay "Figura," Erich Auerbach writes that Christian eschatology in medieval literature is in many ways more compatible with a figural treatment than with a symbolic or allegorical one, for the figural method "provides the medieval interpretation of history with its general foundation and often enters into the medieval view of everyday reality."[15] The method establishes a relation between two real events in Christian history; the first prefigures the second, which in turn encompasses and fulfills the first. The relation is not merely fixed in time: though earthly form is a figure for heavenly fulfillment, the world is already invested with a future reality. The kingdom of God is eternal, and

---

15. Erich Auerbach, *Scenes from the Drama of European Literature* (New York, 1959), p. 61. In the figural view, "this world is only *umbra futurorum*—though indeed the umbra is the prefiguration of the transcendent reality and must recur fully in it," p. 71. "The individual earthly event is . . . viewed primarily in immediate vertical connection with a divine order which encompasses it, which on some future day will itself be concrete reality; so that the earthly event is a prophecy or *figura* of a part of a wholly divine reality that will be enacted in the future. But this reality is not only future; it is always present in the eye of God and in the other world, which is to say that in transcendence the revealed and true reality is present at all times, or timelessly," p. 72.

In this way the figural view of history expresses the essence of Christian eschatology: the kingdom of God is at hand, yet it is still to come. Cf. Löwith, *Meaning in History*, p. 188: "On account of this profound ambiguity of the historical fulfillment where everything is 'already' what it is 'not yet,' the Christian believer lives in a radical tension between present and future." "All history," writes Auerbach, "points to something still concealed," p. 58.

its transcendent timelessness colors events in the concrete present. Yet Auerbach is uncertain about the relation of figural thinking to aesthetic form: "It is not quite clear to me how far aesthetic ideas were determined by figural conceptions—to what extent the work of art was viewed as the *figura* of a still unattainable fulfillment in reality."[16]

Pearl may serve as a model for a figural reading of poetic structure, for it offers a uniquely formal aesthetic experience. The narrator's movement from an illuminated dream of nature to the radiant simultaneity of the New Jerusalem is a visionary movement from figure to fulfillment. This figural verbal drama continues until the poem's entire form—its flawed circle yearning for completion—becomes itself a figure to be fulfilled in the perfect sphere of God's presence. The figural reality of the poem's structure emerges when its story ends; the nature of the narrator's final situation is revealed by the poem's completed form. A figural reading of *Pearl* satisfies an elegiac interpretation of either the narrator's or the poet's situation. The poem may well have its source in a deep sense of loss—either actual grief or its poetic exploration is an earthly *figura* no less real than what it prefigures: transformed by Christ's agony, earthly suffering foreshadows the perfect understanding achieved after death.

The figural structure of the poem is unfolded in the visionary expansion of the narrator's perception. Grief-stricken, he falls to the ground and finds in his own dreams a maiden with calm spiritual conviction. As she warns him, he trusts entirely to his senses, he lacks faith and humility, he is reckless and covetous, he mistakes the nature of the earth and his earthly body, and he misunderstands the conditions of salvation. His dream visions partly

16. Auerbach, *Scenes from the Drama*, p. 62. One medieval conception viewed the artist's work as "an imitation or at least a shadowy figuration of a true and likewise sensuous reality," p. 62. Auerbach judges that modern scholars of medieval works have generally confined themselves to symbolic or allegorical interpretations. One exception is Elizabeth Salter, *Piers Plowman: An Introduction* (Cambridge, Mass., 1962), pp. 23–28; she offers a figural reading of the title character, though avoids the figural and prophetic elements of the poem's form—a reasonable decision in view of its dependence on digressive sermon-technique.

represent his growing awareness of this limited understanding. "Fordolked of luf-daungere / Of þat pryuy perle wythouten spot" [Grievously wounded through the power of love / For my own flawless pearl] (11–12)—his grief is a prideful wound of his own making, yet it has opened him to God's grace (63) and allowed him to forsake temporarily the fallen earthly perception to which he is accustomed.

From the beginning, he is unusually responsive to his sur-roundings. His description of earthly paradise (sections II-IV) is highly crafted and deeply appreciative. The vibrant images of light and motion transcend everyday fallen human vision, and as he fol-lows the ceaselessly flowing stream, he is already nearing his ca-pacity for ecstasy: "I bowed in blys, bredful my brayneȝ" [In bliss I went, my brain brimful] (126). But though the landscape is transformed, the dreamer does not yet see its true nature. Though uniquely aware of light and water, he perceives them here as mere light and mere water—beautiful, but not yet the incarnation of salvation. The river retains its earthly meaning: it is a spatial boundary, a physical obstruction, and the dreamer reasons it is too deep to cross (139–44). But his sensitivity grows as he nears the maiden, and in the actual presence of Pearl's burnished whiteness, his brimful brain is almost overextended. His brain trembling, his mind dissolving, he now begs the maiden to guide him across the river so he can remain with her forever. She replies that despite the wonders he sees, his vision is still flawed and earthly. He has mis-taken the nature of the river, of his body, and of salvation:

> Þou wylneȝ ouer þys water to weue;
> Er moste þou ceuer to oþer counsayle:
> Þy corse in clot mot calder keue.
> For hit watȝ forgarte at Paradys greue;
> Oure ȝorefader hit con misseȝeme.
> Þurȝ drwry deth boȝ vch man dreue,
> Er ouer þys dam hym Dryȝtyn deme.
>
> [You wish to move over this water.
> You must first submit to another plan:

> Your body in clay must colder sink,
> For it was ruined in the Garden of Eden;
> Our first father failed to value it.
> Each man must pass through dreary death
> Before God lets him cross this stream.]
>
> (318-24)

Without understanding this entirely, the dreamer yields to the maiden's greater knowledge—a knowledge he has found in himself. His earthly values gradually fall away, until at last he sustains a sudden experience of heavenly bliss. Increasingly sensitized and receptive, he is able to experience a fragile but exquisite vision of the apocalypse. The elegiac situation becomes the occasion for prophecy, as the world is revealed in its figural immediacy. For poet and reader, the vision reveals that the earthly sphere prefigures the perfect bliss of heaven, where natural images will achieve their final rounded form. God's grace mediates natural sensation and its eschatological fulfillment. The birds that sang with sweet harmony in the dreamer's illuminated landscape (94) transcended the musical instruments of his everyday world, but they also prefigure the finer song of the heavenly hosts, music "Lyk floðeȝ fele laden runnen on resse" [Like the sound of many waters in a rushing torrent] (874), a fountain as thunderous and gentle "As harporeȝ harpen in her harpe" [As harpers playing upon their harps] (881).

In the vision of the New Jerusalem, the dreamer fleetingly experiences diffusion in infinity's flowing sphere of light. But the vision radically overextends his consciousness. He is ravished by sudden pure radiance (1088), and his mind begins to melt: "Delyt me drof in yȝe and ere, / My maneȝ mynde to maddyng malte" [Delight flooded me in eye and ear, / My mortal mind dissolved in madness] (1153–54). In the timeless simultaneity of an eternity he experiences in himself, his human history fades: knowledge of mortality and guilt dissolves, and he prepares to risk his mortal body—the only body in which he can achieve eternal life. Now, overcome with desire, he prepares to hurl himself willfully into heavenly bliss. As he gathers himself to plunge into the river—with the suicidal recklessness of Adam, not the humble self-sacrifice of Christ—he is violently reawakened to the reality of his own flesh. Rushing madly forward, he is wrenched back to the body he thought he had left behind, the body that was all the time the secret landscape of his dream.

In the dream landscape of his body, the mortal seed of timeless germination, the dreamer experiences earthly plenitude fulfilled. But earthly plenitude is only a figure for the translucent simultaneity of eternity; it is only a shadow of the apocalyptic roundness to come. He cannot dwell literally in the kingdom of heaven while his flesh lives; the perfect and simultaneous possession of a limitless existence is possible only after death. Heavenly bliss cannot be taken but must be given; it is not willful possession but humble submission to the generous outpouring of God's forgiveness. The earthly body must willingly fulfill its unique and mortal destiny for the resurrected body to be radiant with life (1146). The boundaries between earthly reality and its transcendent form are miraculous (1166), and mediated only by God according to his will. The dreamer confuses figure with fulfillment, but through God's grace (and the poet's) he is saved from the consequences of his reckless act. Instead of drowning in his delusions, he awakes uniquely aware of his figural mortality in the garden where his dream began. The first shall be last and the last first.

In surrendering himself to the figural power of earthly incarnation, he also surrenders to the poem's structure. The poet leaves no grounds for projecting the narrator into a hypothetical future existence. He is unequivocally returned to the earthly garden, and his only meaningful future lies in submission to the figural potential revealed by the poem as a whole. Where the narrator was at the beginning of the poem, where he is at the end, and where he will be until his death have become one time and one place: the garden of human history, awaiting ultimate redemption. The ground on which he wakes has become potentially groundless, for when the human garden with its mortal flesh succumbs to God as "root and ground" of bliss, it will be freed from mere location.

When the narrator finds himself awakened and still alive, he yearns at first to return to his vision, to submit himself to the apocalypse now. But he has grown to understand the shape of his destiny, and submits instead to communion, the earthly figure for participation in the mystical body of Christ. The Eucharist is the supreme figure of Christian eschatology: it is both shadow and substance of a life in Christ, an earthly miracle that invests the concrete present with the greater miracle to come.[17] Surrendering to God the miraculous dream-extension of his perception and accepting in its place the bread and wine, he submits to his earthly enclosure —world, flesh, and poem. The dying grain at the beginning of *Pearl* has ripened into bread invested with the body of Christ—the wine incarnating his blood is the verbal harvest of grapes at the poem's center. The final lines diffuse us through the spherical body of the poem and return us gently to the garden of our history, a garden encircled by words.

The linear progression of the story dissolves, for narrator and narrative have succumbed to the total body of the poem. At this point we can understand that the dreamer's vision of the New Jerusalem was not a moment's grace now lost, but a figure for imminent and ecstatic timelessness. As the dreamer has learned through Pearl, divine consciousness is coextensive with the universe, and submission to God is a total diffusion in the boundless sphere of his being. It is a state of perceptual equality in which the absolute is infinite and "Vchoneȝ blysse is breme and beste" [Each one's bliss is ecstatic and best] (863). Total submission means coming into one's own being. The self dies into life, and individual consciousness diffuses to fill the space of infinity. This total pres-

17. Auerbach, *Scenes from the Drama,* p. 60, remarks that communion "gives us the purest picture of the concretely present, the veiled and tentative, the eternal and supratemporal elements" of an eschatological *figura.* An event may be without historical documentation, however, and still be "real" as a figure derived from the artist's experience. Imagination, dreams, and visions are imbued with figural potential: "an incarnation, a miracle are real happenings; miracles happen on earth, and incarnation is flesh," p. 74.

ence in Christ is a simultaneity of water and flame (769), a marriage washed in blood (766), a crown of thorns and pearls. It is also the pure enclosure of total simplicity (909). Each of Christ's brides shares identically in his blessedness, in the totality of the perfect sphere. God's presence at last subsumes all human action. Submitting to his will prefigures possessing his kingdom. As Pearl advises the dreamer, "Þe oȝte better þyseluen blesse" [You would do better to bless yourself] (341), for to bless oneself is to accept God's will and to merge with his blessedness. "The court of þe kyndom of God alyue / Hatȝ a property in hytself beyng" [The court of the kingdom of the living God / Has a property of its own being] (445–46). Possessing the kingdom of heaven, Pearl possesses the total form of herself. I, who am wholly His, am thereby wholly my own:

> my Lorde þe Lombe þurȝ hys godhede,
> He toke myself to hys maryage,
> Corounde me quene in blysse to brede
> In lenghe of dayeȝ þat euer schal wage;
> And sesed in alle hys herytage
> Hys lef is. I am holy hysse:
> Hys prese, hys prys, and hys parage
> Is rote and grounde of alle my blysse.

> [my Lord the Lamb, through his divinity,
> Took me as his bride,
> Crowned me queen to flourish in bliss
> For a lifetime that will last forever;
> And possessed of all his heritage
> Is his beloved. I am wholly his:
> His virtue, his excellence, and his nobility
> Is root and ground of all my bliss.]

(413–20)

The simple pearl, lost in a garden, is the seed of an infinite bliss figured by the poem's form. As the narrator loses his pearl in the garden of his dream, so the poet surrounds his own loss with the poem he has created. When the dreamer awakens, he relieves his renewed sense of loss by receiving the Eucharist; the poet's desolation is relieved by submitting to the poem's figural space. In the final stanzas, the encircling frame of words is not a prison of earthly sorrow but the "garlande gay," the circling dance of the blessed. "Through a circular room and by a circular staircase we ascend to the upper chamber of the Temple."[18] Like the temple, *Pearl* is round in three dimensions—a microcosmic model of the spherical cosmos. The mere pearl, "so rounde, so reken in vche araye," is finally coextensive with the space the poem encircles and with the redeemed universe it prefigures. The poem's enclosure is ecstatic, for it will be ravaged and transformed; its apocalyptic form is the form given God himself in the common medieval conception—God is a sphere whose center is everywhere and whose circumference is nowhere. The word of God is everywhere present; there is no church in heaven, for the sanctuary is the sacred enclosure of God himself (1061–64).

Pearl is a sphere dense with language, resonant with alliteration, a circle revolving around a center which is nowhere and everywhere. It tempts poet and reader with a space in which the mind can freely dissolve. Possessing the poem, we possess the final and infinite form of ourselves. Unlike the dreamer, the poem as a whole expresses no horror at the reality of the body; it is impossible to imagine a disembodied theology in the presence of this supremely embodied poem. The Pearl-poet makes manifest the shadow of eternity imprinted in his flesh. *Pearl* is a structure of language created to circle and nurture the seed of the poet's innocence.

18. St. Jerome, quoted by Garrett, *The Pearl: An Interpretation*, p. 17.

Reverberation

Like the concentric rings of stones thrown in water,
our senses interweave and overlap.

(C. N.)

The groups of tones in a melody which are harmonically
connected are like the links of a chain; they give the
melody color and sheen. They are the real body of the
melody, strange as it may seem to speak of body in
connection with a linear phenomenon like a melody. It
must not be forgotten that a melody is only primarily
linear, and that the comparison with a curved line applies
only to the most obvious, external aspect of a chain of
tones. The melodic thread has an ever-changing but
ever-present volume or thickness.

Paul Hindemith, in Kepes, *Language of Vision*, 63

Reverberation—"A vegetation, sound waves with long
leaves."

Robert Bly, *Light around the Body*, 41

If, having fixed the original form in our mind's eye, we
ask ourselves how that form comes alive and fills with life,
we discover a new dynamic and vital category, a new
property of the universe: reverberation. It is as though a
well-spring existed in a sealed vase and its waves, repeatedly echoing against the sides of this vase, filled it
with their sonority.

Eugene Minkowski, in Bachelard,
Poetics of Space, xii

I am beside myself with this
     thought of the One in the World-Egg,
enclosed,   in a shell of murmurings,

          rimed round,
          sound-chamberd child.
          Robert Duncan, *Bending the Bow*, 10

A late fugue by Bach comes nearest to the experience of
a pure musical "space." As we keep our attention dispersed over the whole structure of the polyphonic web we
become aware of the constant flux in the density of its
fabric, alternately constricting, swelling and opening up.
There is no need to look out for the fugue subject as
it reappears in the various voices. The volume of the
musical space will be eloquent enough. At times the
vertical tension between the voices will tighten up and
demand to be resolved by another reappearance of the
subject. The actual intonation of the subject, even in the
hidden middle voices, will announce itself by a sudden
change in the vertical density. The fabric of the voices
will open up and expand into the infinite, an experience
not dissimilar to the mystic's oceanic feeling as described
by Freud. Time will seem to stand still. We begin to
live eternally in the present and are given the infinity of
true musical space.
    Anton Ehrenzweig, *The Hidden Order of Art*, 81

Reverberation—to fall into the vertical dimensions of
time.
                           (C. N.)

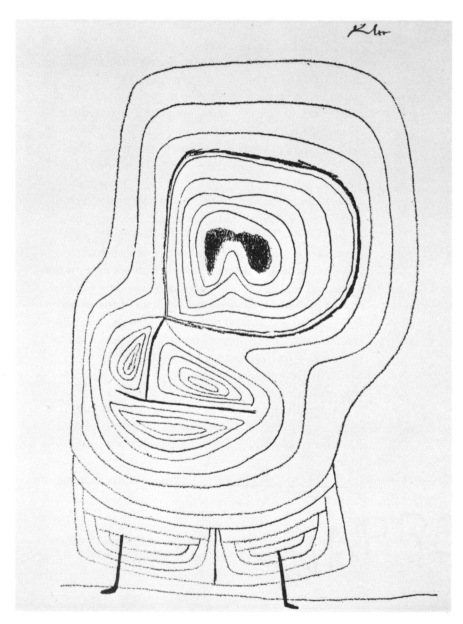

5. Paul Klee, "Heavily Fructified."

THREE

Prospero's island:
the visionary body
of *The Tempest*

There was a man who loved islands. He was born on
one, but it didn't suit him, as there were too many other
people on it, besides himself. He wanted an island all of
his own: not necessarily to be alone on it, but to make it
a world of his own.

> D. H. Lawrence, "The Man Who Loved Islands"

His concentration fixes this
island,
a space figured in language

> Robert Duncan, *Roots and Branches*, 33

There is the sleep of my tongue
speaking a language I can never remember—
words that enter the sleep of words
once they are spoken.

> Mark Strand, *Darker*, 21

Near the end of *The Tempest*, Prospero calls Caliban "as disproportioned in his manners / As in his shape" (V, i, 291–92),[1] echoing his
earlier observation that Caliban's physical and psychological developments are grotesquely alike: "as with age his body uglier
grows, / So his mind cankers" (IV, i, 191–92). Body and mind are
devastatingly fused in Caliban, but the whole play unfolds in

1. *The Tempest*, ed. Northrop Frye, *William Shakespeare: The Complete
Works*, gen. ed. Alfred Harbage (Baltimore, 1969). Quotations are documented
internally by act, scene, and line.

imagery where the body acts out a state of mind and where mind and body interpenetrate.

The Tempest binds emotion to imagery of the body, and even conventional metaphors offer corporeal analogues of consciousness. When Ariel says the king's company is "Brimful of sorrow and dismay" (V, i, 14), we see their bodies as casks filled by their emotions. Prospero suggests that Ferdinand's physical appearance is transformed by grief just as his aimless search for his companions embodies the distractions of sorrow: "he's something stained / With grief (that's beauty's canker). . . . He hath lost his fellows / And strays about to find 'em" (I, ii, 415–18). When Miranda conceives the body as a house inhabited by a spirit, the traditional metaphor becomes fresh in the context of the play:

> There's nothing ill can dwell in such a temple.
> If the ill spirit have so fair a house,
> Good things will strive to dwell with't.
>
> (I, ii, 458–60)

Ariel portrays Gonzalo's sadness as tears falling like cold rain from the thatched roof of his head, offering a delicate image of the head as the mind's house: "His tears run down his beard like winter's drops / From eaves of reeds" (V, i, 16–17). The nobles' repressed guilt erupts like poison stored in their flesh: "their great guilt, / Like poison given to work a great time after, / Now gins to bite the spirits" (III, iii, 104–6); as punishment, they experience the full force of their guilt as an excruciating physical assault. When Caliban rebels, he imagines his master's body covered by an unwholesome dew and blistered by a raw wind. Prospero rebukes him in kind: "thou shalt be pinched / As thick as honeycomb," he warns; "I'll rack thee with old cramps, / Fill all thy bones with aches, make thee roar / That beasts shall tremble at thy din" (I, ii, 328–29, 369–71).

The interaction of physical and emotional identity is not unique to the island, for Prospero tells Miranda that in Milan, Antonio "new created / The creatures that were mine . . . or changed 'em, /

Or else new-formed 'em" (I, ii, 81-83). The special quality of perception on the island is that the body is literally and intensely experienced as a state of mind. Thus Antonio's subjects became new
organisms, but gave no sign they recognized the change. Yet when
Caliban fears his plot will be punished, he is vividly aware that
Prospero could transform the rebels "to barnacles, or to apes / With
foreheads villainous low" (IV, i, 247-48).

Consciousness on the island fuses with the body, and with the
surrounding environment as well. The body incorporates the texture of the external landscape, and the self becomes a function of
its organic setting. In the storm, the trembling elements are given
human form when the nobles rush about the deck half-blind with
terror, and the nobles finally discover their guilt in a physical universe which has become wholly accusatory. Alonso perceives Ariel's
speech as a condemnation by the elements, and hears the winds
and thunder accusingly intone the name of Prospero. These inter-
penetrations of body, mind, and landscape are threatening, yet the
island's special atmosphere is not always tempestuous and guilt-
ridden; Prospero's masque celebrates a graceful human marriage
in a beneficent world where the sky becomes a "Rich scarf to my
proud earth" (IV, i, 82).

Prospero's consciousness controls this atmosphere. He subdues
Caliban at last by threatening him with total perceptual agony,
with suffering unlimited in time and space. If he chose, he could
fill Caliban's mind with endless roaring and suffuse his body with
pain. Like Ferdinand's cry at the height of the tempest—"Hell is
empty, / And all the devils are here!" (I, ii, 214-15)—Prospero's
curses confirm his power to enclose his subjects in a universe of
pain. Caliban quite understands the extent of this power—"From
toe to crown he'll fill our skins with pinches"—and realizes it may
be even greater than he can imagine. He captures the essence of
transformations in this atmosphere where island, mind, and body
become one: he warns his cohorts that Prospero will "Make us
strange stuff" (IV, i, 231-32).

Caliban's use of "strange" invokes the changes rung on the word throughout the play. Prospero tells Miranda of his downfall in Milan, when he to his "state grew stranger, being transported / And rapt in secret studies" (I, ii, 76–77). The "strangeness" of the story puts Miranda to sleep; she succumbs to a "heaviness" of the body. Gonzalo later asks, "Will you laugh me asleep, for I am / very heavy," and Alonso exclaims how "wondrous heavy" he feels (II, i, 182–83, 192). Sebastian describes it as a "strange drowsiness" and advises Alonso not to neglect "the heavy offer of it. / It seldom visits sorrow" (II, i, 193, 188–89). Prospero describes the "heaviness" of their memories of suffering, and earlier refers to his arrival on the island as "the last of our sea-sorrow" (I, ii, 170).

The words "strange," "heavy," "sleep," and "sea" build a network of associations and eventually raise simple description—even with a word normally so unevocative as "strange"—to a level of intense metaphor. Language is drawn into the mutations which occur on the island; all the play's language becomes metaphoric, and the dramatic action becomes verbal music. *The Tempest's* atmosphere, which extends the mind to the landscape of the body, creates as well a radical interpenetration of verbal categories; boundaries everywhere are lost. Even in the comic scenes, verbal playfulness sustains the metaphoric development. At humorous moments, characters unknowingly speak truths which generate the play's cohesive verbal texture.

When Prospero puts the nobles heavily to sleep, he leaves Antonio and Sebastian to their ambitious fantasies. "Art thou waking?" they ask; "Do you not hear me speak?" "This is a strange repose," observes Sebastian, "to be asleep / With eyes wide open; standing, speaking, moving, / And yet so fast asleep" (II, i, 203–9). Extending the exchange with a pun, Sebastian unconsciously characterizes the play's texture: "It is a sleepy language." Sebastian reveals more than the quality of his conversation with Antonio; he describes the language induced by an environment that drenches the body and rises to awareness in speech. As Antonio tells him, "We all were sea-swallowed, though some cast again"

(II, i, 245). Antonio's metaphor is merely playful, but reveals that their experience is more than a change of fortune. As their clothes are unstained and even miraculously freshened by the sea, the nobles themselves have undergone a sea-change.

They no longer exist in a world where time is measured by the public history of Milan and Naples; now they swim to the rhythm of Prospero's purposes. In a comic scene, Trinculo notices the transformation. Stumbling upon Stephano and Caliban under a blanket, taking refuge from the coming storm, he wonders at this bizarre four-legged beast: "What have we here? a man or a fish? . . . A strange fish! . . . this is no fish, but an islander" (II, ii, 24–35). Trinculo's solution, that a fish and a man combine to make an islander, is like Antonio's logic in the scene before: to convince himself that Ferdinand is dead, Antonio makes what seems an incontestable analogy, " 'Tis as impossible that he's undrowned / As he that sleeps here swims" (II, i, 231–32). But Prospero and the audience know Ferdinand lives, and our knowledge lends unexpected credibility to the image of a sleeping swimmer. All the islanders are sleepers, and even those awake seem half-asleep; only the living endure the pain of death.

In *The Tempest*, to sleep is to swim in the body, and all perception is a form of sleep. Antonio tries to make the mystery commonplace and impersonal by blaming this strange sleepiness on "the quality o' th' climate." But the heavy drowsiness of the island, with its strange music and dissolving banquets, is an illusive atmosphere maintained by Prospero's art. Asleep or awake, enchanted or anguished, the waylaid travelers float in the "spongy April" of Prospero's imagination.

Ariel describes the climate of the island in a song that resonates through the play:

> Full fathom five thy father lies;
> Of his bones are coral made;
> Those are pearls that were his eyes;
> Nothing of him that doth fade

> But doth suffer a sea-change
> Into something rich and strange.
>
> (I, ii, 397–402)

The sea-change is a condition of perceptual synesthesia. Indeed, all metaphor in *The Tempest* becomes verbal music resonating toward synesthesia. The nobles have "smelt music"; they absorb the surroundings in their bodies, but their bodies are also diffused through the environment. While they wander, dispersed and suffering, each will "taste / Some subtleties o' th' isle" in himself—for to perceive on the island is to taste or devour. Ariel cries, "I drink the air before me," and Gonzalo muses, "amazement / Inhabits here." The mind's descent into the body is met by bodily vapors rising to the mind. This "strange" synesthesia is a delicate balance of mind and body hovering where consciousness may momentarily give way to organic processes. Under Prospero's control, the shipwrecked men feel their reason overwhelmed by the body's energy: "thy brains, / Now useless, boiled within thy skull" (V, i, 59–60); "ignorant fumes that mantle / Their clearer reason" (V, i, 67–68); "they devour their reason" (V, i, 155).

Ariel identifies the play's central archetype—a symbolic death in the sea followed by drowning the conscious self:

> the never-surfeited sea
> Hath caused to belch up you, and on this island,
> Where man doth not inhabit, you 'mongst men
> Being most unfit to live, I have made you mad;
> And even with such-like valor men hang and drown
> Their proper selves.
>
> (III, iii, 55–60)

As the boatswain puts it, "We were dead of sleep" (V, i, 230). In this death the nobles become unlike their proper selves. But their minds are under Prospero's control, and he can draw a healing power from their experience. When their self-awareness succumbs to the physical rhythms of sleep, Prospero fertilizes their minds with the immense organic energy of his island. Dead of sleep, they feed on the energy of dreams; Prospero quickens death and extends the quality of sleep to the waking hours. Having "drowned his tongue" in the sleepy language of his play, Prospero can create a new language whose "words / Are natural breath."

The metaphoric interpenetration of body and mind makes the island a space where language and thought share biologic rhythms. But the drama of Prospero's role depends on more than this. *The Tempest* is Prospero's world: to understand fully the atmosphere of the play and the regenerated society toward which it moves, one must look to the artist at the center of the island.

In Act V the characters stand "charm'd" in the circle Prospero has drawn before his cell. The circle is an image of both the island and the play under the continuous influence of Prospero's magical art. As his vision radiates from his center to shape his island—its atmosphere and dramatic events—the progress of the play becomes continuous with the texture of his consciousness. *The Tempest*'s vitality arises in part from an illusion that limitless energies are confined within this sharply bounded time and space. Totally enclosed, displacing the abyss of the world and its history, the island is the locus of unassailable creative power. It will never exist again as we know it for the duration of the play—an image of Prospero's dreams, sustained by his will and imagination.

The Tempest displays a self-generated form which depends on a structure limited both temporally and spatially. Time and space act mutually to frame and set apart the events. Only four hours pass between the shipwreck and the end of the play, but it is temporally bounded by vast stretches of public history that reach backward to Milan and forward to the journey home, where Ferdinand and Miranda will marry and eventually rule a new society. The spatial concentration is equally intense, for the island is completely enclosed by sea and sky.

The physical form of Prospero's island is equal to its temporal form; its longitude and latitude are wholly defined by the limits of the play. But the two vast frames of time and space serve a dual purpose: they emphasize the exclusive concentration of energies in the present, and suggest the wider human universe to which the play finally submits its form. Were there no release from Prospero's dream, its immense concentration of energies would be demonic. Instead the dream overflows into waking life; Prospero's control comes to fruition when his vision creates a revitalized society.

For the duration of the drama, the energy is confined to the island. An immeasurable metaphysical distance separates the action from conventional human activity. Prospero asks Miranda if she remembers her past: "What seest thou else / In the dark backward and abysm of time" (I, ii, 49–50). "Canst thou remember / A time before we came unto this cell?" (I, ii, 38–39). " 'Tis far off," she answers, "And rather like a dream" (I, ii, 44–45). Caliban's past is also remote, and only a "celestial liquor" can inspire him to reclaim his original freedom; as for Ariel, Prospero must once a month remind him what he was, for he too forgets (I, ii, 262–63).

The events just prior to the play sever the nobles from their immediate past. The voyage to Tunis stretches "ten leagues beyond man's life" to a point thirty miles from nowhere (II, i, 241), "A space whose ev'ry cubit / Seems to cry out 'How shall that Claribel / Measure us back to Naples?' " (II, i, 251–53). They arrive after a final metaphysical removal: they are "sea-swallowed, though some cast again," and believing the king's company drowned, the rest of the fleet sails home in despair. During the play the king's company *is* dead to the world; *The Tempest* takes place in a nowhere of the imagination—"the tune of our catch, played by the / picture of Nobody" (III, ii, 123–24), "Thou dost talk nothing to me" (II, i, 166)—which occupies no time and space but the present.

Public history takes place in the stretches of time and space which frame the play. Before the storm, public history at Milan was continuous with but separate from the private world of Prospero's island. When the common mortals who now inhabit it sail home, the island will resume a private existence irrelevant to the history of Milan and Naples. But for the duration of the play, Prospero fuses these two histories and directs their progress. Though his power radiates from his island to the surrounding seas, it does not literally extend to Milan; instead Milan is temporarily displaced to the domain of his influence. Only on the island can Prospero manipulate the nobles, but once there they serve his purposes.

Like the human world set in the heavens, Prospero's domain is an island of mind surrounded by water; here his powers fill the perceptual universe: "I have bedimmed / The noontide sun, called forth the mutinous winds, / And 'twixt the green sea and the azured vault / Set roaring war" (V, i, 41–44). Prospero's plan depends on carefully manipulating elemental forces, though at most he can direct them toward the island and temporarily give them conscious form. His project also requires staging characters and personalities. His power to create illusions extends not only to the storms and rainbows of the island and to its insubstantial atmosphere, but also to the emotional agony and melancholy of the shipwrecked travelers. Knowing they act in Prospero's play does not diminish our sense that they experience illusions as reality. With dexterity and craft, Prospero sustains whatever beliefs are required to work his purposes upon the characters while arranging all the play's events. For four hours, through either his own invisible presence or the reports of his agents, he watches everything. "Hast thou, spirit," he asks Ariel, "Performed to point the tempest that I bade thee?" (I, ii, 193–94). Ariel replies in detail, confirming as well the arrangement of the characters: "as thou bad'st me, / In troops I have dispersed them 'bout the isle" (I, ii, 219–20). Prospero eases Ferdinand's suffering and stages a meeting with Miranda: "It goes on, I see, / As my soul prompts it" (I, ii, 420–21). He orders Ariel to create a "strange drowsiness" for all the nobles but Antonio and Sebastian, permitting their own natures to nurture a plot against the others; at the necessary moment foreseen by Prospero (II, i, 291), Ariel awakens Gonzalo.

Like a dramatist, Prospero creates situations where the characters' personalities will predictably bring about the required action. He also structures their perceptual worlds, shaping the horizons

of their perceptions as his gentle direction to Miranda most delicately expresses: "The fringed curtains of thine eye advance / And
say what thou seest yond" (I, ii, 409–10). Under Prospero's direction, Miranda and Ferdinand are reflected in each other's vision,
and "At the first sight," Prospero observes, "They have changed
eyes" (I, ii, 441–42); the transformation invokes the sea-changes
of Ariel's song. As the song's texture echoes through the island's
atmosphere, Prospero's vision suffuses the play's language. Since
Ariel performs his commands "to th' syllable," the events he stages
double as immediate translations of Prospero's speech. In both of
Prospero's symbolic roles—deity and poet—words are acts and
speech becomes flesh.

Thus, though Shakespeare often links the beginning and the
end of his later plays, his artist-surrogate performs the linking
action in *The Tempest*. The play begins with Prospero's tempest
and ends with his charge to Ariel to provide calm seas and auspi-
cious winds for the return voyage. When Ferdinand observes,
"Though the seas threaten, they are merciful. / I have cursed them
without cause" (V, i, 178–79), he invokes the beginning and the
end of the play as well as the purpose which unifies the intervening
hours. For Prospero, sea and land are more than metaphorically
compatible; his island transforms and raises the sea around it so
that the landscape becomes an elevated seascape. When Gonzalo
offers to trade "a thousand furlongs of sea / for an acre of barren
ground" (I, i, 60–61), he foreshadows the structural space of *The
Tempest* where men "hang and drown their proper selves."

The symbolic drowning of the nobles that begins the play is
balanced by another drowning at the end, when Prospero symbolically pledges to give up his art:

> I'll break my staff,
> Bury it certain fathoms in the earth,
> And deeper than did ever plummet sound
> I'll drown my book.
>
> (V, i, 54–57)

Prospero's speech obviously echoes Alonso's despairing need to join his drowned son: "Therefore my son i' th' ooze is bedded; and / I'll seek him deeper than e'er plummet sounded / And with him there lie mudded" (III, iii, 100–102). Between the two symbolic drownings, Prospero transforms drowning into an act of self-discovery. Separated, Alonso and Ferdinand believe each other dead, yet unknowingly they lie bedded together in the deep sea of Prospero's imagination. Here their bodies undergo a transformation that prepares them to return as jewels in the crowned society of Milan. "Those are pearls," sings Ariel, "that were his eyes"; "Full fathom five thy father lies." The play's surrounding structure explains why Ariel's song relieves Ferdinand's distress at his father's death rather than taunting him with his loss. For though dead to the world and to each other, the characters are wonderfully alive to Prospero.

Prospero permeates the environment. "The wind did sing it to me," Alonso agonizes of the tempest, "and the thunder, / That deep and dreadful organ pipe, pronounced / The name of Prosper" (III, iii, 97–99). As Ariel announces, the original crime offended the elements and "Incensed the seas and shores" (III, iii, 74). Alonso's agony links the storm's noise and fury with Prospero's vengeance. Prospero has imprinted his image on the face of matter.

Waves, wind, and thunder are drawn into Prospero's vision, yet the island's music subdues the clamorous resonance of the seas. "This music crept by me upon the waters," marvels Ferdinand, "Allaying both their fury and my passion" (I, ii, 392–93). Airy music diffuses Prospero's blessing invisibly about the island in counterpoint to the threatening elements; Ariel's music transforms the storm. More than anything else, this music distances the island from the world beyond it—a world which must seem irrecoverable to the travelers, where storms are nothing supernatural and men can die only once. Prospero orchestrates wind and thunder for the hounds' pursuit and arranges them in judgment at the tantalizing banquet. This elemental turbulence finds human form in the agonized madness of the nobles. Yet even while the nobles' brains are boiled within their skulls, Prospero fills the atmosphere with a merciful grace. Unlike Antonio, who with inhuman detachment "set all hearts i' th' state / To what tune pleased his ear" (I, ii, 84–85), Prospero orchestrates an enveloping and dazzling music: "I have required / Some heavenly music . . . / To work mine end upon their senses" (V, i, 51–53).

The island is a visionary body politic energized by Prospero's mind; his consciousness suffuses the material form of his island stage. Having used his time "most preciously," he describes the progress of his plans in bodily terms:

> Now does my project gather to a head.
> My charms crack not, my spirits obey, and time
> Goes upright with his carriage.
>
> (V, i, 1–3)

When the nobles awaken, he reminds us that they were "sea-swallowed" for a purpose:

> Their understanding
> Begins to swell, and the approaching tide
> Will shortly fill the reasonable shore,
> That now lies foul and muddy.
>
> (V, i, 79–82)

The image of a "shore, / That now lies foul and muddy" suggests a confused consciousness awash in a distracted body. But the shore is essentially "reasonable"; the body is a graceful form, and the approaching tide will bring not vengeance but understanding. The nobles are now at the point where sea meets land, at the moment of awakening to enlightened bodies. As the tide of understanding approaches, it fills not only the bodies of the nobles but also the body of Prospero's island play.

Dense with terror and romance, Prospero's island is a world fertilized by music and the pounding sea. Amazement inhabits there, for it is an island of mind, "a maze trod indeed / Through forthrights and meanders" (III, iii, 2–3). Like the human mind, the island is a small space, "as strange a maze as e'er men trod" (V, i, 242), where men can wander infinitely. Prospero directs their wandering until their minds are enlightened by the motion their bodies have made. They are completely swallowed in the island's space and time, lost in themselves and in a dream; in this place where "no man was his own" (V, i, 212), they discover themselves.

The boundless sea, swallowing and belching up the shipwrecked travelers, gives way to the bounded sea of Prospero's devouring imagination. His island seems alive, an organism with lungs; it swallows the nobles, nurtures them in its bowels, and disgorges them. The formal metaphor is buried in a satiric exchange: Adrian —"The air breathes upon us here most sweetly"; Sebastian—"As if it had lungs, and rotten ones" (II, i, 46–47). Reborn from the sea they thought would be a grave, the nobles experience breathing as walking in the field of the body. "I have been in such a pickle, since I saw you / last," puns Trinculo (V, i, 282–83), but "pickle" describes the state of his mind and body as well as the preservative qualities of liquor and the horsepond. The briny atmosphere of *The Tempest*, where sea and land are concentrated in Prospero's domain, has pickled all the characters. Wandering in the body of one man's imagination, they have suffered a sea-change.

"My spirits," says Ferdinand wonderingly, "as in a dream, are all bound up"; his nerves, Prospero has told him, "are in their infancy again" (I, ii, 487, 485). The characters succumb together to a dream of the body's infancy; the island brings forth a new body politic. As Ferdinand finds "a wife / Where he himself was lost," so all the nobles receive "a second life" in death, "and second father" (V, i, 210–11, 195). Prospero is father to more than Miranda, for a new society is to be born as well. As this father, whose body nurtures the birth of a visionary society, Prospero participates in the action; far from being the omniscient creator or the detached manipulator, he is uniquely vulnerable. Though the island embodies his vision, he inhabits it with the rest of the characters. If his role is godlike, he is a god incarnate; through his island-body he must himself enact the dream he imagines.

When the tempest abates, Prospero assures Miranda the travelers are safe, yet she finds the storm still beating in her mind. Her anxiety foreshadows the tempest in Prospero's own mind, for he too becomes infected by the "strangeness" of the isle. The swift development of Caliban's plot arouses in him an uneasy "passion / That works him strongly," and forces him to curtail the masque and reassert control. Severely distraught, he tells the bewildered lovers, "my old brain is troubled," and he must walk awhile to still the tempest in his "beating mind" (IV, i, 143–44, 159, 163).

Prospero cannot escape being an actor in his own play; he must wander a maze between vengeance and forgiveness. Thus the nobles suffer dreams of unearthly transcendence alternating with a waking sleep where death is always present. The transcendent mercy of the final scene must be set against the punishment Prospero inflicts and the vengeance toward which he is tempted. The agony the nobles undergo is genuine: they are as threatened by Prospero's manufactured tempest as by a natural hurricane at sea;[2] as Ariel points out, their suffering on the island is no less real for being deluded—they truly believe each other dead. The bereavement that drives them mad is fully enacted by the imagination as a death. Their mazed wandering is inflicted as a punishment: "Ling'ring perdition (worse than any death / Can be at once) shall step by step attend / You and your ways" (III, iii, 77–79). Prospero enjoys seeing them "all knit up / In their distractions," and relishes his control: "they now are in my pow'r" (III, iii, 89–

2. The tempest must be staged to be convincingly frightening. With clever direction, realistic stage storms are possible without massive props and mechanics, and in this way the genuine fury of the storm can disappear in an instant. The stage tradition has ranged between extremes—between the misguided realism of elaborate productions on the one hand, where whole ships have been constructed onstage, and on the other, stylized shipwrecks with sea nymphs brandishing scarves and dancers mimicking waves around a tiny rocking-horse ship.

90). Having usurped each character's will and consciousness, his revenge takes the form of symbolic murder.

Yet Prospero extracts a healing virtue from suffering: having metaphorically died and experienced the madness of intolerable bereavement, the nobles enter a vital space which is both their grave as individuals and the source of their rebirth as members of a new society. This image of the landscape as womb and tomb becomes explicit when Ariel describes the sorrowing ships continuing the voyage: "for the rest o' th' fleet, / Which I dispersed, they all have met again" (I, ii, 232–33). Dispersing the ships and then regrouping them for the journey home, Ariel metaphorically seeds the sea with loss and harvests its despair. This reenacts Prospero's own "sea sorrow," his exile which "decked the sea with drops full salt" (I, ii, 155), and foreshadows Ariel's distribution of the sea-washed nobles—"as thou bad'st me, / In troops I have dispersed them 'bout the isle." Thus dispersed, the sorrowing nobles fertilize Prospero's island-body with life symbolically dead; sown about the island, they atone for the outraged seas and compensate for Prospero's tears. Yet in his devouring art he repudiates the methods of Antonio, who "new-created" his subjects. Prospero nurtures his characters within himself: when the king's fleet approaches, he cannot "new-create" his island to receive them; instead, for twelve years he prepares to extend himself radically and dangerously to an entire landscape.

For the duration of the play, Prospero has no ordinary body; his merely human flesh is transformed by his art. His sterile manner is the emptiness left under his cloak after he has exchanged his body for an island. The masque, his one attempt at explicit sexuality, is fleshless and transcendent despite its imagery of fertility. It is the only direct sexuality left to the artist engaged in the body of his dream. Unlike the masque of stage tradition, in which the audience participates to celebrate the play, the masque in *The Tempest* never leaves the stage. Prospero's drama cannot be opened to the world until its fulfillment—the birth of the body politic must await its appropriate time. All varieties of human potency flower on the island, yet all must be restrained for the drama to achieve its form. Having embraced his island-body with his mind, Prospero must channel all his sexuality to its growth.

This benevolent prospect is juxtaposed with more threatening germination. Dispersed about the island, Antonio and Sebastian bear in their heads the seeds to father a grotesque organism—a body politic based on actual murder. Sebastian calls their plot "a birth, indeed, / Which throes thee much to yield" (II, i, 224–25). In their dreams, all sexual potency is centered in Antonio's unnatural power, for even in the island's innocent atmosphere they can contemplate schemes of murder. In their unwavering lust for power, Prospero's own temptation toward unbounded power is externalized and left to play its part in his island drama. In Milan, Prospero's trust in Antonio—"which had indeed no limit, / A confidence sans bound"—"Like a good parent, did beget of him / A falsehood" (I, ii, 96–97, 94–95). But on the island, fully aware that, as Miranda says, "Good wombs have borne bad sons" (I, ii, 120), Prospero can tolerate the treachery of Antonio and Sebastian and allow their plot to unfold in all its demonic potential. As the storm infects the nobles' reason for Prospero's purposes, and Ferdinand and Miranda "art infected" with each other's love, so Prospero in his power can allow Antonio to infect his island-body. But with his play near completion and the birth of a new society imminent, Prospero—returned to his private body—must repudiate Antonio's falseness and satanic corruption: "to call him brother / Would even infect my mouth" (V, i, 130–31). Though Antonio can be tolerated by an enlightened body politic, Prospero cannot personally forgive him, for to embrace Antonio would corrupt his body just as it would infect his speech.

Gonzalo, whom Prospero most admires in the king's company, has the guileless innocence Prospero remembers in himself, and Gonzalo's idealized vision of the island might have risen out of Prospero's own past. "Had I plantation of this isle" (II, i, 139), Gonzalo muses, there would be no hierarchy of subjects or of social roles and possibilities:

No occupation; all men idle, all;
And women too, but innocent and pure;
No sovereignty. . . .
All things in common nature should produce
Without sweat or endeavor. Treason, felony,
Sword, pike, knife, gun, or need of any engine
Would I not have; but nature should bring forth,
Of it own kind, all foison, all abundance,
To feed my innocent people.

(II, i, 150–60)

Antonio and Sebastian identify the latent fantasies in this idealized sexuality: "I think he will carry this island home in his pocket and give it his son for an apple"; "And, sowing the kernels of it in the sea, bring forth more islands" (II, i, 86–89). Appropriately, they find the flaw in Gonzalo's thinking: "The latter end of his commonwealth forgets the beginning," for there will be "No marrying 'mong his subjects" (II, i, 153–54, 161). The head has forgotten the loins. Gonzalo's vision of self-sustaining creation without human intervention reflects Prospero's temptation to retain total if just control through his art. He knows that innocence proves fruitful under inspired leadership; indeed, it once supplied him with food and books. But as he has learned, Gonzalo's naïveté is unrealistic and unsafe. When Antonio and Sebastian mock Gonzalo's vision, they voice their own metaphoric roles: "He'd sow't with nettle seed" (II, i, 140). Uncontrolled, the island's innocent sexuality would fall prey to lust and avarice; "Good wombs have borne bad sons." Only on Prospero's island—where all sword arms are powerless under his control, where no man can wield the conventional symbols of social potency—may Gonzalo dream of a golden age without engine, sword, or penis. Prospero's temptation to godhead accompanies the vision of a headless race of men.

While Prospero's masque and Gonzalo's dream are at the still center of the island, Miranda's sexuality lies on the horizon. When the island achieves its final form, Prospero exchanges his magic cloak for ordinary clothes; he returns to his own body. Only then does he repudiate Antonio, and only then may Miranda be given in marriage. For twelve years Prospero has directed her education; while the island becomes the child of his imagination, she remains the child of his body, and he will allow neither to be violated prematurely. Until his island bears fruit and he can resume his personal role as father, Miranda must remain under his protection. Prospero's concern for her "virgin-knot," which diverts Ferdinand from the "sad knot" in which he sits "in an odd angle of the isle," is well known. But Prospero's extreme warnings against lust do not deny the prince's bed-right forever; the repressive effect is temporary. Eventually Miranda and Ferdinand will rule the new society: Prospero, in freeing the seed of his private body to fertilize Milan, thereby bestows a final grace upon the island's abundance. As he realizes when he watches the two lovers playing chess, they fulfill the artist's dream of a mind and body perfectly fused: they may wrangle for a score of kingdoms, but they will do so playfully, with grace. As king and queen crowned in marriage, they will rule by a decorous foreplay; for them, the head and the loins will be one. But this is in the future. When Miranda pleads that Ferdinand no longer be put to trial, Prospero exclaims, "What, I say, / My foot my tutor?" (I, ii, 469–70). In his island-body, Ferdinand must occupy a lesser place. And only after the play is over may Caliban once again rule the island; until then he must remain a "footlicker" for imaginary kings.

In celebrating conscious play, the new society fuses innocent sexuality and benevolent will. This society is created in a suspension of historical time where Prospero's vision is externalized at its extreme limits. Though his private body is desexualized during his play, his visionary body is anything but sterile. An organic energy animates the island and the human possibilities which now inhabit it. Prospero couples his detached will to a total sexual contact with nature, and the island enacts an imaginative biology whose sexuality is extended to every perception. Through its actors, Prospero's drama encompasses his naïveté and his innocence, his temptation to unbridled power and his impotence. He wields his artistic power and his deepest sexuality through agents far more fabulous. During the play, Ariel and Caliban serve these imaginative purposes, but they have past histories, and as limbs of Prospero's island-body, they are sometimes rebellious.

Anxious for freedom, Ariel is contained in the drama only by his love and fear of Prospero. As Prospero's agent, Ariel is a function of the time and space in which he fulfills Prospero's purposes. When he is almost free, his love song to the elements he will possess reveals how deeply and ecstatically sensuous he is:

> Where the bee sucks, there suck I;
> In a cowslip's bell I lie;
> There I couch when owls do cry.
> On the bat's back I do fly
> After summer merrily.
> Merrily, merrily shall I live now
> Under the blossom that hangs on the bough.
>
> (V, i, 88–94)

Through his delicate agent, Prospero can claim immediate access to every fertile inch of the island. Known to the king's company only in disguise and to Caliban as a mysteriously powerful music, Ariel carries out Prospero's will and actualizes his plans. Through him Prospero creates illusions and manipulates the island's atmosphere. Ariel calls Prospero "my lord" and "my potent master." Prospero calls Ariel "my spirit," "my diligence," "my industrious servant," "my delicate Ariel," and "my bird." He addresses him as "my tricksy spirit," "my dainty Ariel," "my chick," and "thou, which art but air." This dainty spirit is both the playful music of the island and the noise of the tempest that drives men mad. He can create rapturous effects at Prospero's command or commit symbolic murder. Yet he is never more than a tenuous and insubstantial presence; his role is a continual effervescence.[3] John Gielgud

3. These qualities are difficult to produce onstage. Romanticist interpretations, diffusing the play with allegory, produced heavily ornamented, mechanical extravaganzas with Ariel a kind of frozen Peter Pan. With gauze and wire wings, spangles and painted cheesecloth, and a mask always more literal than the human

once acted Prospero without looking at Ariel: the magician sees his invisible servant only in the mind's eye.

The parallels between Ariel and Prospero's staff fix the spirit within his master's role. When Ferdinand draws his sword, Prospero disarms him with his staff; later Antonio draws his "obedient steel" and is disarmed by Ariel, who wakes the others at Prospero's bidding. When Caliban urges Stephano to attack Prospero with a knife, log, or stake, Ariel provides distracting music. When the nobles draw swords against Ariel's harpy, their weapons prove "too massy" and "will not be uplifted." As Prospero's agent, Ariel taunts the impotent nobles with his invulnerability, boasting that their swords "may as well / Wound the loud winds, or with bemocked-at stabs / Kill the still-closing waters" (III, iii, 62–64). Prospero wields his spirit in a kind of sexual sword-play.

Though Prospero has relinquished ordinary sexuality, Ariel underlines the ecstatic fertility of his art. When Prospero gives up his magic, he changes his magic garment and his staff—symbols of his island power—for traditional clothing, the hat and rapier of a public man with only conventional power. Ariel performs this exchange of phallic symbols—staff for sword; then the Ariel we know vanishes into Prospero's memory. During the play, he is Prospero's image of a creative power so transcendent it can do no permanent harm. Ariel—whose elemental desire is to be free of all control, to revel at random in nature's sensuality—transcends flesh, weight, and earth. He is Prospero's dream of artistic sensuality—

---

face, Ariel was either trivial or fanciful. Suspended in air by complex mechanics and encrusted with a surfeit of costume, Ariel became emphatically everything his producers wanted to transcend—flesh, weight, earth. Suspended in air, the human body can only be heavier than air and slower than the wind. Lionel Abel, *Metatheatre* (New York, 1963), suggests that Ariel is too delicate for visual representation and should not be seen at all. Jan Kott cautions against the temptation to give Ariel the meticulously disciplined flesh of ecstatic ballet: "Ariel moves faster than thought. Let him appear and disappear from the stage imperceptibly. But he must not dance or run. He should move very slowly. He should stand still as often as possible. Only then can he become faster than thought." *Shakespeare Our Contemporary* (Garden City, N.Y., 1966), p. 274.

an imaginative potency that uses all the body's energy, the invisible penis of his fertile island-body. But when Ariel rebels, Prospero's threat challenges our image of his delicate insubstantiality: "If thou more murmur'st, I will rend an oak / And peg thee in his knotty entrails" (I, ii, 294–95). Prospero knows that this invisible sword, his transcendent and magical power, could become a purely physical weapon. Knowing this of Ariel's potency, Prospero must believe that his magical penis never violates the womb of nature and that the pain he causes will ultimately nurture good.

To maintain faith in his creative purity, Prospero projects a character whose sensuality is so gross and physical that Ariel's playfulness becomes entirely benevolent in comparison. Caliban wants to possess "every fertile inch o' th' island"; he knows "all the qualities o' th' isle, / The fresh springs, brine-pits, barren place and fertile" (I, ii, 337–38). Caliban, whom Prospero calls "hag-seed," acts with a will wholly procreative; his gnarled body views all experience through the dense medium of his flesh. When he learns to name the bigger light, when his mind is seeded with words, he turns and tries to rape Miranda: "Thou didst prevent me; I had peopled else / This isle with Calibans" (I, ii, 350–51).

Miranda teaches Caliban language; his profit on it is knowing how to curse. But Caliban will not always curse; when Prospero's play concludes, he will again be lord of his island. Though different from Ariel's playfulness, Caliban's sensuous perception of the island is neither destructive nor essentially incompatible with Ariel's spiritual ecstasy. Caliban, who perceives the island's abundance in all its particularity—its pignuts, jays' nests, and clustering filberts —hears Ariel's music and, when waking from rich dreams, cries to dream again (III, ii, 140). Caliban, who was once lord of the island, was deposed by Prospero. His attempts to regain control provide an extravagant contrast to Prospero's decorously staged recovery of his dukedom. Yet that is not the only sense in which Caliban sets off Prospero's art. Caliban is also the dark clown of flesh. He reveals all the animal properties of the human body, which Prospero hides under his magic garment. Caliban translates Prospero's generalized and imaginative abundance, his potency of thought, into explicit sexuality.[4]

Caliban's desire consequently not only distinguishes but also mirrors Prospero's own creative sexuality. When Prospero says of Caliban at the end of the play, "This thing of darkness I / Acknowledge mine" (V, i, 275–76), it is—as the greatest reach of his mercy—the most hopeful sign that he has grown. For Caliban is not simply the externalized fact of Prospero's fleshly existence. As much as Ariel, the Caliban we know is a function of the unique time and place designed for Prospero's drama. As Ariel embodies the artistic manipulation of the nobles, Caliban embodies the sexual ravishment of swallowing and devouring them. Caliban is a projection of the darkest areas of Prospero's sexuality, yet his lust for Miranda expresses more than a father's desire for the body of his daughter. Rather it expresses what, in this strange island atmosphere, has in a sense already happened; it is a threatening image of Prospero's existing intimacy with the daughter he has so carefully educated in seclusion. Caliban is Prospero's buried knowledge that he cannot help having slept with the daughter of his thoughts. In acknowledging his kinship with Caliban, with appetite, aggression, and formless matter, Prospero does more than accept responsibility for his actions toward the nobles; he acknowledges, too, a guilt which is ultimately sexual.

At the end of *The Tempest*, Prospero pledges to drown his book and break his staff; he takes on not only a human and public role,

4. Stage versions of Caliban have too often treated him either as an amiable teddy bear or as an evolutionary throwback—with huge canine teeth and jaws, fins or vestigial limbs with claws, and sometimes even tusks. But simpler makeup frees the actor for his own inventive body movement. The revealed animal properties of the human body are far more startling than a papier-mâché behemoth. Abel, *Metatheatre*, p. 69, describes a Caliban who would probably do damage to the play but at least suggests the character's paradoxical qualities: Caliban "is too gross for us to look at. There is something sublime about his grossness; and what is sublime, as Kant noted, lacks form. We should never see more than some part of Caliban's body—a tremendous foot, a huge hand, perhaps for one moment a masklike head covering the whole stage. His voice should be not unlike the tempest which caused the shipwreck of the treacherous Duke."

but also the burden of the guilt he wished to spare Miranda. He accepts Caliban, his unnurtured flesh, and—almost ironically—extends his forgiveness to the much manipulated nobles. His island-body, the generative space of his mind, lies surrounded by the archetypal womb and tomb of the sea and framed by an abyss of space and time. Poised at its edge, he knows that every third thought will be his grave (V, i, 311). He has been far from invulnerable. Yet the fruits of his art—a mixture of organic and aesthetic control—are an enlightened society blessed by the betrothal of Miranda and Ferdinand, the artist's dreamed-of marriage of thought and action. Prospero arrived at the island in a "rotten carcass" of a boat, sailing from a decaying society; now he has created a new society for a maid who "quickens what's dead." It is Shakespeare's wise and somewhat bitter vision that he might witness youth and innocence married in Prospero's wisdom.

To the extent that the reader possesses the play, Prospero is not merely Shakespeare's artist-surrogate; he is also the presence of the reader in the play. All the archetypes tentatively joined in *The Tempest*—archetypes of sea and forest, island and globe, a rite of passage toward both unconsciousness and divinity—have universal resonance. When Prospero stands at the center of his island, he stands for a moment at the center of our world; his cave reaches down to the sea, as his imagination embraces the heavens. But there is a limit to what the mind can control, except as repression, or the imagination enchant, except in the dissolving towers of fantasy. In the freely chosen drowning of his art, Prospero establishes kinship between renewal and death; the artist has given an irrecoverable third of his life. At this point even the ultimate human artificer must appeal beyond his own inventions to mercy that overarches his island as the sea surrounds it.

Sensual knowledge

The Lord said: This body is called the Field, and he who knows it is called the Knower of the Field.

Bhagavad Gita, xiii

The body-image incorporates objects or spreads itself into space.

Paul Schilder, *Image and Appearance of the Human Body*, 213

I am always enveloped by all the *seeing-movements* of my body, which are transformed one into another, and inevitably carry me back to the same central situation. . . . every moment is formed of an infinite number of roots that plunge to an unknown depth in an *implicit space*—in the past—in the secret structure of this our machine for perceiving and combining, which returns incessantly to the *present*.

Paul Valéry, *Selected Writings*, 126

Valéry is pursued by the idea that he might come to "see" his own body. He has accepted with rare consistency that all knowledge is of one's body: between person and person there is simply visibility. If one's own body, the locus of perception, should become the subject of perception, the virtual act of consciousness would become the perfect act of knowledge, mind and body knowing each other's function.

Geoffrey Hartman, *Unmediated Vision*, 152

> my body is polarized
> hangs

         My body is earth.
     Felix de Mendelssohn, in Horovitz, ed.,
                     Children of Albion, 58

All experience of space and world starts from physical
sensation. This also explains the deformation of my
figures. They are not at all distortions of the body's shape.
I think, rather, that in the image of the human body
one can also express something nonhuman—landscape,
for instance—in exactly the same way as we live over
again mountains and valleys in our bodily sensations.
                 Henry Moore, in Neumann, *Archetypal
                     World of Henry Moore*, 83

For me sculpture is based on and remains close to the
human figure. That works both ways. We make the kind
of sculpture we make because we are the shape we are,
because we have the proportions we have. All those
things make us respond to form and shape in certain
ways. If we had the shape of cows, and went about on
four legs, the whole basis of sculpture would be entirely
different.
                 Henry Moore, *Henry Moore on
                     Sculpture*, ed. James, 115

The constant of Rilke's mystical experiences is that
the eyes are forgotten and the body itself made one
subsuming penetrable sense to accommodate the earth
and to make it invisible.

the very text of Rilke is the "body," its weight and
balance. There is hardly a metaphor or simile that does
not in some way derive from his sense of the physical: . . .
this speculation is as essential to him as to the sculptor.
His conception of "thing," moreover, tends to negate
the generic difference between the objects of nature,

man, and art. Whether a tree, a young girl, or a column, Rilke will always understand it as an object in which a physical force has sought a certain kind of weight and balance, so that the contour of visible things is not conceived as static and predetermined, but at the mercy of some perpetual inner fountain which, although achieving momentary balance, continually endangers the object's contour and enclosed nature, liable at any moment to burst forth.

Hartman, *Unmediated Vision*, 140, 91

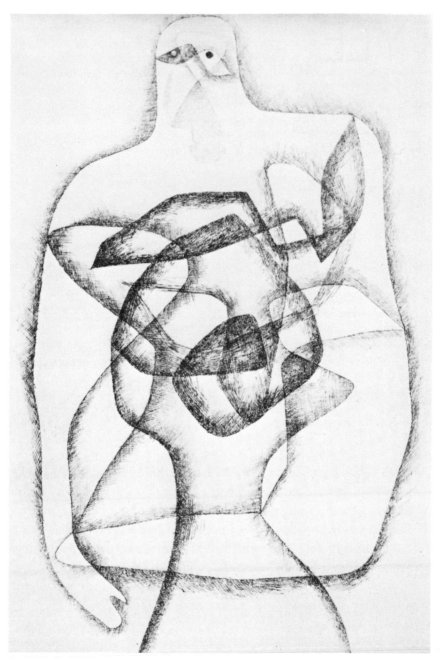

6. Paul Klee, "Figure."

FOUR   Christ's body
and Satan's head:
incarnate space in
Paradise Regained

> then wilt thou not be loath
> To leave this Paradise, but shalt possess
> A paradise within thee, happier far.
>   *Paradise Lost* (XII, 585–87) [1]

> And now began the threading of a maze so labyrinthine
> as to suggest that the builders of these sunless walls
> had been ordered to construct a maze for no other
> purpose than to torture the mind and freeze the memory.
>   Mervyn Peake, *Gormenghast*, 422

> Lace, interlace—what interlaces Infinity is serpent.
>   Frédéric Benrath, in Pellegrini,
>   *New Tendencies in Art*, 71

In *Paradise Lost* Milton projects his mythology against the background of cosmic space. From the description of creation out of the void to the image of the universe circumscribed by golden compasses—from Eden's green enclosure across the terror of chaos to the abyss of hell—the immense space of the poem surrounds us. We are given a heaven "extended wide / In circuit, undetermin'd square or round" (*PL*, II, 1047–48), where God from above sees all history simultaneously spread before him:

---

1. John Milton, *Complete Poems and Major Prose*, ed. Merritt Y. Hughes (New York, 1957). Quotations from *Paradise Lost* and *Paradise Regained* are documented internally by book and line, with the former additionally cited *PL*.

> About him all the Sanctities of Heaven
> Stood thick as Stars, and from his sight receiv'd
> Beatitude past utterance; on his right
> The radiant image of his Glory sat,
> His only Son; On Earth he first beheld
> Our two first Parents, yet the only two
> Of mankind, in the happy Garden plac't,
> Reaping immortal fruits of joy and love,
> Uninterrupted joy, unrivall'd love
> In blissful solitude; he then survey'd
> Hell and the Gulf between, and *Satan* there
> Coasting the wall of Heav'n on this side Night
> In the dun Air sublime, and ready now
> To stoop with wearied wings, and willing feet
> On the bare outside of this World, that seem'd
> Firm land imbosom'd without Firmament,
> Uncertain which, in Ocean or in Air.
>
> (*PL*, III, 60–76)

God's transcendent perception of the universe, "Wherein past, present, future he beholds," contains infinite space; but the anguished space of fallen perception is the limited measure of Satan's alienation: "Nine times the Space that measures Day and Night / To mortal men, hee with his horrid crew / Lay vanquisht, rolling in the fiery Gulf" (*PL*, I, 50–52).

These are general environments of the poem that set the stage for violent movement upward and downward and the dramatic opposition of particular enclosed spaces. Vertical movement includes insurrection, fall, incarnation, and tortured ascension. The frozen enclosure of Satan's wounded pride—his incoiling psychic landscape—contrasts with the appealing green enclosure of Eden. The dramatic conflict between satanic and innocent spaces makes space the focus of the epic's continuing tension.

We arrive at the opening lines of *Paradise Regained* filled with the dense residue of this cosmos, for our experience of *Paradise Lost* does not free us of its presence. *Paradise Regained* immediately establishes its continuity with the earlier poem: the image of "*Eden* rais'd in the waste Wilderness" and the poet's desire to range "through height or depth of nature's bounds" (I, 7, 13) alert us to the spatial setting; the entrance of the Son of God incarnate, the dove's descent from heaven, and the Son's rise from the baptismal waters introduce vertical movement which culminates at the conclusion of the fourth book. Yet *Paradise Regained* duplicates neither the setting nor the spatial conflicts of *Paradise Lost*. Though ascent and descent are anticipated throughout *Paradise Regained*, vertical movement does not become even relatively vast or violent until the last book. The poem's spatial structure does generate dramatic tension, but its spatial contrasts are subtle and considerably more difficult to resolve.

The drama of *Paradise Lost* has prepared us for the limited space we enter in the fallen world of *Paradise Regained*. The narrative soon reveals the environment's new spatial configuration. The air now lies within Satan's kingdom, and he may circle the earth concealed from the eyes of men. His fallen angels remember well whose "fierce thunder drove [them] to the deep" (I, 90), yet they are now "to that hideous place not so confin'd" (I, 362); free to vex man, they "enjoy / Large liberty to round this Globe of Earth, / Or range in th' Air" (I, 364–66). But they favor the same psychic landscape; they still seek out dark, obscured, coiling spaces. Demonic councils take place "Within thick Clouds and dark tenfold involv'd, / A gloomy Consistory" (I, 41–42), and in "the middle Region of thick Air" (II, 117). Above all, Satan himself is still the spatial dissembler of the earlier poem, "involv'd in rising Mist," gliding obscurely in "midnight vapor" (*PL*, IX, 75, 159). It is a familiar figure who roams through *Paradise Regained*, "His easy steps, girded with snaky wiles," who "bowing low / His gray dissimulation, disappear'd / Into thin Air" (I, 120, 497–99).

From these shadowy, dank spaces we move to the physical and psychic landscape where the dramatic confrontations between Satan and Christ begin. The wilderness setting for the Son's fasting and trial recalls the "wild surrounding waste" of *Comus:* "He enter'd now the bordering Desert wild, / And with dark shades

and rocks environ'd round, / His holy Meditations thus pursu'd"
(I, 193–95). In this bleak, alien enclosure—the implacable setting
we associate with initiatory trials—the self must struggle to sustain
its human identity:

> And looking round on every side beheld
> A pathless Desert, dusk with horrid shades;
> The way he came not having mark'd, return
> Was difficult, by human steps untrod
> $\qquad\qquad$ (I, 295–98)

For forty days Christ wanders through a landscape without human
sustenance; it is unclear whether he even finds physical shelter:

> Full forty days he pass'd, whether on hill
> Sometimes, anon in shady vale, each night
> Under the covert of some ancient Oak,
> Or Cedar, to defend him from the dew,
> Or harbor'd in one Cave, is not reveal'd
> $\qquad\qquad$ (I, 303–7)

Christ's progress is continually related to the immense surrounding
waste, the dark convoluted expanse of successive dens. The wilderness is wide, barren, and savage, and Christ wanders "from shade
to shade," "tracing the Desert wild."

Satan designs his traps as alternatives to the barren and inhuman
qualities of this landscape. Disguised as "an aged man in Rural
weeds," he first offers merely to guide Christ back to civilization
and its human comforts. Undeceived, Christ replies calmly, "Who
brought me hither / Will bring me hence" (I, 335–36). Satan attempts to goad him into making bread from stone, but Christ puts
this aside—"Think'st thou such force in Bread?" (I, 347)—and goes
on his way. He sleeps that night in a bower of trees, and dreams,
"as appetite is wont to dream," of food. Rising in the morning, he
climbs a hill to "ken the prospect round"; in a valley he sees a
tempting forest enclosure: "Nature's own work it seem'd (Nature
taught Art)" (II, 295). The Son of God "view'd it round":

> Only in a bottom saw a pleasant Grove,
> With chant of tuneful Birds resounding loud.
> Thither he bent his way, determin'd there
> To rest at noon, and enter'd soon the shade
> High rooft, and walks beneath, and alleys brown
> That open'd in the midst a woody Scene
>
> (II, 289-94)

Satan at once appears dressed in court clothes, and tempts Jesus with a table of food so rich it parodies abundance, enclosed seductively "In ample space under the broadest shade."

In spatial terms, this temptation sets a crafted, superabundant, and protective enclosure against the immense and essentially empty wilderness. It is quite unlike the dramatic confrontations in *Paradise Lost*, where contrasted spaces represent two sets of theological or spiritual values at war—where a character's external, physical landscape clearly embodies qualities of his internal, psychic landscape. The images of Satan's temptation of Eve simultaneously contrast landscape, flesh, and consciousness. Satan enters Eden "wrapt in mist" to seek cover in serpent's flesh—"in whose mazy folds / To hide me, and the dark intent I bring" (*PL*, IX, 161-62) —and lies in wait for Eve "with hellish rancor imminent" (*PL*, IX, 409). Against this are set the idealized garden landscape of Eden and the innocent body and mind of Eve herself: "her look sums all Delight. / Such pleasure took the Serpent to behold / This Flow'ry Plat, the sweet recess of *Eve*" (*PL*, IX, 454-56).[2]

2. The contrast of innocent with satanic spaces is particularly clear in *Comus*, whose "usurping mists" and "thick shelter of black shades imbow'r'd" are contrasted with images of the Lady as a chaste and graceful enclosure. Following the pattern of "those immortal shapes / Of bright aërial Spirits [who] live inspher'd" (2-3), the Lady invokes Echo, a nymph living in an "airy shell," a "violet-embroidered vale," who may have led the Lady's brothers to "some flow'ry Cave." Echo is a "Daughter of the Sphere"; her pure, innocent wandering is bordered by margent green and the airy shell of the heavens. The Lady's chastity is represented as a civilized *hortus conclusus*, an enclosed and courtly garden. Comus couches his schemes of seduction in visions of the forest as a benevolent, dense enclosure, alternatively foreboding and enchanting—a "hideous Wood, / Immur'd in cypress shades" (520-21), a "close dungeon of innumerous boughs" (349), or a gentle "green mantling vine" (294) surmounted by "the spreading favor of these Pines" (184).

The temptations in *Paradise Regained* do not establish the poem's spatial structure by simply contrasting landscapes. In the banquet temptation, Satan's rich setting is no clear analogue for "the hot Hell that always in him burns" (*PL*, IX, 467); nor is Christ's final inwardness revealed by the barren wilderness he first inhabits, though it may mirror the unformed quality of his self-perception. The later temptations, which come to encompass all of earthly time and space, even less clearly represent opposing spaces within the world. For *Paradise Regained* takes place not in vast cosmic space but entirely in the fallen world of flesh: its internal and external landscapes are created by the limits and conditions of each character's perception.

Neither Christ nor Satan ever really sees space in the other's terms, though the same spaces lie before them both. There is no real conflict, because their alternative visions of incarnate space (or of the entire horizon of the fallen world) are mutually exclusive. What tension the poem generates directs us to Christ's growing self-awareness—Satan's doomed posturing helps educate the reader and Christ himself to a divine perspective. Satan thus proves "serviceable to Heaven's King" (I, 421). Presumably *Paradise Lost* has made us feel the need both to anticipate and participate in Christ's arrival. When we understand what it means for him to be the Son of God and man, our fallen world will cease to be a demonic enclosure. Like Satan's rejected banquet, it will vanish in thin air. When we can see the temptations as more of Satan's shape-changing, the fallen world will be emptied of his image and simultaneously illuminated by the presence of Christ.

"I know thy scope," Christ tells Satan: "compos'd of lies / From the beginning, and in lies wilt end" (I, 494, 407–8). For all Satan's rhetorical skill, his offers cannot exceed the scope of his own perceptions; he is fatally limited by his vision of time and space. His sense of passing time is frantic and desperate; he must constantly "on Occasion's forelock watchful wait" (III, 173). History is cacophonous for him, a series of moments to be captured and possessed before they pass away. Thus he can feel only contempt for

God's transcendence of time, and Christ's coming suggests only that no time is to be lost, that disaster is imminent:

> Long the decrees of Heav'n
> Delay, for longest time to him is short;
> And now too soon for us the circling hours
> This dreaded time have compast
>
> (I, 55–58)

He attempts to impose on Christ this sense of temporal anxiety and threat. Though Christ's reign is to be "endless," Satan argues that "The happier reign the sooner it begins" (III, 178–79). Fawning, he urges Christ to recognize himself matured "to a Kingdom's weight" (IV, 282), and warns him that "Thy years are ripe, and over-ripe" (III, 31). This fallen perception mirrors the anxiety of a world where even Christ's disciples begin to doubt him during his absence in the wilderness ("And as the days increas'd, increas'd thir doubt," II, 12). Christ, however, can expose Satan's visions on temporal grounds alone, for his own perception is shaped in the eschatological fullness of heavenly time, the eternity of God, "in whose hand all times and seasons roll" (III, 187). History for him is the rhythmic unfolding of all things in their appointed hour. The word of God is written, and Satan has no power over it. "What concerns it thee," Christ asks Satan ironically, "when I begin / My everlasting Kingdom?" (III, 198–99); "My time I told thee (and that time for thee / Were better farthest off) is not yet come" (III, 396–97); "I shall reign past thy preventing" (IV, 492).

Satan, "compos'd of lies," counterfeits his mounting fear in "the persuasive Rhetoric / That sleek't his tongue, and won so much on *Eve*" (IV, 4–5); he is admiring, threatening, abusive, self-pitying. His growing certainty that Christ really is the Son of God only goads him into renewed attack:

> as a swarm of flies in vintage time,
> About the wine-press where sweet must is pour'd,
> Beat off, returns as oft with humming sound;
> Or surging waves against a solid rock,

> Though all to shivers dash't, th'assault renew,
> Vain batt'ry, and in froth or bubbles end;
> So Satan, whom repulse upon repulse
> Met ever, and to shameful silence brought,
> Yet gives not o'er though desperate of success,
> And his vain importunity pursues.
>
> (IV, 15–24)

But their ostensible combat is not the genuine one. The danger is never that Christ will accept Satan's offers, but that he will accept the role of Adversary which Satan assigns to him—that he will see his choices, even for an instant, in satanic terms. It is not his integrity that Satan hopes to destroy, but his inaccessible inwardness, his calm refusal to open himself to Satan's vision of the confrontation. When Satan tempts Christ to use his powers as the Son of God, he tempts him to interact satanically, to respond as he would himself.

Satan sees himself at war with heaven to possess and conquer earth. To win, he must draw Christ out and engage him on familiar terrain—the embattled space of the fallen world which lies "Between two such enclosing enemies" (III, 361). But Christ is certain of his destiny as "heir of both worlds"; his detachment denies any other possibility. His responses not only expose Satan's offers as illusory visions, but they also deny the existence of confrontation. When Satan urges him to make bread from stones, he coolly answers, "Think'st thou such force in Bread? . . . Man lives not by Bread only, but each Word / Proceeding from the mouth of God" (I, 347–50). He unmasks Satan's rhetoric—"lying is thy sustenance, thy food"—as "dark, / Ambiguous and with double sense deluding" (I, 429, 434–35), and finally refuses any combative posture: "Thy coming hither," he tells Satan, "I bid not or forbid" (I, 494–95). In vain Satan tries to gain access to this supposed Adversary, to probe his nature and limits, to learn "In what degree or meaning thou art call'd / The Son of God" (IV, 516–17). His grandiose offers are not literal temptations, but provocations made in growing desperation. At last he makes a direct and explicit offer that is actually the most subtle of all: he tempts Christ to "fall down, / And worship me as thy superior Lord" (IV, 166–67). It is not the seductiveness of the offer that is dangerous, but its outrageousness. Christ would never fall down and worship the serpent, and Satan does not expect him to, but he might be goaded into punishing a blasphemous outrage. Satan again tempts Christ to act as he would himself: to accept the role of Adversary long enough to damn Satan for eternity, to wield then and there all the power of divinity alone. To do so would betray himself and disobey the will of God. But Christ remains unmoved by Satan's challenge: "I endure the time, till which expir'd, / Thou hast permission on me" (IV, 174–75). The Son ripens in God's time, not in Satan's.

As Satan's temptations escalate, Christ's responses begin to prefigure his final victory over sin and death on the cross. God's plan has been "To exercise him in the Wilderness; / There he shall first lay down the rudiments / Of his great warfare" (I, 156–58). Toward the end of the poem, Satan launches a furious assault on Christ's mind and body by turning on him all the negative force of his earthly enclosure. Under Satan's shadowy nighttime gaze, Christ settles down to sleep in an interwoven bower of trees, "Whose branching arms thick intertwin'd might shield / From dews and damps of night his shelter'd head" (IV, 405–6). Satan then wields supernatural power in a driving, elemental attack: "the Clouds / From many a horrid rift abortive pour'd / Fierce rain with lightning mixt, water with fire / In ruin reconcil'd"—"Infernal Ghosts, and Hellish Furies, round / Environ'd" (IV, 410–13, 422–23). But Jesus remains unthreatened and untroubled by the howling storm; through it all he remains "unappall'd in calm and sinless peace." Enraged by his lack of fear, Satan declares that the storm was never intended to threaten physical harm, but rather to foreshadow some darker and more terrifying fate, "Whereof this ominous night that clos'd thee round, / So many terrors, voices, prodigies / May warn thee, as a sure foregoing sign" (IV, 481–83). The storm is a sign, though it is anything but ominous to the Son of man, for it prefigures the dark night on Calvary when he will suffer and triumph as God incarnate in a human body. The storm brings to an end Christ's movement through the wilderness, for his preparation is complete: the wilderness has become the "Victorious Field" (I, 9). Though Satan cannot know it, the world can be threatening only by the illusory measure of fallen perception; the earth is a negative enclosure only to a consciousness that feels constricted by "the pillar'd frame of Heaven" and "the Earth's dark basis underneath" (IV, 455-56).

All Satan's offers reflect his image of the self. He envisions the self as limited and enclosed in its own space; he dreams of being "a King complete / Within thyself" (IV, 283-84). Even his flattery is framed in this image of isolated and self-sufficient identity: "thy heart," he tells Jesus, "Contains of good, wise, just, the perfect shape"; "in thee be united / What of perfection can in man be found" (III, 11, 229-30). When he offers space, whether of food or world, he offers an enclosure to be conquered and supplanted by the self: "as thy Empire must extend, / So let extend thy mind o'er all the world" (IV, 222-23). He soon realizes that so narrow an enclosure as a table in a shady bower will not tempt Christ; with this awareness he rejects Belial's advice to tempt Christ with a woman, luring him into some seductive glade. "These haunts / Delight not all," says Satan contemptuously; "Therefore with manlier objects we must try / His constancy" (II, 191-92, 225-26).

Satan offers worldly power, glory, and wisdom, and finally the inevitable bait of the world itself. "The world thou hast not seen, much less her glory," he tells Christ (III, 236), and from a mountaintop he lays out for Christ the whole world of nature and man: plains, rivers, seas, fertile fields of abundant crops, animals, birds, and "Huge cities and high tow'r'd, that well might seem / The seats of mightiest Monarchs; and so large / The Prospect was, that here and there was room / For barren desert fountainless and dry" (III, 261-64). Before Christ's eyes, the history of men and nations at war unfolds, while Satan fills his ears with strategies for conquest —"that thou mayst know / How best their opposition to withstand"

(III, 249–50). When this vast panorama ends at last, Christ calls it "Much ostentation" and "Plausible to the world, to mee worth naught" (III, 387, 393).[3]

Satan's visions of world conquest now culminate in the offer of Rome itself with all its wonders. "These having shown thee," he tells Christ, "I have shown thee all / The Kingdoms of the world, and all thir glory" (IV, 88–89):

> there the Capitol thou seest,
> Above the rest lifting his stately head
> On the *Tarpeian rock*, her Citadel
> Impregnable, and there Mount *Palatine*
> Th'Imperial Palace, compass huge, and high
> The Structure, skill of noblest Architects,
> With gilded battlements, conspicuous far,
> Turrets and Terraces, and glittering Spires.
>
> (IV, 47–54)

When Christ again responds that the vision is hollow and illusory, he responds to what Satan really offers: the literal space of his fallen perception. The golden city is Satan's richest vision of enclosure, his dream of worldly conquest at its peak. Yet the vision is firmly rooted in "Hell's deep-vaulted Den" (I, 116), where he inhabits the satanic temple described in *Paradise Lost:*

> The Roof was fretted Gold. . . .
>   Th' ascending pile
> Stood fixt her stately highth, and straight the doors

3. Beginning as space, Satan's vision becomes increasingly temporal and frenzied. This point has been noted by Jackson I. Cope, who suggests it illustrates the different symbolic structure of space and time in *Paradise Lost* and *Paradise Regained:* "At the ideational crisis of *Paradise Lost* time becomes space; at the ideational crisis of *Paradise Regained* space becomes time." *The Metaphoric Structure of "Paradise Lost"* (Baltimore, 1962), p. 68. But despite Christ's historicity, the anxious sense of passing time is Satan's. *Paradise Regained* as a whole, which Cope describes as "the exfoliation of the eternally given into time" (p. 69), is not urgent but permeated with Christ's calm. John Carey notes that the frequency of participles in the poem reinforces this quality, e.g., "the past participle freezes action into posture." John Milton, *Poems,* ed. John Carey and Alastair Fowler (London, 1968), pp. 1071–72.

> Op'ning thir brazen folds discover wide
> Within, her ample spaces, o'er the smooth
> And level pavement: from the arched roof
> Pendant by subtle Magic many a row
> Of Starry Lamps and blazing Cressets fed
> With *Naphtha* and *Asphaltus* yielded light
> As from a sky.
>
> (*PL*, I, 717, 722–30)

As the temple of Pandaemonium was built in hell in parody of heaven's beauty, the Roman Capitol that lifts its stately head above the gilded battlements is only the roof of fretted gold, the glittering pinnacle at stately height, rising above the brazen folds and ample spaces of Satan's demonic enclosure. The pillars of the hellish temple and the ascending pile become the turrets and terraces, the glittering spires, of Satan's vision of Rome. The vision lies wholly within the realm of his own experience: what he has made in hell he makes on earth. Christ sees this clearly. Satan says the conquest of Rome would expel the Emperor, "A brutish monster" and "Hated of all, and hating"; but Christ retorts, "what if I withal / Expel a Devil who first made him such?" (IV, 128–29). Rejecting Rome and its "sumptuous gluttonies," he rejects all satanic space; he rejects its psychic hollowness and ravenous greed, however "Plausible to the world" its illusory glitter. For, finally, the realm of Satan's perception is no more than the space of his own head, "enclos'd / In Serpent":

> Circular base of rising folds, that tow'r'd
> Fold above fold a surging Maze, his Head
> Crested aloft, and Carbuncle his Eyes;
> With burnisht Neck of verdant Gold, erect
> Amidst his circling Spires, that on the grass
> Floated redundant
>
> (*PL*, IX, 498–503)

Satan's brazen head, surfacing above thick coils of ingrown space, is the landscape of each temptation. The Capitol's stately head, lifted above the city's gilded battlements and glittering spires, is Satan's own, crested aloft above the burnished neck of verdant gold. The turrets and battlements of Rome, the brazen folds and ample spaces of Pandaemonium, are illusions, once more the coiling redundancy of serpentine flesh. This impenetrable maze of serpent flesh gives the temptations their increasing sense of dense overabundance, of almost suffocating excess. Far richer than the banquet, Rome is a whole city ripening with abundance, near rotten in its plenitude. And rising above its "mass of sinful flesh" is the deadly head "erect / Amidst his circling Spires," the image behind every temptation. Satan's final offer of himself as an object of worship only makes literal and manifest what has been true all along—that he creates his temptations from himself. He offers Christ the whole world, but any world he offers must begin and end in the enclosed space of his own head.

Christ's rejections prefigure his final victory over Satan and his demonic visions—the final moment, foretold in *Paradise Lost*, when the seed of Eve will bruise the serpent's head:

> And on the Serpent thus his curse let fall.
>   Because thou hast done this, thou art accurst
> Above all Cattle, each Beast of the Field;
> Upon thy Belly groveling thou shalt go,
> And dust shalt eat all the days of thy Life.
> Between Thee and the Woman I will put
> Enmity, and between thine and her Seed;
> Her Seed shall bruise thy head, thou bruise his heel.
>
>   (*PL*, X, 174–81)

In the fullness of time, Satan's monarchy will be dashed to pieces by the Son of God. The ultimate bruising of the serpent's head will evacuate its illusions with the influx of eternity. At the height of its thick, flowing opulence, Satan's head will be dissolved (II, 438). The world will be emptied, its wiles void (III, 443). "So well," Satan tells Jesus in the Rome temptation, "I have dispos'd / My Airy Microscope thou mayst behold / Outside and inside both" (IV, 56–58). If one chose to look, he would discover no more than a glittering shell enclosing outraged space. The "conflux issuing forth or ent'ring in" is another illusion, again the serpent's "well couch't fraud, well woven snares" (I, 97). He hopes in vain that Christ could be "A shelter and a kind of shading cool / Interposition, as a summer's cloud" (III, 221–22), an obscuring haze protecting selfhood from the light of God. But it is the serpent's head that will become at last "an empty cloud."

The prophecy that Christ will bruise the serpent's head is also the prophecy that he will "dissolve / *Satan* with his perverted World" (*PL*, XII, 546–47), that he will "obstruct the mouth of Hell / For ever, and seal up his ravenous Jaws" (*PL*, X, 636–37). When Satan's temptations are seen in this most world-devouring sense, the world of the poem takes clearer shape. Increasing energy is focused on the psychic landscape of *Paradise Regained* as the entire fallen world raises its glittering head against its own salvation. Satan returns from Christ to tell the demonic council he has encountered the enemy—"found him, view'd him, tasted him" (II, 131), "And now I know he hungers where no food / Is to be found" (II, 231–32). The mouth of hell sees itself everywhere, ravenous and insatiable. Satan can offer a world of fallen flesh because it is himself and what he feeds upon. The serpent is self-devouring: he reveals a satanic image of nature as an open-mouthed leviathan, a fallen world that plots to devour its own Son.

But Christ need not take the world as Satan knows it, or the fallen order of nature that Satan possesses. Though Christ is to encounter the same physical world, his submission to it creates an altogether different psychic space. The world, turning on its Son, will turn upon itself and be undone.[4]

4. That Satan and Christ inhabit, and inherit, the same world is apparent in the verbal structure of their encounters. As Northrop Frye writes, "good and evil are inseparable in the fallen world, and, in a world where all instruments are corrupted, one must either use corrupt instruments or not act at all." "The Typology of *Paradise Regained*," *Milton: Modern Essays in Criticism*, ed. Arthur E. Barker (New York, 1965), p. 433. Hence "all the elements of the dialectical conflict are attached to a material context by Satan and to a spiritual one by Christ," p. 436. Milton constructs "a double argument on the same words, each highly plausible and yet as different as light from darkness," p. 440.

We learn in Book II that Christ, "tracing the Desert wild, / Sole, but with holiest Meditations fed, / Into himself descended" (II, 109–11). This descent is at once physical and mental, walking and thinking—"Thought following thought, and step by step led on" (I, 192). To himself he muses, "now by some strong motion I am led / Into this Wilderness" (I, 290–91). It is the motion of his divine mind in the maze of human flesh: "led, but with such thoughts / Accompanied of things past and to come / Lodg'd in his breast" (I, 299–301). Christ journeys as the Son of God incarnate. He wanders in the wilderness of the flesh, the "woody maze" of his body; as he walks, he seeds this human body with his mind.

Satan's perception of Christ's wandering is that "he hungers where no food / Is to be found"; to Christ, feeding his body with thoughts, hunger is no part of what he suffers:

> I feel I hunger, which declares
> Nature hath need of what she asks; yet God
> Can satisfy that need some other way,
> Though hunger still remain: so it remain
> Without this body's wasting, I content me
> (II, 252–56)

"Enshrin'd / In fleshly Tabernacle, and human form, / Wand'ring the Wilderness" (IV, 598–600), Christ's body becomes the book of nature. For the Son of God and man is the Word incarnate, the word from which the book of nature is written and to which it will return.[5] As Christ walks, the book of nature reveals its movement toward the word of God; in his own flesh, he reads the meaning of his incarnation.

What Satan never imagines, what he is never prepared for, is Christ's growing understanding of his incarnation. The body, for Christ, is no fallen enclosure, no despised boundary which confines his consciousness. This is beyond the comprehension of Satan, who sees all incarnation as he sees his own:

5. Cf. John 1:14: "And the Word was made flesh, and dwelt among us"—literally, pitched his tent or tabernacle among us.

> O foul descent! that I who erst contended
> With Gods to sit the highest, am now constrain'd
> Into a Beast, and mixt with bestial slime,
> This essence to incarnate and imbrute,
> That to the highth of Deity aspir'd
>
> (*PL*, IX, 163-67)

Flesh is what Satan makes of it, flesh without freedom or re-demption. The fall from angelic ecstasy must remain for him a frantic battle against time and space, against the intolerable and galling confinement of his poisoned perception. There is no al-ternative vision for the Prince of Darkness; though scorning Belial because "in much uneven scale thou weigh'st / All others by thy-self" (II, 173-74), his only measure of Christ's experience is his own. Satan's experience is self-perpetuating: as he finds his physi-cal envelope repugnant, it becomes so, and imprisons him forever in bestial slime. Flesh is the boundary Satan seeks to overcome; for Christ it is the space he must illuminate, the boundary to which he must submit himself totally. Satan cannot understand this. For him the divine vision of incarnation as pure light "enshrin'd / In fleshly Tabernacle, and human form" does not exist.

In *Paradise Lost*, wandering was under Satan's control: the doomed wandering of Adam and Eve was, for the Tempter, merely a measure of his success. But Christ's wandering is a pro-cess of self-discovery that remains a mystery to Satan. Though he closely follows its progress, it leaves no track on his barren space, for "Hard are the ways of truth, and rough to walk" (I, 478). He never perceives the nature of Christ's journey: "think'st thou to regain / Thy right by sitting still or thus retiring?"; "Why move thy feet so slow to what is best" (III, 163-64, 224). Again and again he is amazed, perplexed, confounded, mute—the qualities which once were Eve's and now describe mankind as well. As Christ wanders his woody maze, remaining calm under trial, his increas-ing enlightenment accompanies Satan's growing confusion. Their encounters move toward the final confrontation in Book IV, when Satan "smitten with amazement fell" (562). This consummate moment prefigures Satan's final downfall, when the serpent's head will be bruised by the seed of Eve and emptied forever of its words and lies, rendered amazed and mute for eternity.

Satan understands this as well as Christ. He has witnessed Jesus' baptism with "dread attending when that fatal wound / Shall be inflicted by the Seed of *Eve* / Upon my head," and warns the demonic council that the "Woman's seed / Destin'd to this, is late of woman born" (I, 53–55, 64–65). God meanwhile proclaims that Satan "now shall know I can produce a man / Of female Seed, far abler to resist / All his solicitations" (I, 150–52). Jesus' resistance takes form as total submission, which is no part of Satan's world. Repeatedly unsuccessful, yet bound by his own nature, Satan must play out the fated role of aggressor in his own defeat. "My rising," Christ reminds him, "is thy fall" (III, 201). But *Paradise Regained* does not include this final vertical displacement. The poem is rather a preparation for Christ's death and resurrection, the upward movement which will empty Satan's head of its devoured content, the world.

The seed of Eve is the fruit of Mary's virginal womb; Jesus has grown "to youth's full flow'r" (I, 67) when he "receives / Light from above, from the fountain of light" (IV, 288–89). Jesus' first act is to nurture the seed of divinity in himself, to seed his body with his mind. Moving through the wilderness, he revolves the law of God in his breast and muses on his role. His circling meditation is not the serpent's coiling movement around a hollow center; as Satan is unable to realize, Christ moves in imitation of angels circling the throne of God (I, 171). He descends into himself to find the plenitude of his flesh: "O what a multitude of thoughts at once / Awak'n'd in me swarm" (I, 196–97). Christ's infinite swarm of thoughts, egg-spawn of cosmic generation, is set against the swarm of Satan's schemes and desires—hive of death and spawn of corruption, the "swarm of flies in vintage time" whose illusory and feverish humming fills the shell of his empty head.

But Christ's head is the fruit of the seed of Eve, planted and nurtured in Mary's virginal womb. Mary's innocence, even then, threatened the pitiless womb of nature's fallen order, Satan's den, the mouth of hell. Since first learning her destiny, she "Meekly compos'd awaited the fulfilling" (II, 108)—the informing potency of the Son of man. Her "heart hath been a storehouse long of things / And sayings laid up, portending strange events" (II, 103–4). Now she has borne her seed, which is putting down roots in the barren waste of the wilderness where Christ prepares himself to transform Satan's sinful world:

> my way must lie
> Through many a hard assay even to the death,
> Ere I the promis'd Kingdom can attain,
> Or work Redemption for mankind, whose sins'
> Full weight must be transferr'd upon my head.
> (I, 263–67)

As an iconographic and phenomenological image, the human head is a seedpod at the end of a spinal stalk. In Christ's head the seed of Eve is born, and flowers in his body as the Son of man. His head is at last the fruit which the cross will bear in heaven, the resurrected seed of Eve. In *Paradise Regained*, Christ nurtures the seed of Eve on earth, making the wilderness fruitful with the word of God; when his preparation is complete, he will return from the wilderness to flower as a "living Oracle" of the Word and be an "inward Oracle" that flowers in the hearts of men. In the fullness of time, this flowering "shall be like a tree / Spreading and overshadowing all the Earth" (IV, 147–48). The kingdom of God will grow to overarch the heavens, an infinite eschatological bower subsuming time and space.

Christ prepares his body for death and resurrection, for its posture of crucifixion and victory. In the fourth book he stands at the still center of the poem, pointed—in calm imitation of his death—toward heaven. This figural posture is achieved by the serpent's last temptation, his last attempt to force Christ to mimic satanic selfhood and isolation. On top of the pinnacle, Satan tempts Christ to fall—in safety if he is the Son of God. Christ can stand only if the posture is the inevitable realization of his body. Later he will use no miracles to save himself from crucifixion. Nor can he be tempted now. No choice, not even the smallest decision, can be sustained in his fragile balance—his prophetic destiny must be embodied in his flesh alone. "Tempt not the Lord thy God," he says, and stands, "But Satan smitten with amazement fell" (IV, 561–62). Christ's words are not spoken in presumption or proud self-assertion: they give witness to his posture as the reflection on Satan's act. In his words is all the natural outpouring of potent life.

But in Satan's amazement and stricken fall, the serpent's head reveals the secret form of its labyrinthine hollowness:

> So after many a foil the Tempter proud,
> Renewing fresh assaults, amidst his pride
> Fell whence he stood to see his Victor fall.
> And as that *Theban* Monster that propos'd
> Her riddle, and him who solv'd it not, devour'd,
> That once found out and solv'd, for grief and spite
> Cast herself headlong from th' *Ismenian* steep,
> So struck with dread and anguish fell the Fiend.
> (IV, 569–76)

The image of the sphinx unveils Satan as both tempter and temptress in one, an emblem for the isolated and sterile self, eternally at war. The snares, the labyrinthine words, "dark, / Ambiguous and with double sense deluding," have had not only the doubleness of disguised purposes but also the doubleness of the hermaphrodite, the aggressively glittering male head and its seductive female hollowness. The only real temptation for Christ, perhaps, was Satan's inhabitable emptiness—the female space within the surface glitter of his cresting head. The temptation of a woman might indeed have been the only appropriate one for Satan to have offered. Christ would have rejected her, but not as he rejected Satan's sterile illusions: he would not have expressed contempt for her body, but placed its ripeness in a context of cosmic femaleness.

The poem ends with Christ poised toward the divine space he has discovered in himself by wandering the labyrinth of his body.

God nourishes his Son with "Fruits fetcht from the tree of life" and "from the fount of life Ambrosial drink" (IV, 589–90), ending the long fast. Christ's preparation is figurally complete. The final lines of the poem return him, the seed of Eve, to "his Mother's house," from which he will "Now enter, and begin to save mankind" (IV, 639, 635). The Son of God has come to understand how flesh can endure the influx of divinity; he has come to understand his incarnation, and thus embodies the ultimate inwardness foretold by Christian theology—the paradise within. To be incarnated is to be both the container and the vehicle, both the tabernacle and the oracle of divinity. Christ incarnate is both the stillness and the wind of God.

Paradise Lost places the fallen world within a cosmic myth that makes death tolerable. *Paradise Regained* opens the world to an influx of eternity that makes death imminent. The space of the poem lies between the Eden where Satan enviously witnessed Adam and Eve "Imparadis't in one another's arms" (*PL*, IV, 506) and the new Eden "rais'd in the waste wilderness."[6] The massing decay of the fallen world, its ripening death, is a source of energy; inhabited by Christ instead of Satan, the world can be transformed and made divine again. Christ's kingdom is the rock that will shatter Satan's and redeem its mass of sinful flesh. *Paradise Regained* prepares us to regain a perfectly integrated sexuality—a sexuality, cosmic and transcendent, bodied forth in the potency of light itself enclosed in human flesh. The protagonist will be Christ

6. The poem's imagery reflects the "flowering of the wilderness between the first book and the last," *Poems*, ed. Carey and Fowler, p. 1076. Christ seeds the barren and sterile land and makes it fruitful. This potency is more than a figure of speech: "O Cross, that art planted in the earth but bearest fruit in heaven," quoted by Hugo Rahner, *Greek Myths and Christian Mystery* (London, 1963), p. 54. In the poem, the potency of the cross enters Jesus at his baptism, which, as Frye writes, symbolizes for Milton the death, burial, and resurrection to come. Pictorial art often shows a cross in the Jordan during Christ's baptism: "This cross . . . is the symbol of the crucified Christ himself who makes the baptismal water fruitful with his blood," Rahner, pp. 80–81. "Baptism is the mystery of the wood in water" through which the cross becomes the tree of life; "Through the sign of the cross you are conceived in the womb of your holy Mother," Rahner, pp. 79, 78.

crucified, and his bed will be the cross. Christ's crucified body is the vehicle through which the seed of Eve will be planted in heaven. Symbolically the poem points the fallen reader in the direction of paradise. Its final posture: Christ standing at the still center of the turning world—a stone phallus in the womb of nature.

Intimate decay

And someone else might feel something scratching in
his mouth. He goes to the mirror, opens his mouth:
and his tongue is an enormous, live centipede, rubbing
its legs together and scraping his palate. He'd like to
spit it out, but the centipede is a part of him and he will
have to tear it out with his own hands.

Jean-Paul Sartre, Nausea, 159

Violet bruises come out
all over his flesh, as invisible
fists start beating him a last time; the whine
of omphalos blood starts up again, the puffed
bellybutton explodes, the carnal
nightmare soars back to the beginning.

Galway Kinnell, Book of Nightmares, 37

that posture of familiar failure, the stomach sagging, the
chest shapeless, the shoulders hunched forward as if it
were easier to walk that way, leaning forward into a
future of pure gravity.

Joyce Carol Oates, Them, 53

If our bodies merely crumpled into unconsciousness
instead of gliding off joint by joint, falling asleep would
be a sudden drop into space while the brain looked on
watching the trunk slip from under like a ripe peach.

Malcolm de Chazal, Plastic Sense, 57

the father of a family might go out for a walk, and,
across the street, he'll see something like a red rag, blown
towards him by the wind. And when the rag has

gotten close to him he'll see that it is a side of rotten meat, grimy with dust, dragging itself along by crawling, skipping, a piece of writhing flesh rolling in the gutter, spasmodically shooting out spurts of blood.

Sartre, *Nausea*, 159

The search for myself is ended, I am buried in the world. . . .

Gurgles of outflow. This tangle of grey bodies is they.

Samuel Beckett, *Three Novels*, 199, 287

The head is all pliable and elastic, as though it had been simply set on my neck; if I turn it, it will fall off. All the same, I hear a short breath and from time to time, out of the corner of my eye I see a reddish flash covered with hair. It is a hand.

Sartre, *Nausea*, 19

It is in the tranquility of decomposition that I remember the long confused emotion which was my life. . . . To decompose is to live too, I know. . . . I listen and the voice is of a world collapsing endlessly. . . . For all things run together, in the body's long madness. I feel it. . . . My body does not yet make up its mind. But I fancy it weighs heavier on the bed, flattens and spreads. . . . the sensation is familiar of a blind and tired hand delving feebly in my particles and letting them trickle between its fingers. And sometimes, when all is quiet, I feel it plunged in me up to the elbow, but gentle, and, as though sleeping. But soon it stirs, wakes, fondles, clutches, ransacks, ravages, avenging its failure to scatter me with one sweep. . . . But this sensation of dialation is hard to resist. . . . my feet are leagues away. And to call them in, to be cleaned for example, would I think take me more than a month, exclusive of the time required to locate them. . . . it is a great smooth ball I carry on my shoulders, featureless, but for the eyes,

of which only the sockets remain. And were it not for
the distant testimony of my palms, my soles, which
I have not yet been able to quash, I would gladly give
myself the shape, if not the consistency, of an egg, with
two holes no matter where to prevent it from bursting,
for the consistency is more like that of mucilage.

Beckett, *Three Novels*, 25, 40,
56, 198, 224, 234, 305

He lay still, in a kind of dream of anguish. His
thirst seemed to have separated itself from him, and to
stand apart, a single demand. Then the pain he felt
was another single self. Then there was the clog of his
body, another separate thing. He was divided among
all kinds of separate things. There was some strange,
agonised connection between them, but they were drawing farther apart. Then they would all split. The sun,
drilling down on him, was drilling through the bond.
Then they would all fall, fall through the everlasting
lapse of space.

It left the soul unburdened, brooding in dark nakedness.
In the end, the soul is alone, brooding on the face of
the uncreated flux, as a bird on a dark sea. . . . The thick
darkness of blood alone.

D. H. Lawrence, "The Prussian Officer,"
"England, My England"

7. Carsten Svennson, untitled.

FIVE

Form and claustrophobia:
intestinal space in
A Tale of a Tub

spend your life looking at yourself in a mirror, and
you'll see Death at work like a swarm of bees storing up
honey in a hive of glass

> Jean Cocteau, *Orpheus*

death. . . . which thogh nauseous to queasier stomachs,
yet to prepared appetites is Nectar and a pleasant
potion of immortality.

> Sir Thomas Browne, *Religio Medici*, 85

I daresay the soil would be quite fat with corpse
manure, bones, flesh, nails, charnelhouses. Dreadful.
Turning green and pink, decomposing. Rot quick in
damp earth. The lean old ones tougher. Then a kind
of a tallowy kind of a cheesy. Then begin to get black,
treacle oozing out of them. Then dried up. Deathmoths.
Of course the cells or whatever they are go on living.
Changing about. Live for ever practically. Nothing to
feed on feed on themselves.

But they must breed a devil of a lot of maggots. Soil
must be simply swirling with them. Your head it
simply swurls. Those pretty little seaside gurls.

> James Joyce, *Ulysses*, 107

When Swift describes satire most conventionally, it is simply a
weapon: "*Ink* is the great missive Weapon, in all Battels of the
Learned." It is "convey'd thro' a sort of Engine, call'd a *Quill*," and

"infinite Numbers of these are darted at the Enemy" (*B*, 221).[1]
When this "malignant Liquor" compounded of "Bitterness and
Venom" (*B*, 221) is compressed in a book, the satiric text becomes
"an *offensive* Weapon," "a Vessel full of *Ordure*" (*B*, 251), whose
contents are flung at the enemy. When the enemy is sufficiently
bespattered, when even his self-image has been eaten away by the
acid of satire, then—presumably—the satirist can withdraw and
wash his hands. If not altogether unsullied, he is at least victorious.
Of course the danger is that the pleasures of combat will outweigh
its moral purposes; like Bentley and Wotton in *The Battel of the
Books*, the satirist may grow addicted to the flavor of "some *Carcass*
half devoured, the Refuse of gorged Wolves, or ominous Ravens"
(*B*, 253). Compromised by the offensive manner he is forced to
assume, he himself can eventually become infected by the corruption he attacks; he can become his enemy's double.

These pitfalls can be avoided if the satiric weapon is superbly
efficient. The effective satire directs all its fire toward the enemy;
it calls no attention to itself, because its style is purely functional
and its form is essentially invisible. Political satire achieves this
effect easily when the reader shares the writer's political or moral
assumptions. The reader assumes himself unscathed because he
wants to be: he cooperates in burning up the language as he reads—
it leaves no residue.[2] At the least, however, we require a satire to
keep its object clearly in view and to maintain a consistent logic
and accelerated pace. We must be given no chance to lose our bear-
ings, no pause for contemplation. Frustrated or confused, our rage
might turn upon itself; a satire which retains the energy it generates becomes, inevitably, a repellent object itself.

Notoriously, *A Tale of a Tub* displays almost none of the characteristics of an efficient satire. Its style is self-assertive, its progress

1. Swift's works are abbreviated as follows and documented internally: *B—
The Battel of the Books*; *D—A Discourse Concerning the Mechanical Operation
of the Spirit*; *T—A Tale of a Tub*. All quotations are from Jonathan Swift, *A
Tale of a Tub*, ed. A. C. Guthkelch and D. Nichol Smith (Oxford, 1958).

2. Cf. Roland Barthes's analysis of political writing in *Writing Degree Zero*,
trans. Annette Lavers and Colin Smith (London, 1967), pp. 25-34.

labyrinthine. Its formlessness is noted by all its critics. Despite references to contemporary quarrels, the *Tale*'s satiric object is no timely enemy but rather timeless human vice; the book reveals no uncorrupted values. The reader feels that the *Tale* satirizes *everything* and at the same time manages to create the satiric object entirely within its own boundaries.[3] Moreover, this self-created object swells to fill the entire text; retaining all the energy it generates, the *Tale* is its own enemy. Swift's book is a single repellent object which, in its universality, embodies everything we affirm and everything we revile. It achieves this effect not through deliberate contradictory assertions but through its very formlessness: we cannot find our way through its mass of digressions without succumbing helplessly to an overwhelming sense of claustrophobia. A convoluted mass of sameness begins to fill our minds.

Two aspects of the text, related to the interaction between the central allegory and the surrounding metaphors and digressions, contribute to this experience. The protagonists of the splintered narrative are virtually interchangeable and offer us no straightforward pathway through the text; still, the fragments of narrative—digressive and inconclusive though they are—imply that the tale will eventually reach a definitive conclusion. At the same time, the book builds a dense and increasingly ubiquitous field of metaphoric associations which, diffusing and dispersing us through the text, continually subvert the suggestion of linear narrative. The narrative, moreover, though initially discrete, soon takes on the characteristics of the rambling metaphors; because they are discontinuous and arbitrarily bounded, the narrative segments lose their temporal movement and no longer seem to take us anywhere.

3. As Northrop Frye observes in his essay on satire, "a kind of parody of form seems to run all through its tradition." *Anatomy of Criticism* (New York, 1966), p. 233. Yet self-parody is not enough to make us this uneasy. Many contemporary satirists—George Orwell, Iris Murdoch, and Anthony Burgess are examples—undermine every point of view within a book while sustaining our sense of the author's secure control over his materials and his craft. The same can be said of *Gulliver's Travels*. Swift, however, is not the only satirist with an early work whose form is demonically anarchic. Compare Ben Jonson's *Every Man Out of His Humour* with a later work like *The Alchemist*.

But the metaphors, as the tale progresses, become increasingly explicit and concise. As Swift suggests, this tenuous balance succeeds only through our participation: "the Assembly has a considerable Share, as well as the Preacher. . . . They violently strain their Eye balls inward, half closing the Lids; Then, as they sit, they are in a perpetual Motion of *See-saw*" (*D*, 271).

The introductory material and appended satires might be expected to mitigate our experience. Yet the clarity of form and imagery in *The Battel of the Books* and *A Discourse Concerning the Mechanical Operation of the Spirit* makes our memory of the *Tale*'s formlessness disturbingly persistent. Similarly, an ironic preface could help us view the central text in terms of the open discourse of the world; its external perspective could reduce the *Tale*'s amorphous immensity to a pathetic trapped space, the pitiful refuge of a solipsistic mind denying itself the world's diversity. But the safe distance that prefaces ordinarily achieve is utterly lost in the veritable riot of frames before the text: the apology and its postscript, the dedications, disclaimers, preface, and introduction —with their changing and ambiguous points of view and different composition dates—only serve to blur the edges of the text and allow its texture into the outside world. It intrudes upon us across its boundaries—we are given too many entrances; the *Tale* has too many mouths. Even after we have entered it, we do not simply remain there, for the text itself displays an unpredictable pattern of excursus and return; Swift continually carries us out to the public domain for objective data that he draws back into the language of his private world. The book's form is filled by devouring the content of our world and replacing it with a subjective arrangement all Swift's own. In this sense he can indeed claim that he writes about nothing, for inside the tub the familiar world no longer exists. The book's uncompromising self-assertion lets the mind move at will from no thought to all thought, for the *Tale* unfolds its thought in a vacuum.

In typically disarming fashion, Swift disguises his own obsession with the book's demented form—he remarks innocently that "some

Authors inclose Digressions in one another, like a Nest of Boxes"
(*T*, 124), but describes "an ill-bred People" who "pronounce the
Example it self, a Corruption and Degeneracy of Taste. They tell
us, that the Fashion of jumbling fifty Things together in a Dish,
was at first introduced in Compliance to a depraved and *debauched
Appetite*, as well as to a *crazy Constitution*" (*T*, 143–44). By such
devices—or by pranks like admitting glibly that the *Tale*'s structure is often entirely whimsical—Swift can pose as the cool observer
who studies the world's madness only to mimic it; in the midst of
madness, he can claim his mimicry is detached, deliberate, method-
ical. Having dissected our carcass, he has since in his book "been
at a great Expence to fit up all the Bones with exact Contexture,
and in due Symmetry" (*T*, 123). No matter that the book's symmetry is formless and the texture appalling, for he pleasantly assures us we will feel entirely at home. Swift's story of Jack's coat
may offer a fitting parable for our perception: Jack, tired of being
confused with his overdressed brother, attempts to emphasize the
contrast by tearing his own coat and grinding away every bit of its
lace and trimmings; but observers continue to mistake him for his
brother, because "it is the Nature of Rags, to bear a kind of mock
Resemblance to Finery . . . which is not to be distinguished at a
Distance, in the Dark, or by short-sighted Eyes" (*T*, 200). If we
force a great distance between the book and ourselves, or if we im-
merse ourselves in it entirely and grow blind in its lightless depths,
or if we mistrust our own reading experience and accept Swift's
disclaimers—we will be deceived.

Despite Swift's self-effacing and often superficial evasions, *A
Tale of a Tub* maintains its recurrent motifs and obsessions with
unsettling consistency. When we understand the book as a reading
experience, we realize that these motifs recur in the midst of un-
relenting formlessness. And accordingly, our need for critical control over the *Tale* expresses less an impulse toward clarity than a
justified defense against genuine threat. For all its savage wit and
universal humor, *A Tale of a Tub* is a deeply frightening book.
Oddly, it seems longer than its objective length; it hovers un-

nervingly between total shapelessness and potential resolution—between the doubtful relief of disintegration and the threat of some conclusive horror that promises no security at all. We become lost in reading the *Tale*, yet we are afraid to be found.

No wonder we quail at Swift's invitation to become one with the writer, to enter the text and place ourselves at its voracious center (*T*, 44). Yet it is Swift's way to mock our terror. When we can finally see the exit from this tub of vapors, Swift audaciously asks that the reader "not expect to be equally diverted and informed by every Line, or every Page of this Discourse; but give some Allowance to the Author's Spleen . . . as well as his own" (*T*, 209). Coming as it does at the end of his book, this request is anything but ingenuous; it is too late to undo what has already happened to us, and if instead his words seem a generous invitation to read the book again, they become almost sinister. We may celebrate the end of this book, but in a different way: "The Conclusion of a Treatise, resembles the Conclusion of Human Life, which hath sometimes been compared to the End of a Feast" (*T*, 208). A feast, yes, a feast for worms, and the verbal rhythms of the *Tale* are no less insinuating. If we have any doubts about Swift's designs on us, we should place the repeated invocations to our gentleness and intelligence beside his boasts of power over us. With double-edged frankness, he admits to many ploys for keeping "a firm Hold upon my gentle Readers"—not the least of which is curiosity, "that Ring in the Nose, of a lazy, an impatient, and a grunting Reader. By this *Handle* it is, that an Author should seize upon his Readers" (*T*, 203).

When we acknowledge the unique verbal texture of the *Tale*, when we submit to the alarming virulence of its scatology and the pervasive quagmire of its form, it becomes almost impossible to believe that the book exists simply to unmask fraudulence and apply moral censure. Yet it is not surprising that critics have worked hard to pin down the elusive objects of the satire. By clearly delineating what is wrong with the institutions and individuals Swift attacks, we can imply that their reverse is the book's positive vision.[4] Swift would recognize this response to his book, for satire is *"a sort of* Glass, *wherein Beholders do generally discover every body's Face but their Own"* (*B*, 215); "even, I my self, the Author of these momentous Truths, am a Person, whose Imaginations are hard-mouth'd, and exceedingly disposed to run away with his *Reason"* (*T*, 180). Perhaps Swift is merely displaying the kind of humility that validates even the most uncompromising moral censure. Yet the book is his creation, and as the bee tells the spider, *"if we may judge of the Liquor in the Vessel by what issues out, You possess a good plentiful Store of Dirt and Poison in your Breast"* (*B*, 232). In satiric books, Swift tells us, there "is wonderfully instilled and preserved, the Spirit of each Warrior, while he is alive; and after his Death, his Soul transmigrates there, to inform them" (*B*, 222). Its timeless quality leads us to see *A Tale of a Tub*, with its consuming dread of corruption, as a prophetic autobiography. If, as Swift suggests, we "have a Way of reading a Man's Destiny, by peeping in his *Breech"* (*D*, 284), and if a man's life is

4. Development in the concepts of mask and persona provides some critics with a compromise view that allows Swift to remain essentially rational while the *Tale* itself becomes nihilistic. They conclude that Swift intentionally made the *Tale* a model of madness; it contains no real system of positive values, because it fully embodies everything Swift despised. Of course some surgery then has to be done on the reading experience; otherwise the critic appears to be a doctor who cures his patient by helping him forget he is diseased. So the *Tale* becomes a delirious extravagance that makes its corruptions absurd by exaggerating them. The most straightforward version of this thesis is in Irvin Ehrenpreis, *Mr. Swift and His Contemporaries*, vol. I of his *Swift: The Man, His Works, and the Age* (Cambridge, Mass., 1962), particularly pp. 185–246.

The approach is somewhat useful in allowing critics who must dominate the *Tale*'s destructive vision to give some credence to the form. Ronald Paulson, *Theme and Structure in Swift's "Tale of a Tub"* (New Haven, 1960), is able to describe many of the metaphoric relationships. Jay Levine, "The Design of *A Tale of a Tub* (With a Digression on a Mad Modern Critic)," *English Literary History* 33 (1966), 198–227, concludes that Swift deliberately imitates the egomania of a modern sacred critic in order to satirize it; but Levine is nonetheless able to make valid observations about the *Tale*'s form: "The allegory of the *Tale* is not the center, or kernel but the enveloping shell; within that shell is the Worm, the Self, the Nothingness (all suggestively satanic in implication) of the digressions. The meaning of the *Tale* resides precisely in its emptiness, in its dose of wormwood," p. 214; "In the last pages the ascendant Critic is left writing upon Nothing [*T*, 208]—that is, quite frankly spinning the words out of his inner void," p. 217.

best understood from the perspective of its end, then this demented and brilliant book compels us to regard its "*Posteriors*."

If *A Tale of a Tub* embodies the satirist's fury against those who take the word in vain and those who wish to build a world entirely of words, it also embodies Swift's gracious assurance that "the true ultimate End of *Ethicks*" is "my Reader's *Repose, both of Body and Mind*" (*T*, 140). When he elsewhere expresses the desire to have "contributed to the *Repose* of Mankind" (*T*, 208), he does not make clear, perhaps, what repose he has in mind. But in *The Battel of the Books*, the malevolent goddess deceives a verbal warrior and leads him into a "peaceful Bower," where he is "disarmed, and assigned to his Repose" (*B*, 248). The ultimate repose is death, though in Swift even death has unsuspected ambiguities: "The Torture of the Pain, whirled the valiant *Bow-man* round, till Death, like a Star of superior Influence, drew him into his own *Vortex*" (*B*, 244). Whether we are drawn into the vortex of this book or whether we withdraw defensively into our own, we will be undone. Whether we accept Swift's dark vision or reject it, whether we construct positive values for him or substitute our own, our response will be violent enough to destroy our security. For the reader cannot avoid the words which seed the text—"which, however scattered at random, when they light upon a fruitful Ground, will multiply far beyond either the Hopes or Imagination of the Sower" (*T*, 186). Swift's writings are "*fruitful* in the Proportion they are *dark*" (*T*, 186). However we read it, *A Tale of a Tub* hurls us unwillingly toward an intimate knowledge of our own mortality.

In its wandering movement away from and back to a central cluster of metaphors, *A Tale of a Tub* effectively creates an interconnected, if unstable, field of images. Spirit, soul, brain, wind, and air are set against matter, desire, body, corpse, vermin, and earth. These conventional polarities have their typical vertical alignments: spirit and wind are associated with height, matter and body with depth. But Swift does not invoke these polarities to reinforce the usual distinctions; rather he activates their natural associations for a dialectic of union by mutual infestation. It rapidly becomes clear that each image is penetrated and violated by every other and that any image can therefore stand for the totality of permutations. In the stifling and noxious density which results, forms accumulate associations not by reaching parallel fulfillment but by degenerating to a common ground.

Somewhat deceptively, Swift describes circular interchanges between the winds of inspiration and their fraternal flatus in the bowels. *"Words are but Wind"* that puffs us up, and our "Bodies" are "their *Vessels*" (*T*, 153): "The same Spirits which in their superior Progress would conquer a Kingdom, descending upon the *Anus*, conclude in a *Fistula*" (T, 166). Human language, whether embodying the airy flights of religious zeal, the fantastical schemes of scholars, or the fictional moralisms of politicians at war, becomes too heavy for this rarified atmosphere of disembodied truth. Words cluster, clump together, and plummet to the bottom of the vertical spectrum. There they lie among the noxious refuse of our verbal lives—the misdirected venom of abuse and the decaying bodies of our enemies destroyed in a battle of books. In time this compost of verbal sediment generates its own potent vapors, which rise to assert their supremacy among abstractions: "Mists arise from the Earth, Steams from Dunghils, Exhalations from the Sea, and Smoak from Fire; yet all Clouds are the same in Composition, as well as Consequences: and the Fumes issuing from a Jakes, will furnish as comely and useful a Vapor, as Incense from an Altar. . . . so Human Understanding, seated in the Brain, must be troubled and overspread by Vapours, ascending from the lower Faculties, to water the Invention, and render it fruitful" (*T*, 163). Thus Swift describes the *"Phænomenon of Vapours,* ascending from the lower Faculties to over-shadow the Brain, and thence distilling into Conceptions" (*T*, 167). "The Seed or Principle, which has ever put Men upon *Visions* in Things *Invisible*, is of a Corporeal Nature" (*D*, 287). Indeed, the resulting excitations of spirit agitate "the inward Mass. . . . by their Turbulence and Convulsions" (*T*, 154), so stimulating the rise of new and even ranker vapors.[5] Thus our desires become our dreams, our bodily needs having "been refined from a Carnal, into a Spiritual Extasie" (*T*, 157):

> AND, whereas the mind of Man, when he gives the Spur and Bridle to his Thoughts, doth never stop, but naturally sallies out into both extreams of High and Low, of Good and Evil; His first Flight of Fancy, commonly transports Him to Idea's of what is most Perfect, finished, and exalted; till having soared out of his own Reach and Sight, not well perceiving how near the Frontiers of Height and Depth, border upon each other; With the same Course and Wing, he falls down plum into the lowest Bottom of Things; like one who travels the *East* into the *West;* or like a strait Line drawn by its own Length into a Circle. (*T*, 157–58)

All human enthusiasms and ambitions share a common source with those of the great prince Swift describes, in whom "the collected part of the *Semen,* raised and enflamed, became adust, converted to Choler, turned head upon the spinal Duct, and ascended to the Brain" (*T*, 164–65). These universal vapors are "in perpetual Circulation" (*T*, 165); our "own Ordure, which exspiring into Steams, whirls perpetually about" (*T*, 178) and at last reinvests our bodily imagination. Yet the circular process leaves space to hope for at least a flawed and momentary transcendence. All human reason is either patently voracious or successfully self-deceiving, but perhaps the book of faith (whatever its source) may

5. Cf. Robert M. Adams's description of Swift's image of the spirit: "What precisely is the spirit? It is agitated air, 'a redundancy of vapors,' whether denominated enthusiasm, hysteria, or inspiration; its exponents are the learned Aeolists, a set of inflated gapers after air; it is the effective cause of conquests and systems, of faction and madness. Its normal seat is in the lungs, the belly, and the genitals; denied adequate expression here, it may rise to the brain and afflict that organ with a vapor. What the difference is between overt, acknowledged madness and those forms of undeclared madness which are socially rewarded Swift half offers to make clear; but the explanation dissolves into a *Hiatus in MS*, and the satiric edge of his wit is turned against all forms of wind, because all make, or are capable of making, man turbulent and fantastic." *Strains of Discord: Studies in Literary Openness* (Ithaca, 1958), p. 151.

be fully "spiritualized and refined . . . from the Dross and Grossness of *Sense* and *Human Reason*" (*T*, 61–62).

We might wish there were qualitative distinctions hidden within the fumes and damps of human sense and senses, but *A Tale of a Tub* will not permit them. We cannot schematize or stabilize the perceptual theory in Swift's book of the body, his "Physico-logical Scheme of Oratorial Receptacles or Machines" (*T*, 61): there are no relative degrees of pollution along the vertical scale strung between man's soul and his dung. Meaning decays as a function of the digressive, dazed, and wandering language. No listing of logical associations communicates the sense of gradual but inexorable pollution of categories. The allegory of the three coats, interspersed throughout the book with Swift's vision of assault by bodily vermin, is absorbed in the general fermentation of language; accordingly, it loses its purported purity as a satire on religious decay. In Section VI Swift playfully announces that his reader should have been told fifty pages earlier of Peter's decision to retain for his coat *all* the trimmings and ribbons dictated by the series of passing fashions. The announcement is apt, for the *Tale*, too, retains and absorbs all its embroidery until it is impossible to decide whether its disease is "Inlaid *or* Embossed" (*T*, 183). Inside and outside are indistinguishable, for all form has become intestinal.

When we move from the surface and rind of the *Tale* to its sweeter and thicker interior, when we "descend to the very *bottom* of all the *Sublime* throughout this Treatise" (*T*, 44), we learn that "to a judicious Palate, the *Maggots* are the best" (*T*, 66). But maggots are also an eighteenth-century image for crazy schemes, and in either sense have a way of taking over the whole of a body; whatever they infest does not long retain its "beautiful Externals for the Gratification of superficial Readers" (*T*, 67). Having laid open the body of his *Tale* by "Untwisting or Unwinding," drawn up its suffocating meanings "by Exantlation," and displayed its malignant structures "by Incision" (*T*, 67), Swift leaves us no light of our own by which to view the corpse.

In Swift, the body—the human body, the body politic, and this book with its biology of words—achieves its form through in-testinal process. It is a form continually in motion, "a sensless un-savory Carcass" (*T*, 80) animated by any mind imprisoned in it. Thought moves through it like a demented and insatiable worm devouring the subject of all knowledge: the body. "The *Spirit*," Swift writes later, "is apt to feed on the *Flesh*, like hungry Wines upon raw Beef" (*D*, 280). Drowned in sensation, the mind, whose unquenchable curiosity Swift compares to that of the mob and of his readers, is attacked and butchered by its own perceptions: "This I mention, because I am wonderfully well acquainted with the present Relish of Courteous Readers; and have often observed, with singular Pleasure, that a *Fly* driven from a *Honey-pot*, will immediately, with very good Appetite alight, and finish his Meal on an *Excrement*" (*T*, 207). Swarming journalists and critics, in-sects swarming indiscriminately over honey-pot and excrement, the swarming mob—all are externalized versions of Swift's tor-tured self-perception. Sensation becomes infestation, and infesta-tion is talk.

The author and the world echo each other's vices in a cacophony of demented speech. At last it becomes impossible to remember a single unpolluted moment, for either the self or the world. Even Martin, wanting to strip his coat of all its mad embellishments, finds that without some ornamentation the whole coat would fall apart; we have fallen so far that our coats are held together by their very corruptions. In this sense of absolute decay, Swift declares "the Universe to be a large *Suit of Cloaths*, which *invests* every Thing: That the Earth is *invested* by the Air; The Air is *invested* by the Stars; and the Stars are *invested* by the *Primum Mobile*. Look on this Globe of Earth, you will find it to be a very compleat and fashionable *Dress*. . . . To conclude from all, what is Man him-self but a *Micro-Coat*, or rather a compleat Suit of Cloaths with all its Trimmings?" (*T*, 77–78). All we can know of the world is its omnipresent quivering, the pulsating fermentation of enlivened substance which seeps into our consciousness from within and without. The horror in Swift is a contamination phobia, an image

of Swift himself frozen in the knowledge that he has already succumbed to corruption, terrified by his suspicion that the dream of
cleanliness is a fantasy generated in slime. *"The Corruption of the
Senses,"* he writes, *"is the Generation of the Spirit"* (*D*, 269), but
the phrases are reversible, for there is no simple causality in a world
universally degraded.[6] The verbal process in Swift is not linear
but labyrinthine; the language is a multidirectional assault on the
book that contains it. He writes "by feeling the World's Pulse"
(*T*, 210), but it is a pulse which drums incessantly in his own chest.

   Everything is drawn into this vortex of the self; the will "to reduce the Notions of all Mankind, exactly to the same Length, and
Breadth, and Height of his own" (*T*, 166) is inescapable. The
spider and the bee—the spider that spins a web out of its own substance and the bee that gently plunders the world for the substance
of the hive—are the same. Swift's only relief is to write, but his own
book reinfects him, for satire is the fatal mirror in which, dimly,
he sees himself. One look and a *"Person's* Brains *flie out of his
Nostrils"* (*T*, 100), but he cannot resist looking. He cannot resist
tasting his own satiric venom, for his soul is a serpent addicted to
its own vomit (*T*, 100). So the bursting, swarming froth, the universal pickle, has nowhere to go but back into the circulation of
his blood.

   Despite its arbitrary digressiveness and assertion of demented
selfhood, Swift's book frequently purports to be a comprehensive
view of the world. He calls *Reynard the Fox*, a book used for political satire, a "compleat Body of Civil Knowledge" (*T*, 68), im-
plying that a satiric point of view will tell us all we need to know
about political structures and their advocates. "I cannot but be-
wail," he writes, "that no famous *Modern* hath ever yet attempted

6. I would therefore take issue with Norman O. Brown's interpretation in *Life
against Death* (New York, 1959) that the spirit is generated by the repression of
physical desire. Swift's causality is endlessly (and simultaneously) cyclic; it has
no point of origin and no history. There is no evidence that the body was ever
redeemable. Despite the criticism it has received, Brown's considerable sensitivity
to Swift's anality is otherwise quite valuable.

an universal System in a small portable Volume, of all Things that are to be Known, or Believed, or Imagined, or Practised in Life" (*T*, 125). After claiming that his own reflections take "in the whole Compass of Human Nature" (*T*, 97), and that he has indeed dissected its entire carcass, he prepares us to receive "a very compleat Anatomy thereof" (*T*, 123). Toward the end of the book he asserts that "the Reader truly *Learned* . . . will here find sufficient Matter to employ his Speculations for the rest of his Life" (*T*, 185). The claim is genuine enough in retrospect, but Swift goes on to predict that seven scholars locked for seven years in separate chambers would find diverse and perhaps contradictory meanings in his miraculous and comprehensive volume: "whatever Difference may be found in their several Conjectures, they will be all, without the least Distortion, manifestly deduceable from the Text" (*T*, 185). This final irony is less relevant to the diligence and single-mindedness of modern scholars than to the particular qualities of the text in question. Swift's boast that there is sufficient "matter" for a lifetime's speculation invokes not only the wandering enthusiasms of human consciousness but also his sense of all substance, all "matter," as essentially corrupted.

The book at many points implies a suppressed pun on order as ordure, which on inspection it does indeed resemble. All order— all form and structure—is a distillation of ordure. "The Judicious Reader," he promises, "shall find nothing neglected here, that can be of Use upon any Emergency of Life. I am confident to have included and exhausted all that Human Imagination can *Rise* or *Fall* to" (*T*, 129). Swift's italicized verbs are crucial; he invokes the cycle of bodily vapors with its interchangeable height and depth, spirit and body. The book is comprehensive not as an encyclopedia of separate subjects but as a model of all perceptual processes and their ends. It is as though Swift offers Sir Thomas Browne's graceful labyrinths—no longer illuminated by faith, they are shrouded in an eschatology of growing darkness.[7]

7. As *A Tale of a Tub*, ed. Guthkelch and Smith, p. lix, notes, Swift curiously borrows some of Browne's vocabulary from his *Vulgar Errors*, though Swift

Although the anatomy of his book, its *"own Guts,"* is drawn into *"a reasonable Compass"* (*T*, 46), it lies pulsing unspeakably around us; its revealed structure is altogether boneless. When Swift writes repeatedly that his book is a complete anatomy of man, he has in mind not an austere skeleton supporting a few unpleasant organs and framing bodily functions, but a network of tubes which conduct bile and corruption. "Besides, the Spinal Marrow, being nothing else but a Continuation of the Brain, must needs create a very free Communication between the Superior Faculties and those below" (*D*, 287). An anatomy externalizing all the objects of human knowledge would be superfluous, for all knowledge simply mirrors the human knower: *"An Universal Rule of Reason, or Every Man his own Carver"* (*T*, 130). Elsewhere we may find evidence of Swift's faith in a superior reason, but we cannot use it to relieve the suffocating atmosphere of his *Tale*; within this echoing tub there is no escape from the demonic self-sufficiency of the writer and his book. Perception is a rhythmic activity that fulfills itself, a book whose flawed argument is somehow complete and coextensive with the universe.

The pervasive sense of solipsistic and claustrophobic isolation gives all the images of enclosure their promise of completed form. References to finished structure ("erecting certain *Edifices in the Air,"* *T*, 56) and to hollow vessels of various types and functions may appear absurd and insubstantial from a detached perspective. Yet from within the *Tale* they provide unsettling glimpses of the total field of words that surround the reader. Many images are definitively resolved in the two appended satires, where we find the spider swollen to bursting inside a castle built out of itself, and the malignant female deity of criticism feeding upon her own bile. These are final images of stark horror. The experience of reading the *Tale*, however, allows only a perception of structure like that

---

makes Browne's delicately physical imagery demonic. Many critics have observed that Swift's book serves a purpose exactly opposite to such seventeenth-century anatomies. See the index to the Guthkelch and Smith edition for additional notes on Swift's borrowings from Browne.

of the guardian at the disordered library: "by walking much in the dark about the Library, he had quite lost the Situation of it out of his Head" (*B*, 226). What *we* have lost, of course, is whatever placid faith in structure we brought with us to the *Tale;* we gain the shadowy intuition of an infectious form whose mechanical perfections are suspiciously organic—indeed, horribly "enlivened" (*T*, 76).

Swift's Preface compares his tale to an empty tub that sailors throw out to divert a whale "from laying violent Hands upon the Ship" (*T*, 40). The ship endangered is given as the commonwealth, whose abstract religious and governmental structures "are hollow, and dry, and empty, and noisy, and wooden, and given to Rotation," and "apt to *fluctuate*" (*T*, 40–41). But the *Tale* is both the diverting tub and the whale which swallows the ship. For the reader, the book itself is the omnipresent vessel that contains the world's fluctuating abstractions. Yet such abstractions alone are far too inorganic for Swift's purposes. If we are to be truly threatened (and we truly are), the book's ascetic pages will themselves have to be more than ideologically corrupted. Swift must make his book physically "loaden and press'd down by Words" (*T*, 60)—words with more than conceptual density, which will make us literally gasp for air. Book must become body: recurring metaphors must acquire the execrable redundancy of flesh (cf. *T*, 98).

Thus, after Swift pretends regret that no modern has produced a small, universal volume, he confesses that one philosopher on a mythical island did attempt one; the method, a process of physical and chemical reduction, suggests that books literally are bodies: "*YOU take fair correct Copies, well bound in Calfs Skin, and Lettered at the Back, of all Modern Bodies of Arts and Sciences whatsoever, and in what Language you please*" (*T*, 126). This mock-alchemical recipe produces a potent substance that can inspire the kind of thinking such a volume requires: "*This you keep in a Glass Viol Hermetically sealed, for one and twenty Days. Then you begin your Catholick Treatise, taking every Morning fasting, (first shaking the Viol) three Drops of this Elixir, snuffing it strongly up your Nose. It will dilate it self about the Brain (where there is any) in fourteen Minutes, and you immediately perceive in your Head an infinite Number of* Abstracts, Summaries, Compendiums, Extracts, Collections, Medulla's, Excerpta quædam's, Florilegia's *and the like, all disposed into great Order, and reducible upon Paper"* (*T*, 126–27). The order, of course, will be insane. The mind will be flooded by every variety of rational system —consciousness will be consumed in a delirium of classification. Swift's demented alchemist, bottling and imbibing the noxious odor of all Order, will synthesize a book resembling the cancerous body of Swift's "malignant Deity, call'd *Criticism*," who is "extended in her Den, upon the Spoils of numberless Volumes half devoured" (*B*, 240). It will be a book whose perfection is its overripeness, "whereof to a judicious Palate, the *Maggots* are the best."

The perceptual processes embodied here and elsewhere in the *Tale* are offered as a compressed image in *The Battel of the Books*. The malignant female goddess, her body a triumphant cluster of corruptions, transforms herself into a book:

> Her Diet was the overflowing of her own *Gall:* Her *Spleen* was so large, as to stand prominent like a Dug of the first Rate, nor wanted Excrescencies in form of Teats, at which a Crew of ugly Monsters were greedily sucking; and, what is wonderful to conceive, the bulk of Spleen encreased faster than the Sucking could diminish it. (*B*, 240)

> And now she reach'd the fatal Plain of St. *James*'s Library. . . . she cast about to change her Shape. . . . She therefore gathered up her Person into an *Octavo* Compass: Her Body grew white and arid, and split in pieces with Driness; the thick turned into Pastboard, and the thin into Paper, upon which, her Parents and Children, artfully strowed a Black Juice, or Decoction of Gall and Soot, in Form of Letters; her Head, and Voice, and Spleen, kept their primitive Form, and that which before, was a Cover of Skin, did still continue so. (*B*, 242–43)

It is not unusual that Swift makes the blank whiteness of the page female, a conventional contrast to the masculine creative will. What is distinctive is the image of the page as a thinly veiled mask for fleshly corruption; its purity and passivity are the spider's trap, the deceptive mask of ravenous female hunger. The *Tale* is a tub in which we as readers and probably Swift himself are swallowed and dismembered. Its metaphors are not logical persuasions but perceptual events which enter to possess us. Swift's words empty us of the world by filling us with their own reverberations: "she took the ugliest of her Monsters, full glutted from her Spleen, and flung it invisibly into his Mouth; which flying strait up into his Head, squeez'd out his Eye-Balls, gave him a distorted Look, and half overturned his Brain. . . . she vanished in a Mist, and the *Hero* perceived it was the Goddess, his Mother" (*B*, 243). Reading a page, we are infested by images and infected by a plague of associations that echo in the "hollow Vault" of our heads (*T*, 186). The book is a product of the "Satyrical Itch" (*T*, 48); Swift's moral convictions are an epidemic, his "hard-mouth'd" faith a disease. "Books, the Children of the Brain" (*T*, 71), are born "From a Head broken in a hundred places and from a Body spent with Poxes ill cured" (*T*, 70).

"It is the Quality of rotten Wood," writes Swift, "to give *Light* in the Dark," but "its Cavities are full of Worms" (*T*, 62). Swift's images of book as body and body as book mask a demonic inversion of Christian incarnation—as though the Word could only be embodied satanically: "I have deduced a *Histori-theo-physilogical* Account of *Zeal*, shewing how it first proceeded from a *Notion* into a *Word*, and from thence in a hot Summer, ripned into a *tangible Substance*" (*T*, 137). Swift's book and his body make up a thick and malodorous incarnation of all the world's discourse. The *Tale* is a total gastro-intestinal system, a digestive tract in which the intestines empty into the mouth. Wholly self-enclosed and self-generated, it is simultaneously a small object and the complete space of its own terminal universe. For the only complete anatomy is an anatomy which begins and ends in itself, a body closed to the outside world. Within this trough of fermenting thought, this book-body buggered by its own words, there is no relief and no release of tension. Even if we can remove ourselves to a perspective of humble and self-critical censure toward the text, its vision will reinfect us. As soon as we attempt a disinterested judgment, its grotesquely swollen word-bag bursts in our faces. Swift's *Tale* leaves no hope that our flesh is even potentially susceptible to redemption; in the fullness of time we will awaken only to a lingering suffocation.

The intolerable irresolution of our experience results from the simple, inescapable realization that the book was *written* and the book is *read*. Its absolute self-sufficiency is logically incompatible with its external existence as an experienced object. If the book is to be the world's body, we must see in it the immense volume of the world. Yet there is no way to place ourselves perpetually at its center. In this gelled form whose motion comes from us, there is no final moment of stasis. The repose of the gentle reader can never be complete. Swift's *Tale* is the nightmare of an immortal paralytic who daydreams obsessively of suicide.

The perfect circle of time lies overlapped and looped in knots; eternity has become intestinal. Our only salvation is to replace the world with ourselves and thus protect mankind from all self-knowledge. So the book unfolds its hydra-headed form in a hall of mirrors. With its continual return to metaphors of unspeakable contamination, it seems to be cautiously circling a nameless but definitive central image. We wait for the mirrors to reveal the final image of horror which Swift offers elsewhere. But no single reflection resolves itself. *A Tale of a Tub* lacks the definitive, terminal image which absorbs all its antecedents. Nevertheless, "this Physico-logical Scheme of Oratorial Receptacles or Machines, contains a great Mystery, being a Type, a Sign, an Emblem, a Shadow, a Symbol, bearing Analogy to the spacious Commonwealth of Writers" (*T*, 61). As the fan of horror movies knows, the unseen and anticipated horror is usually more frightening than its often amusing realization—and Swift's failure to be explicit in his book only increases its power. It does not really matter whether Swift deliberately evades and obscures the central horror or simply fails to control the material. For the reader it is an inescapable quality of the resulting text. Simultaneously self-reflexive and chaotic, the book holds our complete attention with an image whose very proximity obscures its form.

A Tale of a Tub is indeed "a compleat Body of Civil Knowledge, and the *Revelation*, or rather the *Apocalyps* of all State-*Arcana*" (*T*, 68). Its form resembles the idol who "did daily create Men, by a kind of Manufactory Operation" (*T*, 76). Reading it, we continually sacrifice pieces of "the uninformed Mass, or Substance, and sometimes whole Limbs already enlivened" (*T*, 76). It is not Swift's discredited nihilism that makes this masochistic violence demonic—it is his Christianity. The book of revelation is an image of the body fulfilled: resurrection as dismemberment. Eternally reincarnated in this book, the world's womb and tomb, our dismembered limbs retain their self-awareness. The figural meaning of the *Tale* lies in its power to act as a vortex that swallows time past and time future.

As Swift tells us in his famous anatomy of knowing, we enter the palace of learning (the body) through the back door. To discover it is where we already are would be terrifying enough. It is perhaps worse to fear, as Swift does in his image of intercourse as catalyzed corruption ("the fermenting of the *Male* and *Female Dragon*," *T*, 68), that the anal doorway was the one through which we were born. But faith is required to believe it is where we shall be reborn in the end of time. "Physicians discover the State of the whole Body, by consulting only what comes from *Behind*. . . . Thus Human Life is best understood by the wise man's Rule of *Regarding the End*" (*T*, 145). It is not Swift's anality that shocks us. It is the anal vision of eschatology. His book, with its corporate body composed of cannibalistic minds, the corrupted flesh that the spirit feeds upon, incarnates in its verbal space one body outside time. The final horror is an image which prophetically resolves the conflict between the world and the self.

For there is only one source for the image of a single mind "reducing, including, and adjusting every *Genus* and *Species* within

that Compass, by coupling some against their Wills, and banish-
ing others" (*T*, 57); hidden at the inaccessible center of *A Tale of
a Tub* is an image partly revealed in the last of the satiric trinity:
"the Brain is only a Crowd of little Animals, but with Teeth and
Claws extremely sharp, and therefore, cling together in the Contexture wc behold, like the Picture of *Hobbes*'s *Leviathan*, or like
Bees in perpendicular swarm upon a Tree, or like a Carrion corrupted into Vermin, still preserving the Shape and Figure of the
Mother Animal" (*D*, 277). The mother animal—Swift's satire was
more double-edged than his contemporary readers thought when
they saw in it a hidden image of the Church. His boast that the
book contains all that man can *"Rise* or *Fall* to" extends the image
of perception as bodily process to infect the theology of man's
fall and resurrection. In death the whole body becomes rigidly
phallic, "ejaculating the Soul" (*D*, 267) toward heaven and planting in God's mind a corporeal seed of human corruption. The
formal archetype for the *Tale* is a demonic vision of the mystical
body of Christ.

Self-creation

It is in sensation that everything begins: flesh, objects, moods, compose for the self a primal space, an horizon of density or dizzying emptiness.

> Jean-Pierre Richard, in Miller,
> "The Geneva School," 318

I would know the red *thee* of the enclosure
where thought too curls about, opens
out from, what's hid

> Robert Duncan, *Bending the Bow*, 3

It is not a little thing, he thought, this writing that lies before me. It is the telling of a creation. It is the story of birth. Out of him had come another. A being had been born, not out of the womb, but out of the soul and the spinning head.

> Dylan Thomas, *Adventures in
> the Skin Trade*, 107

Michelangelo depicted on the Sistine ceiling the creation of the world. He ended up by depicting . . . his own creativity in the biblical panel closest to the mural of the *Last Judgement*. . . . Before creating the world, the great creator had to create himself. Far from being the potent virile father figure of the creation scenes, a feeble old man tries to emerge from the womb of a whirling cloud which envelops him like a chrysalis. . . .

We call it "God dividing Light and Darkness"; Michelangelo's contemporaries gave it the heretical meaning of God creating himself, delivering himself as it were from his own womb.

Could the image of the "self-creating god" on the ceiling represent Michelangelo in the act of painting the ceiling?

There a womb is being prepared to receive, nurse and ultimately return the artist's projections, an inner space that both contains and repels the spectator.

Anton Ehrenzweig, *The Hidden Order of Art*, 208, 147, 209, 94

From time to time thinkers ranging from ancient philosophers to modern psychotherapists have expressed their conviction that man projects into his creations only that which is within himself. The key words of this premise are "within himself." Men, facing words like these, are apt to see them as metaphors, pointing to some tenuous, spiritual, wraith-like self. To only a few has it occurred that such words pertain to a tangible flesh and a material blood. . . .

Ida P. Rolf, *Structural Integration*, 3

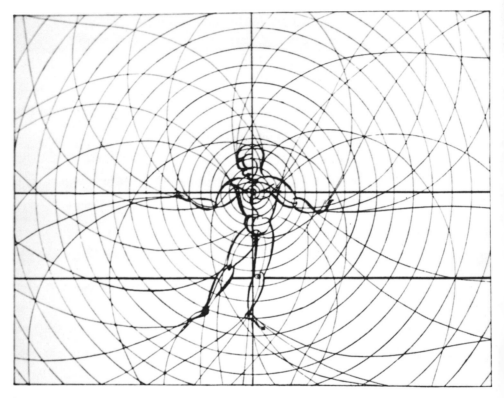

8. Anonymous, "Creating an Imaginary Space."

<table>
<tr><td>SIX</td><td>

Blake's *Jerusalem:*
a fourfold vision
of the human body
</td></tr>
</table>

I have shaken hands with delight in my warme blood
Sir Thomas Browne, Religio Medici, 52

The reality of body is not given, but to be made real, to
be realized; the body is to be built; to be built not with
hands but by the spirit. It is the poetic body; the made
body; Man makes Himself, his own body, in the
symbolic freedom of the imagination.
Norman O. Brown, Love's Body, 226

Metaphoric readings of Freudian psychology describe the artist
projecting womb-receptacles appropriate to his psyche.[1] The artist
creates an external home for a secret and inward self from which
he is estranged. The art object, becoming both antagonist and lover,
springs from the sexual power of ripe states of mind. "We express
ourselves there," William Carlos Williams puts it, "as we might on
the whole body of the various female could we ever gain access to
her."[2] We can never fully assimilate the world's femaleness or
wholly possess our own, but we can create particularized versions
of it indefinitely. The female archetype never entirely subsumes its
individual incarnations: the artist remains interested in phenomena
and committed to continued creation.

In Anton Ehrenzweig's analysis, the Freudian metaphor for
creation distinguishes between productive, viable projections and

1. Anton Ehrenzweig, *The Hidden Order of Art* (Berkeley, 1967).
2. *Selected Essays* (New York, 1954), p. 259.

those which repress consciousness in impenetrable enclosures. So
the metaphor need not be constrictive. As a poet who consciously
and frequently uses wombs, eggs, orbs, globes, balls, and fur-
naces, Blake appears to be a likely representative for the theory. In
the most general terms, Blake's poetic world is an egg which the
imagination fertilizes. If we apply this image to *Jerusalem*, the
poem becomes an englobed and englobing space, a self-encircling
or self-creating act for poet and reader. The poem is an enticing
structure through which we may deliver ourselves from other
wombs—personal or universal, always sterile.

Jerusalem's verse and illuminations are among the most patterned and mutually supportive work in the history of art. With
its immense range of narrative detail, only the iconographic tour
de force binds the poem into a cohering structure. Gesture, posture,
movement, and block form sustain each page as a field of force.
The text's physical presence is apparent at once. The first plate of
Jerusalem [20][3] is the literal and figurative entrance to the poem
for both poet and reader: a human figure warily carries a luminous
sphere through a dark doorway. The inscription over the archway
to this ambiguous space, removed in most copies of the poem, both
sustains and complicates our movement into the poem:

> There is a Void, outside of Existence, which if enterd into
> Englobes itself & becomes a Womb
>
> (1, 1–2)[4]

The poem establishes its spatial setting and alerts us to our act of
entrance. We can fill this initial emptiness with our presence. But
the phrase "outside of Existence" is unsettling and problematic.

---

3. Numbered illustrations in brackets are reproduced at the end of this chapter.
Numbered plates in *Jerusalem* are cited in the text or in parentheses; these numbers correspond to those of the Blake Trust color facsimile, which reproduces
copy E.

4. *The Poetry and Prose of William Blake*, ed. David V. Erdman (Garden City,
N.Y., 1970). *Jerusalem* is documented internally by plate and line (for chapter 2,
Erdman follows the numbering in copies A, C, and F), *Milton* (*M*) by plate and
line, and *The Four Zoas* (*FZ*) by page and line.

Moreover, the human figure seems to have a multiple role; he can be interpreted variously (and not exclusively) as poet, reader, protagonist, or the formal energy of the poem itself. Though here this ambiguous effect is reinforced by the dark and inconclusive quality of the space behind the door, Blake's other and more explicit womb images are equally complicated.

Though many of Blake's paintings use circular iconography, the implications vary widely. The popular print "God Blessing the Seventh Day" [9] and the famous frontispiece to *Europe* [10] share this womblike iconography but arouse different ranges of response. The illustration to Genesis, glowing with light, shows a creator enclosed in an oval shell formed by the arms and wings of six angels. The deity is benign and fruitful, his hands spread in a gesture of innocence while women are spawned in his cosmic egg. It is a self-generative image of the place where new life grows. The plate of "The Ancient of Days," with its blinding light trapped in darkness, creates an entirely different atmosphere. The forceful creator, his hair stiffly streaming, his hand shaping a fixed compass, demonstrates the arc and thrust of his power from a center of will. For this figure, patterned after Blake's Urizen, creation reproduces an even more frozen version of his womblike environment.

Both prints are nevertheless engaging and satisfying. It was no accident that "The Ancient of Days"—the creator of a fallen and limited world of Newtonian reason—makes a deceptively attractive frontispiece to *Europe.* Blake's intended irony has been repeatedly fulfilled, for "The Ancient of Days" (along with the obdurate old man from *The Book of Urizen*) is often used to illustrate editions of Genesis—clearly with no conscious decision to picture a God who is restrictive and domineering as well as powerful and creative. Yet the double image is painted into the picture, and it runs through Blake's whole verbal-visual use of womb images. He manipulated these archetypes deliberately and consistently in his work, with a strong sense of their ambiguous power. Not one failed to travel through incarnations sacred and profane, ecstatic and debased. All the forms his mind engendered were turned inside out, taken to apocalyptic consummation, and finally inverted and mocked.

This ecstatic and ironic doubleness, which may have begun in a Romantic self-consciousness, became part of Blake's visionary posture. Irony is available for any image; it is an incarnation through which any form can pass. Like even bitter satire, it has its source in the biological or somatic situation of thought itself. Blake's particular genius was to link this ironic ambiguity to the physical presence of the page. (Indeed, as an engraver, he literally had to invert an image to print it in an uninverted form.) Blake's work engages our senses physically and holds us to an experience of the page. This fact of his art continually works against any tendency to distance ourselves from it, to see it abstractly. All Blake's circular or womblike images in *Jerusalem* help enclose the reader in the total space of the poem, and we cannot work only with his lean and geometrical figures. He moved easily from circle or sphere to egg, womb, cave, or shell to achieve similar effects; each figure of enclosure derives its particular meaning from the situation and images it encloses. The womb can generate a circumference either ecstatic or repressive:

There is a Void, outside of Existence, which if enterd into
Englobes itself & becomes a Womb
(1, 1–2)

all within is open'd into the deeps
(5, 56)

He saw now from the outside what he before saw & felt from within.
(8, 25)

There is an Outside spread Without, & an Outside spread Within
Beyond the Outline of Identity both ways, which meet in One:
An orbed Void
(18, 2–4)

utter'd from the Circumference into Eternity.
(23, 28)

What is Above is Within, for every-thing in Eternity is translucent:
The Circumference is Within: Without, is formed the Selfish Center
And the Circumference still expands going forward to Eternity.
And the Center has Eternal States! these States we now explore.

                                                            (71, 6-9)

Blake's redeemed man experiences an opening outward of his
most inward center; but the regenerated body is more than an
expansion of its center to the circumference of the world. This
single metaphor lacks the drama enacted by the poem itself, which
renders even the absolutes of the fallen world in the same pattern.
There "is the Great Selfhood / Satan . . . / Having a white Dot
calld a Center from which branches out / A Circle in continual
gyrations" (29, 17–20). Even the circle in its most immutable form,
the "Concave Earth wondrous, Chasmal, Abyssal, Incoherent! /
Forming the Mundane Shell" (13, 53–54), is ravaged and transformed when the world's mundane egg is fertilized and incubated
in the poet's body.

The human figure of plate 1 enters an imaginative womb which
intensively models the whole human perceptual universe, the
mundane shell. The mundane shell is the sky that encloses the
earth and is its inverse reflection: by day "the lovely blue & shining
heavenly Shell," it is actually a region of "dark and intricate caves":

The Mundane Shell, is a vast Concave Earth: an immense
Hardend shadow of all things upon our Vegetated Earth
Enlarg'd into dimension & deform'd into indefinite space.
                . . . It is a cavernous Earth
     Of labyrinthine intricacy

                                      (*M*, 17, 21–23, 25–26)

This is the fallen world where man incubates and at last hatches
into eternity. This world of vegetative generation, the mundane
egg, is the only locus for the birth of a regenerated body. The
visionary body will arise from this womb, where the vegetated
body is already diffused in the woof of nature. To provide the

dramatic setting for this myth of rebirth, *Jerusalem* invokes the ultimate form of a vegetated universe: an egg cluster that proliferates endlessly in serpentine coils. It is a world of massive vegetable groupings, of weighted flesh woven on Enitharmon's looms:

> As a beautiful Veil so these Females shall fold & unfold
> According to their will the outside surface of the Earth
> An outside shadowy Surface superadded to the real Surface;
> Which is unchangeable for ever & ever
>
> (83, 45–48)
>
> Let Cambel and her Sisters sit within the Mundane Shell:
> Forming the fluctuating Globe according to their will.
>
> (83, 33–34)

Female looms weave a damp suffusion, a cloud body trembling with vegetable doubt, and the flesh of this body is enfolded in female space. The flesh of the looms is soft and diffuse. Its ultimate form is the polypus, a demonic parody of the ecstatic body: "Out from his bosom a mighty Polypus, vegetating in darkness" (18, 40). This is the circumscribed body which hoards its center and draws back from its circumference, but this symbolic geometry is less immediate than its blind proliferation and vegetable texture: "the Great Polypus of Generation covered the Earth" (67, 34). This moulding body is the world of generation, "From the blue Mundane Shell, reaching to the Vegetative Earth" (13, 33)—an earth that shares its texture with the serpentine coils of Satan's flesh and the noxious density of *A Tale of a Tub*, where "Life lives upon Death & by devouring appetite / All things subsist on one another" (*FZ*, 87, 19–20). It is the vast female womb of nature, "Vegetated beneath / Their Looms, in a Generation of death and resurrection to forgetfulness" (17, 8–9).

Yet it is the male who shapes the spaces of generation. The abstract male will forms the hard shell to an interior female diffusion. "The Male is a Furnace of beryll; the Female is a golden Loom" (5, 34). Male wills "are opake hardnesses covering all Vegetated things" (67, 5), and the body is a "vegetable mould: created by the

Hammer and Loom" (36, 56). "Shadowy generation," webs of
life rolling in darkness, "soft affections," "evanescent shades"—
these flesh textures in a "globe of blood" are condensed by the
male into opaque bodies of stony form and substance:

> Shadowy to those who dwell not in them, meer possibilities:
> But to those who enter into them they seem the only substances
> For every thing exists & not one sigh nor smile nor tear
>
> (13, 64–66)

In the encircling womb of nature, the Spectre—self-seeking male
reason, "opake blackening Fiend" (7, 8)—encompasses trembling
clouds of terror in a circle of definition. The "Spectre / Stands
between the Vegetative Man & his Immortal Imagination" (32,
23–24), confining the body to its condensed globe of blood and
covering

> His face and bosom with petrific hardness, and his hands
> And feet, lest any should enter his bosom & embrace
> His hidden heart
>
> (34, 1–3)

This hardened perceptual horizon makes the body a stone wielded
in power. Its "hard restricting condensations" (73, 21) lead the
world of generation into war. The war is endless, bringing forth
stone fruit and decaying generation. The body of male will is an
opaque and terrible condensation whose hardening form negates
the void of terrified female diffusion.

This contrapuntal vegetative war reaches its peak in *Jerusalem*.
But it cannot in itself release the world's energy. Instead it extends
the sexuality of endless bodily strife across the globe: "Wine-press
of Love & Wrath double Hermaphroditic" (89, 4). The vegetated
body maintains its form by antagonistic sexual warfare: "She wove
two vessels of seed . . . / Giving them bends of self interest & selfish
natural virtue: / She hid them in his loins" (80, 74–76). As the war
intensifies, the world of generation becomes a direct expression of
the fallen will:

> Enitharmon answerd. No! I will seize thy Fibres & weave
> Them: not as thou wilt but as I will, for I will Create
> A round Womb beneath my bosom lest I also be overwoven
> With Love; be thou assured I never will be thy slave
>
> (87, 12-15)

Images of bodily vegetation extend increasingly to the whole mundane egg. The generated body, always a hermaphroditic self-negation, now negates the whole womb of nature. The imagination, which is the divine body of man or Jesus, comes face to face with the Antichrist: "His Head dark, deadly, in its Brain incloses a reflexion / Of Eden all perverted" (89, 14-15). "A Vegetated Christ & a Virgin Eve, are the Hermaphroditic / Blasphemy" (90, 34-35). The dialectic of opposition and inversion continues until subsumed images of absolute negation fill the fallen world and bring an end to generation, "the whole Creation which groans to be deliverd" (16, 26). No movement is possible without reciprocal annihilation: Albion sacrifices himself, but the act is transformed into mutual forgiveness. The mundane egg is consumed and regenerated.

In the womb of the natural mind, all generation becomes a dialectic of negation. The iconographic circle is really two interlocking, self-negating spheres. Brooding on the human body as the vehicle of this divided womb, Blake desires a visionary doubleness—contraries without negation: "Negations are not Contraries: Contraries mutually Exist: / But Negations Exist Not" (17, 33-34). The apocalyptic consummation becomes fourfold—a balanced double opposition, each within the other, equal and identified.

Seen with fourfold vision, even the world of generation and death has organic unity to its shape. "The Stygian Lake, with the Ireful Sinners Fighting" [14] enacts two rows of three angry figures, face to face, fists upraised, their bodies reduced to massive heads and limbs, almost without torsos. The composition has organic force, as if the six bodies were generated by a single point of fury at their feet. The image suggests a six-headed, two-halved body of anger, each half (like the vegetable body of hermaphroditism) utterly negating the other. The body is fulfilled by the fruits of its negation—three dead figures at its feet. The whole plate duplicates Blake's vision of a single mind consumed by rage that transforms the imaginative body.

We discover in the womb of the poem a concentrated organic form—the visionary body, woven naturally into the vegetable fibers of generation and death; it must be reenergized from the center outward. This potential for the redemption of the human body, for the actual transformation of the vegetable body into the fourfold vehicular body of the imagination, is the crucial force of the poem:

> And every Man stood Fourfold. each Four Faces had. One to
> the West
> One toward the East One to the South One to the North. the
> Horses Fourfold
> And the dim Chaos brightend beneath, above, around! Eyed
> as the Peacock
> According to the Human Nerves of Sensation, the Four Rivers
> of the Water of Life
> South stood the Nerves of the Eye. East in Rivers of bliss the
> Nerves of the
> Expansive Nostrils West, flowd the Parent Sense the Tongue.
> North stood
> The labyrinthine Ear. Circumscribing & Circumcising the ex-
> crementitious
> Husk & Covering into Vacuum evaporating revealing the
> lineaments of Man
> Driving outward the Body of Death in an Eternal Death &
> Resurrection
> Awaking it to Life among the Flowers of Beulah rejoicing in
> Unity
> In the Four Senses in the Outline the Circumference & Form,
> for ever
> In Forgiveness of Sins which is Self Annihilation. it is the
> Covenant of Jehovah
>
> (98, 12–23)

The fourfold vision is a vision of four-in-one, of four faces simultaneously in the imaginative body of the poet. If we are to take Blake's world-body metaphor seriously, we must see the generated body (still vegetable, still closed) as the locus of the spiritual body of imagination. This imagination is real not as a principle but as a particular form: the form of the divine body of man. The most frequent feature of the illuminated books, especially of *Jerusalem*, is flesh—the human body. This body undergoes radical metamorphoses in the text and in the paintings. It is a "vehicular" body, a hollow form, a nexus for aesthetic and somatic transformations. It is a vehicle both eternally the same and ever changing, a vehicular form whose permutations Blake enacts in *Jerusalem*.

Each page begins and ends in the image of the whole plate, and the progressive posturing of the words is always enacted within the larger body. The illustrations for *Songs of Innocence and Experience* may complement or comment on the text, which is gently diffused in a wash of color. But in *Jerusalem* the plates bind word and image together in dynamic tension. At times the plate is literally the body in which language proliferates; the calligraphy becomes the nervous fiber of the page. In plate 62 the text shields or replaces the torso of an anguished figure, and plate 57 [17] half encloses the text in a green globe spinning off female figures. In plate 15 [12] a body's outstretched arms frame the page. Plate 35 [18] identifies Christ's stigmata with the wound in Adam's side through which Eve was delivered. Eve rises toward the text, and the page speaks through wounds that will never heal. Eve is speech delivered of Adam the word; the mutual stigmata are a sexual talisman. The text wounds the page, and the word stirs the pulses. The taste of speech roots language to the tongue—perhaps no other poet has so definitively made the word flesh. Each page is a revolution in consciousness that resurrects the imagination in a new body.

Critics tend to respond to Blake's art as though it were simply external sense data, ripe with symbolic intent; transferring the qualities of the verbal environment—what the text says—to the paintings, they ignore the page as a total iconographic form. Hence the illuminated poetry is treated not as an imaginative unity but as a landscape of related objects, as an abstract environment where mythological figures act. Blake's uniquely postured images of the body become conventional and representational images of the human figure. In turn these images serve as the personae or agents of perception for both poet and reader—to borrow Blake's image of the eye, we must then see *with* rather than *through* them. Philosophic abstraction (even when enlightened by catalogs of Blake's analogies) does not evoke Blake; rather it casts him as a poet in the image of Urizen.

The problems of this view are clear in Joseph Wicksteed's discussion of plate 14 [19]: "Man, ALBION (in this case, perhaps, Los himself as representing Blake) is shown slumbering on a promontory, surrounded by gentle waters and guarded by angels . . . and over all the rainbow arch of love and promise. The eyes, although clearly closed, seem to be watching the vision as though to show it as a dream."[5] Such an interpretation of Blake's figures applies the conventions of eighteenth-century rational and descriptive personification much too literally, and combines them with a moral judgment against human flesh. Like the Romantic poets who followed him, Blake inherited a tradition of personification and narrative to which he responded and went on to redefine. In the face of his poetry we have to ask all the primary questions again: Why should mind body forth in multiple personae? How does the poet energize himself through masks? When the plate is viewed instead as a perceptual whole, a visionary field which the imagination has given bodily form, the image is no longer that of a dreamer with his dream conveniently painted behind him. It becomes a particular manifestation of the imagination in its regenerated fourfold body. The dreamer and his dream, the poet and his vision, are four-in-one. The image is simultaneous, an identity. The oval-winged woman and the cranial arc of the rainbow are not even alternate versions of the man's visionary horizon

5. *William Blake's Jerusalem* (London, 1954), pp. 139–40.

or of the mundane egg; they are a simultaneous body that is four-in-one.

Blake's objections to natural objects suggest that he may have encountered people as externalized versions of his own states of mind—that the people in his life came to have the texture of masks, generated in the external world by his own imagination. For in this sense Blake himself was the vehicle for all the masks, the protagonists, of *Jerusalem:* Blake the poet, cosmic man, embodies multiple personae in the poem's vehicular form. Personification occurs dramatically in Blake; it is his technique for giving physical or bodily form to the imagination. Accordingly, not even a character's mood can change without ontological ramifications. When names or sets of names change, an accumulation of energy is released. Narrative tension increases and intensifies until it suddenly precipitates new dramatic characters and new images of the body.

Two plates at opposite ends of *Jerusalem* illustrate the essential transformation of persona and iconographic image. The first plate [20] displays the cautious posture of a clothed figure entering the poem. The later plate [21] celebrates the ecstatic rippling poise of the naked Albion. The overall parallel has been observed before,[6] but the analysis can be taken further. The clothed figure has no dynamic relation to the lamp he carries. The stiff beams of light radiate from an entirely self-contained source, a lamp tightly bound by concentric rings. But the figure at the end of the poem carries a light as powerful as the sun. The bottom of the first lamp is shadowed with red, like a sign of potential flame. In the later image red almost fills the circle; the coloring is off center, and the circle is surrounded by an uneven corona of red, so that the light appears to vibrate with energy. But most striking is the naked figure's dynamic relation to the light he bears. The angle of his arm overlays the rays of light, and the red corona is shaped to the triangle formed

6. Cf. Jean Hagstrum, *William Blake: Poet and Painter* (Chicago, 1964), p. 118: "the humble man who had entered the gate with a flickering light emerges as a heroic nude in a blaze of apocalyptic light, bearing a luminous ball. . . ."

by his arm and torso. The right palm held level over the figure's head gives the body a downward force balanced by the outward thrust of the light. The human body here is the source of the energy that radiates from the sphere.

In this dynamic posture we recognize the human body as the central form that generates the space of the page. The body's outline is not a rigid circumference around an immovable density, but an iconic form susceptible to radical change according to its internal situation. Yet the body is the image of both fallen man and redeemed man. Thus the middle space of the poem, the space which models the world of generation, shows bodies impacted with energy [12, 22, 23]. In these powerful plates Blake adopts the baroque technique of designing a violently twisted torso in which two or more postures can be united at once. Combined with the dynamic use of color and outline, these twisted torsos create an image of agonized bodies in which the entire world of vegetating generation is asserted. Though they have not yet discovered the ecstatic variety of Blake's flaming bodies [24], these figures [22, 23] at least experience the full terror of a fallen world.

With the human body as both a fallen and regenerated form, Blake's iconography becomes obsessed with this body's potential for an ecstatic and expansive bilateral symmetry. His agonized figures torture the self-generating, bipartite thrust of the human body, its double arc unfolding from the spine [22, 24]. In the doubleness of the ironic vision, two halves of the body, springing from and spinning about the same source, make up both the negative world of generation and death and the communality of the transformed body: "And they conversed together in Visionary forms dramatic which bright / Redounded from their Tongues" (98, 28–29). In the world of generation and death, our bilateral symmetry represents the restriction of human vision. The Spectre forces the male to conceive the female genitals (plate 58) as a bat-winged horror—blind and therefore cut off from infinite delight and infinity itself. Yet the webbed wings of the reasoning Spectre

mimic angels' wings and share the posture of ecstatically outstretched arms.[7] The hovering Spectre [13] introduces one of the
first multiple, ironic iconographic patterns in *Jerusalem*.

The wings of the Spectre and the heavy red wings of the Dragon
enclose our limited vision in the blue wings of the mundane shell.
Yet "In every bosom a Universe expands, as wings" (34, 49). The
restricting wings of the reasoning Spectre invoke at the same time
"thy Form O lovely mild Jerusalem, Wingd with Six Wings" (86,
1; cf. plate 2). Ironically, bat wings form a full circle with the wings
Albion would have had in commingling with his emanation. The
consummating embrace of Los and Enitharmon, of man and his
female inwardness, is part of the cycle of wings and outstretched
arms in the fallen world. As flight ranges from reasoning to ecstasy,
so outstretched arms are its multiple vehicle. Outstretched arms invoke the world of generation aching for release—its body massing
toward the arms [12], its shadowy female hovering [22], and its
despair (plate 92)—yet they also celebrate Albion worshiping
Christ (plate 76); outstretched arms are the image shared by
Satan smiting Job with boils and Job blessing his regenerated
communality.

The visionary fusion of wings and arms is perhaps most com-
pelling in Blake's stark drawing of the Trinity [15]. God and
Christ embrace, Christ's arms outstretched beneath the floating
wings of the Holy Ghost. In *Jerusalem* an evolving pattern finally
fuses two images: embracing lovers and a single imaginative body
with arms ecstatically outstretched. One design [16], showing far
more than mere decorative balance, includes a man and woman in
a leaping embrace, as in the frontispiece to *The Marriage of Heaven
and Hell*. Their legs are supported by the right arms of two larger

7. My initial comparison here, between restrictive and ecstatic outstretched
arms, has been observed before. Cf. Jean Hagstrum, " 'The Wrath of the Lamb':
A Study of William Blake's Conversions," *From Sensibility to Romanticism*, ed.
Frederick W. Hilles and Harold Bloom (New York, 1965), p. 318: "Urizen as
the God of Pity is a direct perversion of the good—a reduction to evil of a noble
virtue. With arms extended, he recalls Christ on the cross and the man who stands
before it. . . ."

winged figures below, whose feet touch below the couple's heads. The design, like two pastel petals of a flower, creates a bipartite and fourfold motion—the lovers leaping inward and the winged figures in gentle outward flight. It is a simultaneous fourfold vision of male and female, union and flight.

In the iconographic resolution of *Jerusalem*, the ecstatic body, arms outstretched under the dome of the head, is equal to two bodies embracing under a half-moon. Among flames, and with mutual desire, God and Jerusalem commingle sexually [24], completing the leap Albion would have made to the crucified Christ: "Amidst a circular background of blue, the heads of God and Jerusalem merge into an icon of Jesus, as Jerusalem's upward glance fulfills the motion of her buttocks by enclosing the face of God in the human and triangular space created by her outstretched arms."[8] The fourfold imagination takes joy in the double arc of its body from its source. Blake's visionary body suggests an infinity of postures. Albion's outstretched arms (plate 76) are poised not only to accept Christ's agony but also to celebrate continued life. Thus the embrace of God and Albion reenacts the creation of Adam. *Jerusalem* dramatically enacts Blake's self-deliverance from the womb of his world.

8. Thomas J. J. Altizer, *The New Apocalypse: The Radical Christian Vision of William Blake* (East Lansing, Mich., 1967), pp. 208–9.

9. William Blake, "God Blessing the Seventh Day."

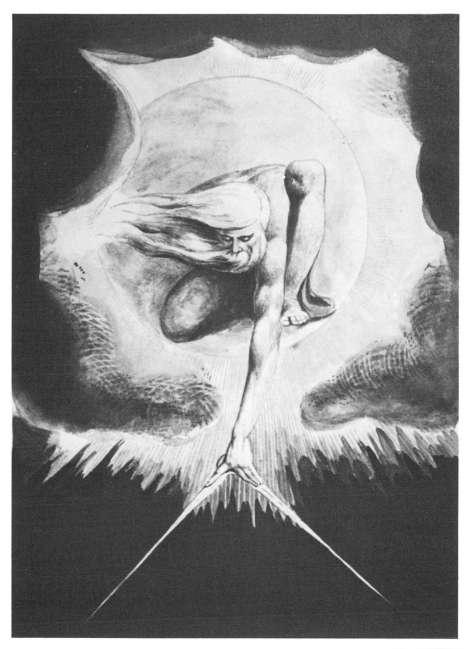

10. William Blake, "The Ancient of Days." Frontispiece to *Europe*.

11. William Blake, *Jerusalem*, plate 8, detail.

12. William Blake, *Jerusalem*, plate 15, detail.

13. William Blake, *Jerusalem*, plate 6, detail.

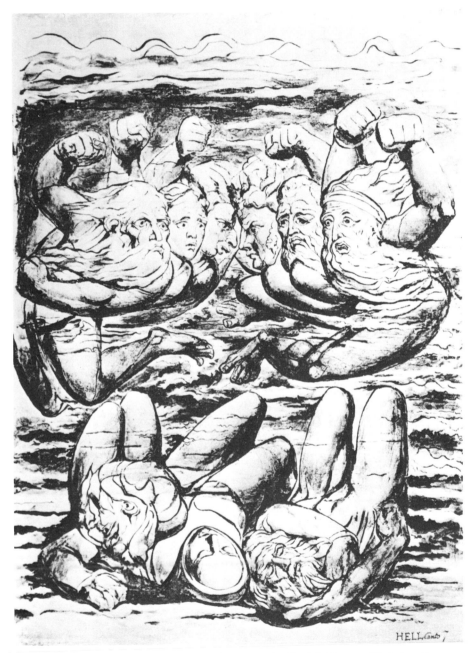

14. William Blake, "The Stygian Lake, with the Ireful Sinners Fighting."
Illustrations to Dante.

15. William Blake, "The Trinity." Rossetti Manuscript.

16. William Blake, *Jerusalem*, plate 18, detail.

17. William Blake, *Jerusalem*, plate 57.

18. William Blake, *Jerusalem*, plate 35.

19. William Blake, *Jerusalem*, plate 14, detail.

20. William Blake, *Jerusalem*, plate 1.

21. William Blake, *Jerusalem*, plate 97.

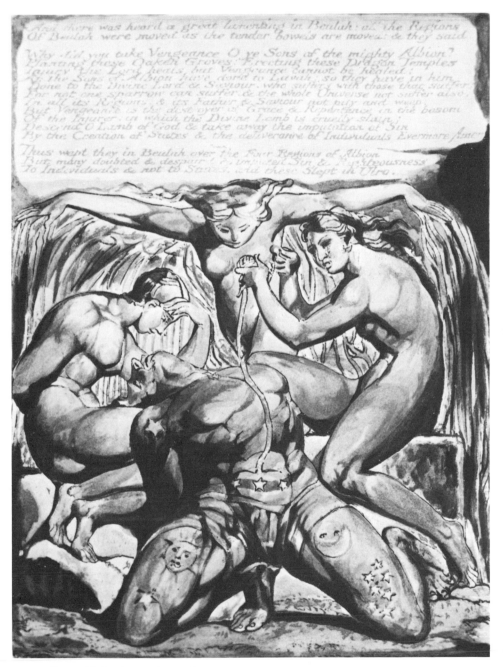

And there was heard a great lamenting in Beulah: all the Regions
Of Beulah were moved as the tender bowels are moved: & they said:

Why did you take Vengeance O ye Sons of the mighty Albion?
Planting these Oaken Groves: Erecting these Dragon Temples
Injury the Lord heals but Vengeance cannot be healed:
As the Sons of Albion have done to Luvah: so they have in him
Done to the Divine Lord & Saviour, who suffers with those that suffer:
For not one sparrow can suffer & the whole Universe not suffer also,
In all its Regions, & its Father & Saviour not pity and weep.
But Vengeance is the destroyer of Grace & Repentance in the bosom
Of the Injurer: in which the Divine Lamb is cruelly slain:
Descend O Lamb of God & take away the imputation of Sin
By the Creation of States & the deliverance of Individuals Evermore Amen

Thus wept they in Beulah over the Four Regions of Albion
But many doubted & despair'd & imputed Sin & Righteousness
To Individuals & not to States, and these Slept in Ulro.

22. William Blake, *Jerusalem*, plate 25.

23. William Blake, *Jerusalem*, plate 47.

24. William Blake, *Jerusalem*, plate 99.

Bodily rapture

On my haunches, eager and alone, casting an ebony
shadow, with the Gorsehill jungle swarming, the violent,
impossible birds and fishes leaping, hidden under
four-stemmed flowers the height of horses, in the early
evening in a dingle near Carmarthen . . . I felt all my
young body like an excited animal surrounding me,
the torn knees bent, the bumping heart, the long heat
and depth between the legs, the sweat prickling in the
hands, the tunnels down to the eardrums, the little balls
of dirt between the toes, the eyes in the sockets, the
tucked-up voice, the blood racing. . . . There, playing
Indians in the evening, I was aware of me myself in
the exact middle of a living story, and my body was
my adventure and my name.

> Dylan Thomas, *Portrait of the Artist*
> *as a Young Dog,* 22–23

The body, delighting in thresholds,
Rocks in and out of itself

> Theodore Roethke, *Collected Poems,* 163

He remembered the hour in that other southern garden,
when, both outside and within him, the cry of a bird
was correspondingly present, did not, so to speak, break
upon the barriers of his body, but gathered inner and
outer together into one uninterrupted space, in which,
mysteriously protected, only one single spot of
purest, deepest consciousness remained. That time he
had shut his eyes, so as not to be confused in so generous an experience by the contour of his body, and the
infinite passed into him so intimately from every side,

that he could believe he felt the light reposing of the
already appearing stars within his breast.

Rainer Maria Rilke, in Hartman,
Unmediated Vision, 140

if the body is a coffin it is also a closet of breath

Mark Strand, *Darker*, 5

The lady I followed, moving her lively body forward
with a motion that caused the folds of her dress in changing taffeta to glitter, graciously placed her bare arm
around a long stem of hollyhock, then started to grow
under a clear ray of light in such a manner that the
garden slowly took her form, trees and flowerbeds
becoming the roses and ornaments of her garment;
while her figure and her arms printed their contours
on the sky's purple clouds. Thus she passed from my
sight in a process of transfiguration, for she seemed to
disappear into her own greatness. "Oh! do not leave
me! I cried . . . for Nature dies with you!"

Gerard de Nerval, in Hartman,
Unmediated Vision, 165–66

Suddenly I realize
That if I stepped out of my body I would break
Into blossom.

James Wright, *Collected Poems*, 135

I was born without a skin. I dreamed once that I stood
naked in a garden and that it was carefully and neatly
peeled, like a fruit. Not an inch of skin left on my body.
It was all gently pulled off, all of it, and then I was
told to walk, to live, to run. I walked slowly at first, and
the garden was very soft, and I felt the softness of the
garden so acutely, not on the surface of my body, but all
through it, the soft warm air and the perfumes penetrated me like needles through every open bleeding
pore. All the pores open and breathing the softness, the

warmth, and the smells. The whole body invaded,
penetrated, responding, every tiny cell and pore active
and breathing and trembling and enjoying. I shrieked
with pain. I ran. And as I ran the wind lashed me,
and then the voices of people like whips on me. Being
touched! Do you know what it is to be touched by a
human being!

Anais Nin, House of Incest, 68–69

and I understood
the unicorn's phallus could have risen, after all,
directly out of thought itself.

Galway Kinnell, Book of Nightmares, 59

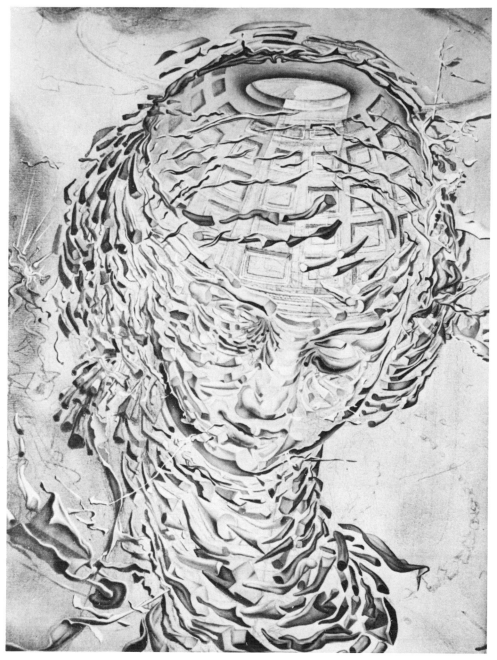

25. Salvador Dali, "Raphaelesque Head Exploding."

SEVEN   To fold the world
into the body's house:
perceptual space
in *The Prelude*

A man's head is an eminence upon
A field of barley spread beneath the sun.

A house for wisdom; a field for revelation.

At the field's end . . .
One learned of the eternal.

On a wide plain, beyond
The far stretch of a dream,
A field breaks like the sea

Theodore Roethke, *Collected Poems*,
13, 90, 199, 124

Often I Am Permitted To Return To A Meadow

as if it were a scene made-up by the mind,
that is not mine, but is a made place,

that is mine, it is so near to the heart,
an eternal pasture folded in all thought. . . .

whose hosts are a disturbance of words within words
that is a field folded.

Robert Duncan, *The Opening
of the Field*, 7

Wordsworth's poetry invests the two recurring spaces of house and
field with descriptive and emotive energy. What Wordsworth will

164

later call the "intermingled work of house and field" (*E*, V, 709)[1] sustains the old shepherd in "Michael," who each morning "to the fields went forth / With a light heart" (*M*, 283–84). His lifetime is gradually enclosed by the space of the fields: "Month followed month, / And in the open fields my life was passed" (*M*, 349–50). Returning home at the end of each day to work in repose on some "implement of house or field" (*M*, 109), he brings the two spaces momentarily together; the rhythm of place becomes a natural and almost ideal mutuality. The house is a haven from which to watch the fields at night, and in shearing time the sheep are brought to the old oak by its door. The fields are harvested beside the house, in its "depth of shade" and "covert." Michael finds a certain freedom in serving only the spaces of house and field, which, over the years, become the core of his experience. The "fields, where with cheerful spirits he had breathed / The common air" (*M*, 65–66) are a home for the shepherd's thought. The sheepfold is "a straggling heap of unhewn stones," and the house "on a plot of rising ground / Stood single, with large prospect" (*M*, 17, 132–33); "As cheerful as a grove in Spring" (*M*, 306), the house is almost an organic outgrowth of the land. Both house and sheepfold are more a tentative humanizing of the mountains than an alien imposition on them.[2]

1. The following poems by Wordsworth are abbreviated and documented internally: *C*—"Calm Is All Nature as a Resting Wheel"; *CB*—"The Old Cumberland Beggar"; *E*—*The Excursion*; *HG*—"To a Highland Girl"; *I*—"Ode: Intimations of Immortality from Recollections of Early Childhood"; *IT*—"I Travelled among Unknown Men"; *L*—"Louisa"; *M*—"Michael"; *P*—*The Prelude*; *R*—*The Recluse*; *RI*—"Resolution and Independence"; *SR*—"The Solitary Reaper"; *TA*—"Lines Composed a Few Miles above Tintern Abbey"; *TY*—"To a Young Lady"; *WB*—"Composed upon Westminster Bridge"; *WT*—"When, to the Attractions of the Busy World"; *YT*—"Yew-Trees."

Quotations are from *The Poetical Works of William Wordsworth*, vols. I-V, ed. Ernest de Selincourt and Helen Darbishire (London, 1954), and *The Prelude*, ed. Ernest de Selincourt, rev. Helen Darbishire (Oxford, 1959). In quoting from the 1850 version of *The Prelude* throughout, I have tried to view this final text as an organic outgrowth, rather than a reversal or qualification, of the earlier versions.

2. Cf. Geoffrey H. Hartman, "Wordsworth, Inscriptions, and Romantic Nature

The common resonance of intimate and open space is the motive power of the poem. But the fusion is not entire. There is an "unbending" quality to Michael's mind, a limit to his working pastoral vision. The unfinished sheepfold is in part an effort to make the fields wholly his own, to possess their distance in the close repose of the fireside. Though roofless, "a heap of stones," the sheepfold is a structure like the house; it is a bridge between house and field. "If these fields of ours / Should pass into a stranger's hand," Michael tells his son, "I think / That I could not lie quiet in my grave" (M, 230–32). As a metaphor, the sheepfold is the temptation to possession that the shepherd cannot overcome. In a corner of the field, it is the field folded. Laying its stones, Michael folds his house in a pasture of thought.

Modulations of house and field permeate Wordsworth's perceptions and his poetry. As he himself wrote, even his early poems "contained thoughts and images most of which have been dispersed through my other writings." Thus even a poem of Wordsworth's early youth (C) contrasts the field, "this blank of things," with "a harmony, / Home-felt, and home-created." In nature, a house of midway shelter suffices—the bower, grove, or cave. Thus the poet finds intimate and protective space "in the houseless woods" (TA, 20). Stirred by the wind, "the fir-grove murmurs with a sea-like sound" (WT, 104). Like the butterfly he watches, the poet feels his mind found out among the trees and called forth again. Wordsworth's ideal women, though more playful than him-

Poetry," *From Sensibility to Romanticism*, ed. Frederick W. Hilles and Harold Bloom (New York, 1965), p. 401: "The [sheepfold], moreover, is a monument almost merged with nature: to interpret the stones of the unfinished sheepfold is to interpret nature itself. We are made to see the naked mind confronting an anonymous landscape, yet drawing from it, or interpolating, the humane story of 'Michael.' The poem begins in an act of the living mind bent over a riddling inscription, perhaps an inscription of death." Hartman's *Wordsworth's Poetry 1787–1814* (New Haven, 1964) is the essential discussion of the balance in Wordsworth's poetry between internal and external perception. It develops at length the relationships Hartman first treats in *The Unmediated Vision* (New York, 1966), p. 165: "The experience of the drowned mind helps to explain how Wordsworth came to his apocalyptic vision of a drowned world, symbol for the immanence of a sustaining spirit."

self and responsive only to the graceful surface of nature, also appreciate the mutuality of grove and field:

> Thy mornings showed, thy nights concealed,
>   The bowers where Lucy played;
> And thine too is the last green field
>   That Lucy's eyes surveyed.
>
> (*IT*, 13–16)

Or as he writes in "Louisa," "She loves her fire, her cottage-home; / Yet o'er the moorland will she roam" (*L*, 13–14). The poet can appreciate the experience both of protective enclosure and of spaciousness, "of the fire-side, or of the open field" (*R*, 361).

But in the growth of the poet's own mind, grove and field acquire much more dramatic and active roles. When the world presses too heavily on the mind, the grove is a retreat: "Dear Child of Nature, let them rail! / —There is a nest in a green dale, / A harbour and a hold" (*TY*). The green dale and its repose for the nesting mind are set against the outside world: "I love the fir-grove with a perfect love. / Thither do I withdraw when cloudless suns / Shine hot, or wind blows troublesome and strong" (*WT*, 87–89). The grove is a home for the self, a natural frame for privacy, a retreat secure from one's own pain.

The intimate space of house or grove and the immensity of the field ("the wide waste") become analogues in Wordsworth's poetry for private and public experience. *The Prelude* begins with the poet's need to harmonize these two areas of experience—the yearnings for contemplative solitude in nature and the cares and demands of the human world. Again the rhythm of recurring spaces is invoked. In nature, the poet is content "to have a house (what matter for a home?)" (*P*, VII, 73). Wordsworth spent his childhood "piping on boughs, or sporting on fresh fields" (*P*, XII, 35), and sought the "deep shelter" of a "sequestered valley" (*P*, II, 113, 111). When he left his childhood home and its pastures islanded with groves, it was to "sing notes of greeting to strange fields or groves" and "range / The field of human life" (*P*, XIII,

135, 16–17). Within the shelter of the university, he learns that the world is "a wild field where [souls] were sown" (*P*, III, 183), though at Cambridge he was "an idler among academic bowers" (*P*, VIII, 503) and often chose to "quit / My comrades, leave the crowd, buildings and groves" to pace "alone the level fields" (*P*, III, 91–93). Eventually the bowers of Cambridge are left forever:

> Returned from that excursion, soon I bade
> Farewell for ever to the sheltered seats
> Of gownèd students, quitted hall and bower,
> And every comfort of that privileged ground,
> Well pleased to pitch a vagrant tent among
> The unfenced regions of society.
>
> (*P*, VII, 52–57)

Cambridge, "that inclosure old, / That garden of great intellects, undisturbed" (*P*, III, 266–67), prompts Wordsworth to meditate on the ideal bower for nurturing youth—a "primeval grove," a "sanctuary" protected by its own spirit,

> A habitation sober and demure
> For ruminating creatures; a domain
> For quiet things to wander in; a haunt
> In which the heron should delight to feed
> By the shy rivers, and the pelican
> Upon the cypress spire in lonely thought
> Might sit and sun himself.
>
> (*P*, III, 438–44)

Removed from the world and its distractions, such an ideal and ancient enclosure encompasses its own awesome internal distances. It is both grove and field. When the poet enters its safe and private enclosure, the grove becomes a natural analogue for the intimate space of meditation:

> ye groves, whose ministry it is
> To interpose the covert of your shades,
> Even as a sleep, between the heart of man

> And outward troubles, between man himself,
> Not seldom, and his own uneasy heart
>
> <div align="right">(<i>P</i>, XII, 24–28)</div>

In a grove, thought flows peacefully in the bowl of the mind. It is the constant renewal of childhood's security, the reenergizing of the womb's silence, and the submission of the mind's hemispheres to sleep. "A grove there is ... / With length of shade so thick, that whoso glides / Along the line of low-roofed water, moves / As in a cloister" (*P*, VIII, 458–62). "Some Hermit, from his cell forthstrayed, might pace / In sylvan meditation undisturbed; / As on the pavement of a Gothic church" (*P*, IX, 442–44).

Truth, Wordsworth writes, has "her sunny glades / And shady groves in studied contrast" (*E*, IV, 590–91). The doubleness "of level pasture, islanded with groves" (*P*, VIII, 191) is appropriate and necessary. Even in nature itself the rhythm of intimate enclosure and ecstatic immensity is inevitable:

> Abroad, how cheeringly the sunshine lay
> Upon the open lawns! Vallombre's groves
> Entering, we fed the soul with darkness; thence
> Issued, and with uplifted eyes
>
> <div align="right">(<i>P</i>, VI, 479–82)</div>

We find "beneath the roof / Of that perennial shade, a cloistral place / Of refuge," a "safe covert" (*WT*, 10–13), not only from the world and the mind's cares but also from the sometimes threatening expanse of the fields. Yet there is no endless stay in the tranquil "house / Of nature" (*WT*, 23–24). For a grove is also the circumstance, the occasion and structure, of the mind's ease in the flow of thought. There are vitality and ancient energy in repose: we feed on a dark silence seeded with unexpected power.

To leave a grove at night is to be "unhoused beneath the evening star" (*P*, VI, 370), but nature's house is also the home we carry in our heads. Unhoused, the mind is unsheathed and opened to the expanse of the world, extended to the abstract covert of the bending sky. There are, as Wordsworth learns, groves and bowers within (*P*, III, 383–85). The mind has "leafy *arbours* where the light / Might enter in at will"; yet "*Caverns* there were within my mind which sun / Could never penetrate" (*P*, III, 246–49). Arbor and cavern both take the shape of the mind's house (the skull); repose in the first resonates in the depths of the other.

The uniqueness of *The Prelude* is grounded in this continual and explicit fitting of the internal to the external world. Wordsworth's first questions are "What dwelling shall receive me? in what vale / Shall be my harbour? underneath what grove / Shall I take up my home?" (*P*, I, 10–12); they pose both the obvious narrative problem and a deeper one—what kind of a home his head will be. Almost at once the first stirrings of his visionary answer balance house and field: "to the open fields I told / A prophecy" (*P*, I, 50–51). Bower and field find a home in his mind, as the poet seeks a home in them. Enclosure and far-reaching fields are made mutual in the only space which at once duplicates the point and the arc of the heavens—the flesh mold of the mind.

As the poet's mind has arbors and caverns, so in the external world the grove is linked emotively to the cave. In this geography of spatial analogues, the hermit who walks in a bower will often make his home in a cave. Seeking a home in the houseless woods, the poet settles for a grove that shelters at least his mind. But the grove is also linked (through the form and motion of the nesting mind) to "subterranean fields" (*P*, XI, 140), the "fields of sleep" (*I*, III, 28); the mind internalizes the field as a deep and spacious cave, a vertical and widening distance.

All tranquil space is therefore a form "of the individual Mind that keeps her own / Inviolate retirement" (*R*, 772–73). "The calm / And dead still water" lies upon the poet's mind: "Thus were my sympathies enlarged" (*P*, II, 170–75). All repose reverberates "In the last place of refuge—my own soul" (*P*, X, 415). The poets who tune their harps in an "echoing cave" have discovered a physical frame for "the mind's / Internal echo" (*P*, XI, 458; I,

55–56). A bottomless dream is externalized in *The Excursion* as the poet, anticipating rest in a cave, begins to meditate on an internal distance: "in caves forlorn, / And 'mid the hollow depths of naked crags / He sate, and . . . in their fixed and steady lineaments / He traced an ebbing and a flowing mind" (*E*, I, 154–61). Standing still before a cave, the poet is "By power of that impending covert thrown / To finer distance" (*E*, I, 16–17).

In a celebrated passage of *The Prelude*, Wordsworth begins reading in stillness, "seated in a rocky cave": "listlessly I sate, and, having closed / The book, had turned my eyes toward the wide sea" (*P*, V, 58, 63–64). Seated alone in the silent cave, his eyes are drawn to the surrounding distance, and he meditates on "poetry and geometric truth" (*P*, V, 65). Cave and sea duplicate the shape and rhythm of his musing mind, and he soon succumbs to a bottomless dream of internal spaces, "voyaging through strange seas of Thought, alone" (*P*, III, 63): "Sleep seized me, and I passed into a dream. / I saw before me stretched a boundless plain / Of sandy wilderness, all black and void" (*P*, V, 70–72). Entering the cave of his head, Wordsworth "sees the vault / Widening on all sides" (*P*, VIII, 564–65). It is what in *The Recluse* he calls the opening of the inward frame (*R*, 472–73). The final pages of *The Prelude* describe the opening outward of this inward frame:

> we have traced the stream
> From the blind cavern whence is faintly heard
> Its natal murmur; followed it to light
> And open day
>
>   (*P*, XIV, 194–97)

The poet has moved naturally from the womb to the sheltered groves of childhood, then to sterile academic bowers and the threatening fields of the world that force his retreat to the bower and deeper cave of his own mind; the movement is fulfilled in a second birth into the "circumambient world" (*P*, VIII, 56). Yet the movement requires all its component steps. The wish to remain a child forever is at the same time a denial of this second, uniquely conscious, birth. The weight of the world must coerce the mind to discover its own power.

As a child romping in the fields and hiding in the woods, absorbing natural things as immediate experience without self-consciousness, Wordsworth needed no special rituals and no attendant language to achieve mutuality of rest and exhilaration. Returning to nature in adult life, the rhythm of cave or grove and field becomes slow and meditative. Then the eye's inclination to possess and evaluate must be overcome in deliberate submission to enclosed and extended space. As the physical responsiveness of youth matures, its energy passes to mental leaps, to the imaginative embrace of a landscape.

The ebbing and flowing mind is what energizes the body no longer spontaneously in physical touch with natural surfaces. But Wordsworth's flesh is not forgotten; indeed his body comes to have a unique role in the meditative journey inward. Random childhood play evolves among the fields and woods into a series of physical postures which accompany and encourage the musing mind. Wordsworth typically chooses to recline by the side of a running stream, to sit in a cave, to walk in a field, "or in mute repose / To lie, and listen to the mountain flood / Murmuring from Glaramara's inmost caves" (*YT*, 31–33). His blood seems to flow in the presence of water; his body becomes "a motion or a shape / Instinct with vital functions" (*P*, VIII, 298–99). It is a relationship of pure mutuality, for "everywhere a vital pulse was felt" (*P*, VIII, 480). The stream flows, the blood pulses, and both move with the ebb and flow of his mind: "Who that shall point as with a wand and say / 'This portion of the river of my mind / Came from yon fountain'" (*P*, II, 208–10).

In nature, body and mind are mutually stimulated by the surrounding environment "By which, and under which, we are enclosed / To breathe in peace" (*R*, 643–44), whether sheltering vale ("Urn-like it was in shape, deep as an urn; / With rocks encom-

passed," *E*, II, 333–34), enclosing cave or grove, or at times even the
sky with "circumambient walls; / A temple framing of dimensions vast" (*E*, IV, 1160–61). There, as Wordsworth writes in his
prospectus to *The Excursion* (*R*, 816–21), "How exquisitely the
individual Mind / . . . to the external World / Is fitted:—and
how exquisitely, too— / . . . The external World is fitted to the
Mind." In *The Prelude* Wordsworth offers an iconic image for
this mutuality:

> Through quaint obliquities I might pursue
> These cravings; when the fox-glove, one by one,
> Upwards through every stage of the tall stem,
> Had shed beside the public way its bells,
> And stood of all dismantled, save the last
> Left at the tapering ladder's top, that seemed
> To bend as doth a slender blade of grass
> Tipped with a rain-drop, Fancy loved to seat,
> Beneath the plant despoiled, but crested still
> With this last relic, soon itself to fall
>
> (*P*, VIII, 392–401)

The isolation of the drooping plant, crested with its final flower,
bends over the poet's imagination; it is a perfect model of the mind
at play in an enclosing environment. Seated beneath the arch of
the solitary flower, the poet releases the flower of his mind in the
curve of his perceptions. The balance is delicate, quaint, and cannot be maintained indefinitely, yet nature offers enough support
for meditation to work.

But this mutuality, this fitting, is not so readily achieved when
the poet "must hear Humanity in fields and groves" (*R*, 829). As
nature alternates between grove and field, Wordsworth's private
meditations are challenged by the outer world. Confronting civilization in *The Prelude*, the poet discovers he needs the support of
another natural enclosure—his own body. When he first entered
the "vast dominion" of the city, "a weight of ages did at once descend" upon him (*P*, VIII, 543, 552). The metaphor recalls Wordsworth's earliest writings, for even then he longed for solitude as the

world pressed in on him, seeking freedom from the world's "offi-cious touch that makes me droop again" (*C*). Elsewhere he refers to the sheer weight of custom (*I*, VIII, 127), and in *The Prelude* soon feels the oppressive weight of the city's past bearing down on his own body: "a sense / Of what in the Great City had been done / And suffered, and was doing, suffering, still, / Weighed with me" (*P*, VIII, 625-28). Coupled with the weight of the city is the "many-headed mass / Of the spectators" (*P*, VII, 434-35), the "huge fermenting mass of human-kind" (*P*, VII, 621) which over-whelms the poet in the bloodletting after the French Revolution: "thus, on every side beset with foes, / The goaded land waxed mad; the crimes of few / Spread into madness of the many" (*P*, X, 335-37). An overloaded "reservoir of guilt," amassed over the ages, "burst and spread in deluge through the land" (*P*, X, 477-80). "When the calamity spread far and wide" (*P*, X, 503), and the fields of the world are sown with blood, Wordsworth fears the immense world will "engulph him soon in the ravenous sea" (*P*, IX, 4). Overcome by violence and human carnage, the poet has a sudden startling vision of a child in a field, ecstatically urging a whirling toy to spin faster and faster (*P*, X, 356-74).

Wordsworth's mind is distracted, his body exhausted: "depressed / By false opinion and contentious thought, / Or aught of heavier or more deadly weight" (*P*, XII, 210-12), "wearied out with con-trarieties . . . I drooped" (*P*, XI, 304-7). Disenchanted with the world and his own perception, he turns to "recoil and droop, and seek repose" (*P*, I, 265):

> When from our better selves we have too long
> Been parted by the hurrying world, and droop,
> Sick of its business, of its pleasures tired,
> How gracious, how benign, is Solitude
> (P, IV, 354-57)

All his external concerns and pleasures alienate him, "and when these had drooped / And gradually expired" (*P*, VIII, 345-46), he moves inward toward nature. "With forehead bent" under the curve of his drooping body, Wordsworth sinks into thought. Though his body is bent, "the mind / Drooped not; but there into herself returning, / With prompt rebound seemed fresh" (*P*, III, 95–97). The poet resists:

> The tendency, too potent in itself,
> Of use and custom to bow down the soul
> Under a growing weight of vulgar sense,
> And substitute a universe of death
> For that which moves with light and life informed
>
>   (*P*, XIV, 157–61)

The very weight of civilization turns Wordsworth toward the reserves of nature in himself, the reservoir stored in his body. His posture is shaped by the world's oppressive presence: the poet "must hang / Brooding above the fierce confederate storm / Of sorrow" (*R*, 830–32). In his love of nature, Wordsworth inhabits his body and finds shelter in its enclosure. The drooping human body, the tranquil corporeal frame, is the space where the disenchanted mind will sink to dream:

> Dreams not unlike to those which once begat
> A change of purpose in young Whittington,
> When he, a friendless and a drooping boy,
> Sate on a stone, and heard the bells speak out
> Articulate music.
>
>   (*P*, VII, 111–15)

At the limit of endurance, the drooping, brooding body imitates the arc of grove or cave, the curve of nature "compassed round by mountain solitudes" (*P*, XIV, 139). Crouched over the cave of his body, the poet's posture duplicates the figures in his memory, in his mind's eye—the Cumberland beggar, "Bow-bent, his eyes for ever on the ground" (*CB*, 52); the father in *The Prelude* (VII, 603–18), sitting on a stone bending over his child; the solitary reaper, "singing at her work, / And o'er the sickle bending" (*SR*,

27–28); the leech-gatherer, who stands "As a huge stone is sometimes seen to lie," his body "bent double, feet and head / Coming
together in life's pilgrimage" (*RI*, 57, 66–67).

"Thy mind," Wordsworth writes, is "a mansion for all lovely
forms," and the memory is "as a dwelling-place" (*TA*, 139–41).
Hanging over his own past, the poet makes his body a house of
time. Like the house at the edge of the field, or Michael's sheepfold, the meditating body is the field folded. "As one who hangs
down-bending from the side / Of a slow-moving boat, upon the
breast / Of a still water . . . now is crossed by gleam / Of his own
image" (*P*, IV, 256–68). Bent over the shape of his past life, the
poet's body is enclosing and enclosed; his posture creates a dwelling
place, a house encircling and enclosing the hearth.

The eye that gathered "pleasure like a bee among the flowers"
(*P*, I, 580) learns that "Our Memory . . . hath eyes" (*HG*, 67).
Hovering over his past, Wordsworth discovers "the ties / That
bind the perishable hours of life / Each to the other" (*P*, VII, 461–
63), "the self-created sustenance of a mind" (*P*, VI, 301). He views
"the things which I had shaped, / And yet not shaped, had seen
and scarcely seen" (*P*, VII, 482–83), the spots of time that nourish
and repair his consciousness. These experiences have flowered in
his body since first sown there in the "seed-time" of his soul,
"doomed to sleep / Until maturer seasons called them forth / To
impregnate and to elevate the mind" (*P*, I, 594–96). He takes those
assorted moments, treating time as a series of objects, and rebuilds
in his body the home of his mind. Through his meditative poem,
Wordsworth has

> played with times
> And accidents as children do with cards,
> Or as a man, who, when his house is built,
> A frame locked up in wood and stone, doth still,
> As impotent fancy prompts, by his fireside,
> Rebuild it to his liking.
>
> (*P*, VI, 289–94)

The Prelude is the process of building and rebuilding the house of time, of reshaping the flesh shape of the mind. It aims at more than simply refining the conscious experience of bliss, and does more than expose worldly suffering to the influence of nature. Wordsworth comes to see the city "Open unto the fields" (*WB*, 7), to see "the curling cloud / Of city smoke, by distance ruralised" (*P*, I, 88–89), but his repaired and restored imagination also has a larger purpose. The poem begins with the poet's attempt to find grounds for enduring the human world; in emotional flight from contact with civilization, he finds sufficient strength in his memory of nature. Yet beyond this, the meditating body—weighted, drooping, and bent—provides a revitalizing energy; through it the poet achieves a remarkable power to reshape and restructure his natural experience.

The light of nature was stored in the hive of his body. There natural objects undergo a dark reconciliation, a secret interfusion which transforms particular pleasures into a generalized perceptual force. His bodily eyes blind, Wordsworth turns inward to view with his mind the abyss of his flesh: "There doth the reaper bind the yellow sheaf, / The maiden spread the haycock in the sun" (*P*, VI, 536–37). The external rhythm of house and field widens into the rhythm of folding and unfolding perception. The poetic mind harvests the fields of sleep. When Wordsworth returns in his poem to the experience of nature, his mind has breathed the "pent-up air" under "splitting fields of ice . . . struggling to free itself" (*P*, I, 539–40). In the last books of *The Prelude*, nature provokes an apocalyptic need to unfold the mind over the fields of the world, to fold the world into the body's house. Through conscious meditation, Wordsworth's body becomes a vehicle for verbal energy.

In Book VII of *The Prelude* Wordsworth recalls first seeing a prostitute:

> I shuddered, for a barrier seemed at once
> Thrown in, that from humanity divorced

> Humanity, splitting the race of man
> In twain, yet leaving the same outward form.
>
> (*P*, VII, 388–91)

Later he speaks unhappily of a division "That almost seems inherent in the creature, / A twofold frame of body and of mind" (*P*, XII, 125–26). The "exterior semblance," he writes, "doth belie / Thy Soul's immensity" (*I*, VIII, 109–10). Remembering his early experiences of nature, he feels estranged from the joyous child he was then; yet the memory fills him, and he is man and child at once, for those days have "such self-presence in my mind, / That, musing on them, often do I seem / Two consciousnesses, conscious of myself / And of some other Being" (*P*, II, 30–33). Returning to nature as an adult, this "twofold frame of body and of mind" is unified through meditation. Only an immense expanse like the spreading sea and sky can shape the soul's aspirations. "Think," he writes in an external figure for body and mind, "how the everlasting streams and woods, / Stretched and still stretching far and wide, exalt / The roving Indian" (*P*, VII, 745–47). Thus a single figure against a vast landscape is one of Wordsworth's most recurrent images. The beggar, the reaper, the leech-gatherer—as the poet watches each figure and listens, the human body becomes a humming stone: "And the whole body of the Man did seem / Like one whom I had met with in a dream" (*RI*, 109–10). Singing or quiet, these bowed figures bend in solitude over the abyss of past time, set off from the immense surrounding landscape. They and the poet, who "hung / Listening" in silence, become vehicles for all the bodies brooding on the earth. Each figure is a reaper, harvesting into his body the dreams of the ages. Once, Wordsworth reveals the wish implicit in the solitary human form: "Oh! what a joy it were, in vigorous health, / To have a body . . . And to the elements surrender it / As if it were a spirit!" (*E*, IV, 508–13).

The meditative posture—crouched over the cave of the body and brooding on dark fields of flesh—cannot itself provide this full submission to nature. Having slept long and deeply in the body's house, the poet is impelled to extend himself in the fields of the world again. "The breath of this corporeal frame / And even the motion of our human blood / Almost suspended" (*TA*, 43–45), the tranquil body has a vitality like "the stationary blasts of water-falls" (*P*, VI, 626). The "still overflow" of somatic meditation gives Wordsworth the energy and power to breathe the air of an immense landscape. The unreleased energy he perceives in his body is fulfilled in the embrace of the world.[3]

The human nature Wordsworth desires is "not a punctual presence, but a spirit / Diffused through time and space" (*P*, VIII, 610–11). "A disappearing line," he recalls, is "like an invitation into space / Boundless, or guide into eternity" (*P*, XIII, 146–51). The illusion of purely linear time that *The Prelude* offers is one manifestation of the straight line. But the perceptual time of an unfolding intellect returns again and again, turning in upon itself until mind and body are fit for a total vision of nature. *The Prelude* is a challenge to follow autobiographical time until it transcends time and space. Consciousness then deals "with the whole compass of the universe" (*P*, XIV, 92), and the poet's awareness is "spread over time, past, present, and to come, / Age after age, till Time shall be no more" (*P*, XIV, 110–11). Then all "time / And seasons serve" the mind, "the elements are potter's clay," and the "earth crouches" beneath an imagination "here, nowhere, there, and everywhere at once" (*P*, V, 528–33).

The ecstatic release of the body's power, the final harvest of the fruit of time, has its forerunner in the most expansive moments of childhood play, when "along the margin of the moonlight sea— / We beat with thundering hoofs the level sand" (*P*, X, 602–3), or

---

3. Following upon meditation, writing is a movement outward—into the world; we may compare Hazlitt's description of Wordsworth's methods of composition: "Coleridge has told me that he himself liked to compose in walking over uneven ground, or breaking through the straggling branches of a copse-wood; whereas Wordsworth always wrote (if he could) walking up and down a straight gravel-walk, or in some spot where the continuity of his verse met with no collateral interruption." Quoted by Kenneth Burke, *The Philosophy of Literary Form* (New York, 1957), p. 10.

When we had given our bodies to the wind,
And all the shadowy banks on either side
Came sweeping through the darkness, spinning still
The rapid line of motion, then at once
Have I, reclining back upon my heels,
Stopped short; yet still the solitary cliffs
Wheeled by me—even as if the earth had rolled
With visible motion her diurnal round!

(*P*, I, 453–60)

The apocalyptic posture of *The Prelude* takes this accidental extension of childhood play and makes it deliberate and conscious. Once again, the child playing with the surface of the world matures to the man whose mind now makes the same contact. Returning to the fields, Wordsworth climbs a mountain to embrace the curve of the world:

Like a lone shepherd on a promontory
Who lacking occupation looks far forth
Into the boundless sea, and rather makes
Than finds what he beholds.

(*P*, III, 516–19)

Or him have I descried in distant sky,
A solitary object and sublime,
Above all height! like an aerial cross
Stationed alone upon a spiry rock
Of the Chartreuse, for worship.

(*P*, VIII, 271–75)

As the poet stands footbound gazing at the upright shape of an unmoving man, he truly discovers the "human form" as an "index of delight" (*P*, VIII, 279–80). On the mountaintop, the mind spreads the body's upright pleasure over the surface of the earth. "My head," Wordsworth writes, "hath its coronal, / The fulness of your bliss" (*I*, IV, 40–41). Struck still by the figure of the lone man on the mountain, Wordsworth sets out to crown his body with a blissful vision of the circling world. In the end he ascends the mountain himself, and his posture recalls Christ's at the end of

Paradise Regained, while his vision of time as space echoes God's perception in *Paradise Lost.* But the poet's posture is not symbolic; instead he performs a concrete and literal act of revelation.

At the top of the mountain, the horizon of his mind overlays the horizon of the world. There the mind frames its book, *The Prelude,* in a moment that spreads out autobiographical chronology like a map of time unfolded into space: "Anon I rose / As if on wings, and saw beneath me stretched / Vast prospect of the world which I had been / And was" (*P,* XIV, 379–82). *The Prelude* begins and ends in itself. The apocalyptic posture enacts all the preceding events of the poem; it continually renews the entire body of the book. For the book then has the double texture of earth and air— of airy thought diffused throughout a human density. As foretold in his cave dream, the poet's book is now both stone and shell.

The poets who were trained in field and grove, "who attuned their harps / In wood or echoing cave," now "stand / On Etna's summit, above earth and sea, / Triumphant, winning from the invaded heavens / Thoughts without bound" (*P,* XI, 453–58). Wordsworth unfolds his body over the fields of the world; he folds the world into his poem's house. If we accept the final vision of *The Prelude*—the poet on the mountaintop—we must be satisfied with an image of the body erect in a bending environment encircled by the mind. This, for Wordsworth, is "the highest bliss / That flesh can know" (*P,* XIV, 113–14): the body erect in the bowl of the mind.

Cove—cave—head

A head is also a sort of ball into which space enters
Jean Hélion, in Kepes,
Visual Arts Today, 103

What is the body covering? The corresponding Old
English terms for the "body" suggest the answer: they
call the "body" *flaesc-homa*, properly "flesh-cover";
ban-cofa, "bone-cave"; *ban-faet*, "bone-vessel"; or
ban-hus, "bone-house." The "house," the "cave," the
"vessel" made of flesh and bones are all "cover" for the
invisible agency that has chosen the house, cave, vessel
for its dwelling place.
Theodore Thass-Thienemann,
The Subconscious Language, 277

Cove, cave, head—shells where the world's wind echoes.
(C. N.)

Terrified, the small boy bears the big bird of the dirty
word into the house, and grunting, puffing, carries it up
the stairs to his own room in the skull.
Karl Shapiro, Poems 1940–1953, 35

Moore, burrowing into his mother figures, created an
inner space that appears bigger and stronger than the
solid stone. His recent work has shifted to the male
figure or head, but retains the same womb symbolism.
The cavity in the phallic helmet is stronger than its
outer shell.
Anton Ehrenzweig, The Hidden
Order of Art, plate 29

It is a place of darkness; it darkens; it stands ever dark.
It stands wide-mouthed, it is wide-mouthed. It is wide-
mouthed; it is narrow-mouthed. It has mouths which
pass through. I place myself in the cave. I enter the cave.

Aztec, 16th century, in Rothenberg, ed.,
Technicians of the Sacred, 26

The conception of the body as a magical vessel, a
transformative retort that is at the same time a mys-
terious cavern and a landscape, gradually brings about
a strange transformation of the head, as though it had
been affected by the symbol of the body cavity. The
head itself becomes the sheltering uterus.

Erich Neumann, *Archetypal World
of Henry Moore*, 143

Animals wake up first facially and then bodily. Men's
bodies wake up before their faces do. For the animal
sleeps inside his body, whereas man sleeps with his
body in his mind.

Malcolm de Chazal, *Plastic Sense*, 49

in our heads
bodies collapse
and grow again

Sam Cornish, *Generations*, 67

But when our heads are planted
under the church, from those empty pods
we rise in the fields of death

Louis Simpson, *At the End
of the Open Road*, 61

My mind floats in the purple air of my skull.
I see myself dancing. I smile at everybody.
Slowly I dance out of the burning house of my head.
And who isn't borne again and again into heaven?

Mark Strand, *Darker*, 12

26. Paul Klee, "Leaning."

EIGHT Suffused-encircling
shapes of mind: inhabited
space in Williams

> But surely, everywhere, from whatever poem, choreographies extend into actual space.
>
> Robert Duncan, *Bending the Bow*, vi

> At his desk, Robert Seaton was bending over one of the little black notebooks, in a pose so rigid, so attentive that Nigel almost expected to see some jeweled flower or insect come fabulously burrowing up out of the blank page before his eyes.
>
> Nicholas Blake, *Head of a Traveler*, 180

> Carrying our seed in our head; like flowers
>
> Norman O. Brown, *Love's Body*, 137

William Carlos Williams is all there at the beginning. His work opens outward in a series of figures. His writings are the unfolding of a poetic, a man, a vision. It is a movement toward fulfillment—the germination and reverberation of a single verbal action: a flower.

The use of flowers as a metaphor for the self and of flowering for all modes of becoming is as basic to Williams as the act of writing. The flower emerges early as a total metaphor, saying all there is to say about the human condition and its permutations. In *In the American Grain* the Indian is " 'right,' the flower of his world" (*IAG*, 138),[1] and Cotton Mather is "a flower in mail, in-

---

1. The following editions of Williams's work are abbreviated and documented internally by page: *A—The Autobiography of William Carlos Williams* (New

185

human" (*IAG*, 113). In Williams's vision the metaphor of flowering expresses two poles of human consciousness—fulfillment and frustration. Through this doubleness the word "flowering" itself comes to embody a reconciliation of joy and pain.

In the American Grain resonates with human versions of the metaphor. Columbus's chaste flower, "pure, white, waxlike and fragrant" (*IAG*, 7), broods throughout his chapter: "if . . . he had undertaken that holy pilgrimage . . . the flower might again, in that seclusion, often have appeared to him in all its old-time loveliness . . . " (*IAG*, 16). Montezuma's personality, about which the "most airily expansive moods of the race did flower," shows all the sensitive modulations of flesh as flower: "He was the very person of their ornate dreams, so delicate, so prismatically colorful, so full of tinkling sounds and rhythms, so tireless of invention. Never was such a surface lifted above the isolate blackness of such profound savagery" (*IAG*, 35). Perhaps from the same floral source issue the Puritans, "condemned to be without flower," whom we know for "their projection of the great flower of which they were the seed" (*IAG*, 65); they anticipate "the brutalizing desolation of life in America . . . yet perversely flowering" (*IAG*, 234). Even "a flower sheared away—nothing" (*IAG*, 64) is a human alternative: "The quality of the flower will then be seen to be normal, in all its tortured spirituosity and paleness, a desert flower with roots under the sand" (*IAG*, 213). Williams's human population is a profusion of flowers; it is such a delicate obsession.

Everywhere—in the most direct and simple gestures—Williams saw the metaphor of flowering extended. He has called "love itself a flower" (*CLP*, 52), and its opposite—the inverse flower of anguish —is expressed in

York, 1967); *CLP—The Collected Later Poems* (New York, 1963); *CP—The Complete Collected Poems of William Carlos Williams: 1906–1938* (Norfolk, Conn., 1938); *IAG—In the American Grain* (New York, 1956); *IWWP—I Wanted to Write a Poem* (Boston, 1958); *KH—Kora in Hell: Improvisations* (Boston, 1920); *P—Paterson* (New York, 1963); *SA—Spring and All* (Dijon, 1923); *SE—Selected Essays* (New York, 1954); *SL—Selected Letters* (New York, 1957).

> virginity
> longing for snow and
>
> a quiet life
> that will (rightly)
>
> blossom as
> a mangled corpse
>   (*CLP*, 139)

Like Daniel Boone's intimacy with the wilderness, a flower is a caress—here and there—of the landscape. The more healthy figures in *In the American Grain* flower both in the environment around them and in the landscape of the self. Thus Williams uses an immense flower to characterize all the time and space he has personalized: "Another petal reaches / into the past . . . when my mother was a child" (*CP*, 292). And "The Crimson Cyclamen" shows how lithe and human Williams can make the immediate visual facts of a flower's behavior.

There is nothing especially unconventional in these uses of flowering as a loose metaphor for becoming and self-realization. Williams catalogs the flowers around him and the flowers in our history, and thereby possesses his landscape. But he seems unsatisfied; indeed the catalog gradually gives way to a larger quest, signaled by a new extension of the metaphor: "this very fine flower of U.S. art is warped out of alignment" (*KH*, 27). Williams's own art, the flower before him, is now more than a possession—it is something he can *do*. Through his poetry, the metaphor finally becomes a special form of consciousness—any moment in which several things in the visual field are appreciated together:

THE FLOWER

> This too I love
> Flossie sitting in the sun
> on its cane
> the first rose

> yellow as an egg the pet
> canary
> in his cage
> beside her carolling
>   (*CLP*, 104)

Identifying sensation or mind with flowering suggests a space of objective validity that can be entered and energized by the imagination. The mind-flower of "The Lesson" (*CLP*, 213) balances a sensuous image of curled, quiescent, almost damp inhabitation with the intimate, resonant space of consciousness. For the flower is both heavy root, familiar to the mud, and seed-packed erection in space. Here the brain is both "intestined / to the invisible root / where . . . thought lies communal / with / the brooding worm" and extended in the air, "the wanton the dancing / that / holding enfolds it." Abstracted, the visual space of the poem is a single, columnar thrust to the last stanza:

> The hydrangea
> pink cheeked nods its head
> a paper brain
> without a skull
>
> a brain intestined
> to the invisible root
> where
> beside the rose and acorn
>
> thought lies communal
> with
> the brooding worm
> True but the air
>
> remains
> the wanton the dancing
> that
> holding enfolds it
>
> a flower
> aloof
> Flagrant as a flag

> it shakes that seamy head
>
> or
> snaps it drily
> from the anchored stem
> and sets it rolling

The stanzas are like segments of a stem that blossoms as "a flower / aloof" in the fifth stanza, and is decapitated or dismembered, snapped "drily / from the anchored stem," in the last. Each stanza as a unit violates the thematic and visual space of the one preceding it, asserting a new image of inhabitation by flowering mind. The succeeding units are approximately small rectangles, an intimate cellular structure sustained by our experience of its space. It moves from the upright hydrangea down to the brain-root-worm, returns then to the air and the flower aloof, and the balance is harmonized by the dismembered flower-head rolling on the ground.

Williams has achieved a complete identification of head and flower—an equation sensuously apprehended. Yet the whole poem does not intrude single-mindedly into our consciousness; it remains a passive structure. Its internal violations are gentle and painless—fraternal unions. For all its brevity and fullness, "The Lesson" resides firmly in a world of reinforcing similitude, and the reader consumes the page without difficulty. Williams has not yet found a technique to prevent the reading situation from being immediately internal.

Nevertheless, this increasingly versatile mind-flower—resonance and intimacy of mind dwelling in a form—accretes various shapes, signs, and gestures. Though the poem's structure does not yet compel us to inhabit its space, it encourages our growing intimacy with the consciousness shaped by the poem. We begin to recognize "flowering minds" (*CLP*, 52) and "a pattern / which is the mind itself . . . that circumstance / of which the speech is poetry" (*CLP*, 12).

If the act of mind-flowering is traced through Williams's poetry, we discover its formal characteristics. Exploring an intimacy between phenomena and his own consciousness, the poet inhabits a space that is distinct from both his own previous experience and the object contemplated. This twofold space—of the object and the poet's perception—is encircled by and suffused with consciousness. We can describe these spaces, circulating in water and about the sea, as suffused-encircling shapes of mind. We witness "the wave / rising or the wave curving to the hollow" (*CLP*, 26) and sense in ourselves an

> immeasurable sea,
>
> unmarred, that as it lifts
> encloses this
> straining mind, these
> limbs in a single gesture.
> (*CLP*, 68)

Explored as analogues to meditation, these sea caves of mental space appear in any drift of air, seed, or water:

> And the mind hesitant
> regarding the stream
> senses
> a likeness which it
>
> will find—a complex
> image: something
> of white brows
> bound by a ribbon
>
> of sooty thought
> (*CLP*, 118)

A circumstance of the same sea speech, Williams's poem "Seafarer" (*CLP*, 170) is about inhabited or violated space in nature:

> the rocks
> seem rather to leap
> at the sea than the sea
> to envelope them. They strain
> forward to grasp ships
> or even the sky itself that

> bends down to be torn
> upon them.

To the mutual tension of rocks, sea, and sky, the poet replies: "It is I! I who am the rocks! / Without me nothing laughs." His gesture of affirmation is openly verbal; the spatial relationships are maintained by human action. Yet once the poem is written, its tensions remain poised forever without our intervention. Both seafarer and poem wholly enclose the field of force, and the result remains primarily descriptive. Like "The Flower" and most of the poems preceding the bulk of *Paterson*, "Seafarer" offers a place the reader may enter or not, at will.

As a description of inhabitation—of thing and consciousness, shape and animation—Williams perhaps never surpassed a phrase from *Kora in Hell:* "that bough-bending time of the mind's florescence" (*KH*, 24). This florescent space is invoked when two lovers wish *"their bodies were two fluids in the same vessel"* (*KH*, 83). We arrive at a "bent backed, ball kneed, cave bellied" (*KH*, 33) shape of meditative habitation, and a texture of liquid suffused in air. Williams's meditating body recalls Wordsworth's body, weighted, drooping, and bent. Wordsworth is committed to the body as a shell that frames the meditative process, while Williams is concerned with perceptual acts that inhabit bodily space and with the subsequent texture of internal fruition. Wordsworth's cave is a bounded space, Williams's a hollow filled by a human presence— yet the latent iconographic image is similar. The imaginative possibility points to the poem as filled space: *"A house is sometimes wine. It is more than a skin"* (*KH*, 75). We can trace the playful permutations of this image to its formal model in the nesting mind —a sensuous double hemisphere with the dream density of milk:

> Full, it moulds itself . . .
> > like a brown breast, full
> not of milk but of what breasts are
> > to the eye, hemispherical
> (2 would make a sphere)
> > to the mind; a view of the mind

that, in a way, gives milk:
>   that liquor that minds
> feed upon. To feed, to feed *now!*
>   *Chuck, chuck, chuck, Toe whee. Chuck!*
> —burdensome as twin stones
>   that the mind alone can milk
> and give again .
>   *Chee woo! etcetera*

                                        (*CLP*, 195)

"*Etcetera*," for we father airy stones in many places. The result is a difficult balance between metaphors that are both the same and different. Yet the balance is crucial, for with it rests all continued interest in the world of phenomena.

In Williams, this world protects itself from the encircling act of mind that would include all its phenomena in a permanently undifferentiated, totally inhabited space. His early poetry repeats images of barren particularity, of desolate wastes and dry fields of stubble. Though sensuously and appreciatively perceived, particular spaces retain an isolate loneliness. In the world of nature, inhabitation hovers between aridity and fruitfulness. Even the innocent flower is complicated by emotional reflexes of exultation and despair. Williams writes of "the clean raked fields of hell where autumn flowers are blossoming" (*KH*, 80), and the doctor elaborates an ironic metaphor of flowering disease: "*Pathology literally speaking is a flower garden. Syphilis covers the body with salmon-red petals. The study of medicine is an inverted sort of horticulture. Over and above all this floats the philosophy of disease which is a stern dance. One of its most delightful gestures is bringing flowers to the sick*" (*KH*, 81).

Later in his career, Williams is explicit about the seductive mask offered by appreciated space: "the quietness of flowers is perhaps deceptive" (*CLP*, 190). A complementary source of despair is evoked by a rose "turning slowly / upon its thorny stem" (*CLP*, 147). A flowery whirlpool also opens "The Crimson Cyclamen" (*CP*, 280):

> the petals flare back
> from the stooping craters
> of these flowers
> as from a wind rising—

These flowers reveal an indifferent vortex invested with consciousness, a structure revolving about emptiness—nil—nothing at all. But the early poems will not draw us into their emptiness unless we have been there already and submit to the poem's form without resistance. As a consequence of this failure, Williams is accused of a sentimentality that is often in us and not in the poem or in its coaxing void.

"The world of action," Williams writes, "is a world of stones" (*KH*, 19). Movement both physical and psychic folds inward on a final and immovable density. Even the most abstract, imaginative gesture—the arc of a falling leaf in the wind, the curve a bird's wing shapes in the air—describes an enclosed space in which sensation resonates to the point of repose: "Calculus is a stone" (*KH*, 80). When calculus projects a curve, we fill the space its line encloses with awareness and sensation, and it solidifies. "The stomach is full, the ocean no fuller, both have the same quality of fullness. In that, then, one is equal to the other. Having eaten, the man has released his mind" (*SA*, 29). Filling the space is an imaginative act, a mental gesture which creates an object. This inhabited space, this object, is a stone.

A poetry of such space—inhabited by consciousness—creates new objects: "Poetry has to do with the crystallization of the imagination—the perfection of new forms as additions to nature" (*SA*, 78). As Williams writes, "It isn't what he *says* that counts as a work of art, it's what he makes, with such intensity of perception that it lives with an intrinsic movement of its own to verify its authenticity" (*SE*, 257). Williams describes his creative act as "a transference—for psychic relief—from the actual to the formal" (*SL*, 226), from the given world to the formal structure of inhabited objects. The inhabited object "*is disclosed by the imagination of it*" (*KH*, 68); its authenticity is proven by our need to dream. But almost any sensation rests comfortably in the twin hollows of the mind—the problem is still to make inhabitation "compatible with frustration" (*SE*, 255).

It is not until *Paterson* that Williams achieves the emotional fullness of inhabited space. Before then his success was limited, for the reader could effortlessly subsume the words on the page. Intimate or antagonistic, Williams's early poetic space was easily internalized, and once internalized it came to rest. But Williams's later poetry resists immediate internality; it asserts itself as an object, a physical presence forcibly experienced by poet and reader.

We approach the page committed to the established boundaries of the self, boundaries which do not yet include the poem. Yet the reading process creates a unique verbal space in which consciousness is identified with the formal properties of the poem. Interaction with poetry gives our consciousness the shape and texture of inhabited space. Confronting the poem as an external object, then possessing the printed page, our consciousness becomes a function of the thing it perceives. Consciousness, then, is known as a thing; for a moment it is a thing with shape and texture, a verbal object subject to contemplation. What we experience at the moment of reading is a verbal object shaped by our interaction with the poem.

Williams's famous phrase "no ideas but in things" identifies ideation with sensation: consciousness is always consciousness of some *thing;* perception is never merely self-reflexive. Yet this interpretation is complicated by the experience of reading *Paterson.* Our continuing struggle with its physical surface is relieved on every page by our subsequent inhabitation. For a moment the distinction between self and object disappears; inhabitation seems wholly self-reflexive. But the effect is temporary, as a confrontation follows in which perception of one object yields to the perception of another. The continuing presence of the poem as an external space keeps the process in motion.[2]

2. J. Hillis Miller, *Poets of Reality* (Cambridge, Mass., 1965), presents a different analysis. He gives Williams a poetic of "copresence," where all objects exist to-

A spatial interpretation encourages a naturalistic notion of Williams's perceptions. He views the world with definite innocence and ease: the texture of one thing may be exchanged poetically for the texture of another. But his vision encompasses both the shocked violation of contact and the stillness of inhabitation that follows. This movement from contact to submission is focused in the symbols which channel Williams's developing vision. For his earlier work, when poetry served to shelter timeless images of becoming, it was the metaphor of an opening flower. Now, when the self can flower in a landscape of words, inhabitation has a larger, more open-ended incarnation: the falls of *Paterson*.

The falls in *Paterson* owe much of their potency to their perfect marriage of form and motion. "A marriage," Williams tells us, "has to be seen as a thing" (*A*, 333), so the falls become a thing, an animated shape whose space is inhabited. But the falls go further as a nexus for inhabitation. The trembling, still shape described by the arc and fall of rushing waters duplicates the posture of meditation: *"What do I do? I listen, to the water falling"* (*P*, 60). The rippling, "bent backed, ball kneed, cave bellied" drift of water is a continually changing suffused-encircling space. Thrust and curl are native to the falls, for the falls are a whirling spill. They gather the raging water into an arc and hurl it out and down, investing it with a moment of stillness before the drop. The falls are a witness to "transmutations from force to body and from body to—nothingness. Light" (*SE*, 262). They possess a suffusing meditative rhythm: "the wave rhythm of Shakespeare watching clowns and kings sliding into nothing" (*SA*, 71).

The falls are a symbol where energy is localized, chosen from

---

gether in close proximity in the poet's mind. The poem, therefore, is not an object that continually asserts its externality; it is absorbed into the poet's internal world. This approach, committed to the all-embracing resonance of the self, denies entrance into the poem as a unique perceptual space. Poetic drama becomes a tension between copresent possibilities of consciousness. In his introduction to *William Carlos Williams: A Collection of Critical Essays* (Englewood Cliffs, N.J., 1966), Miller argues that this total union of the self and the world was enacted once and forever in Williams's early poem "The Wanderer."

among thousands they are brother to, coeval with "the pouring /
waters of their hair," "the gathered spray, / upright in the air, the
pouring air," "the heavy air, whorls of thick translucencies / poured
down" (*P*, 29), "the roar of the river / forever in our ears," "a bud
forever green, / tight-curled" (*P*, 28), "to / fall— / with you from
the brink" (*P*, 35), "the angle of a forehead," "the mind / casts
off / rebelliously / an eagle / from its crag" (*P*, 241), "the water-
fall of the / flames" (*P*, 146), "the poem, / the most perfect rock
and temple, the highest / falls" (*P*, 99),

> and
> in the warm still
> air lets
> her arms
>   Fall
>
> Fall
> loosely
> (waiting)
> at her sides
>   (*CLP*, 121)

This imagery generates the poem, for "the spaces it opens are new
/ places / inhabited by hordes / heretofore unrealized" (*P*, 96);
Paterson is consequently filled with hesitant poised motion, imminent action, precipitous form at the brink of the falls: "the
river, curling, full" (*P*, 30), "the crowd hesitated, bewildered"
(*P*, 61), "and leaned on the parapet, thinking" (*P*, 89), "the falls
of his harangue hung featureless / upon the ear, yet with a certain
strangeness / as if arrested in space" (*P*, 87), "the sight of a human
body hanging over the precipice," "ice bound" (*P*, 48), "the up-
pointed breasts / of that other, tense, charged with / pressures un-
relieved" (*P*, 23), "my failure with you has been the complete
damming up of all my creative capacities" (*P*, 59), "I pretend to
be asleep. He stands there, / I feel him looking down at me, I /
am afraid!" (*P*, 38), "She has run at me with a poker, etc., but I
always told her not to strike" (*P*, 38), "one branch / of the tree at
the fall's edge, one / mottled branch, withheld" (*P*, 31).

As a nexus of verbal energy, the falls have a special role in the structure of the poem. Their open-ended power to accrete shapes, gestures, signs, and images creates an expanding associative context for the poem's action. All movement in *Paterson* takes place as part of this collage or cluster; the reading process invests the associative nexus with intimacy, and participates in the formal leap of the falls. In this context, perception becomes a situational human geometry, a free flow of form rooted absolutely to an object. The leap and fall is from the words to the page; it is an action—our inhabitation of suffused-encircling space. *Paterson* forces the reader's participation in the poem.

A verbal form is created by words, space, and reading. Williams calls poetry of this space a "field of action" (*SE*, 280), and he writes, "the poem is made of things—on a field" (*A*, 333). As poet and reader, "we must create out of the blankness about us" (*SE*, 103); white blankness is the space of the page we structure verbally. It is a feminine space or field, a female silence in which we sow words. "We express ourselves there (men) as we might on the whole body of the various female could we ever gain access to her (which we cannot and never shall)" (*SE*, 259): *"the empty form drops from a cloud, like a gourd from a vine; into it the poet packs his phallus-like argument"* (*KH*, 78). As early as the cover piece to *Kora in Hell*,[3] Williams was literal in describing the feminine space of poetic action:

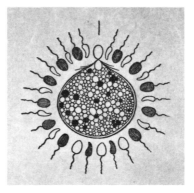

3. "The cover design? It represents the ovum in the act of being impregnated,

Passive and open, feminine space permits both violation and inhabitation. All the metaphors for passivity in *Paterson* are also metaphors for this space and the process of inhabiting it:

> a flower within a flower whose history
> (within the mind) crouching
> among the ferny rocks, laughs at the names
> by which they think to trap it. Escapes!
> Never by running but by lying still—
>
> (P, 33)

> *What do I do? I listen, to the water falling. (No sound*
> *of it here but with the wind!) This is my entire occupation.*
>
> (P, 60)

> What but indirection
> will get to the end of the sphere?
>
> (P, 246)

The world toward which Paterson the man directs his thoughts is at rest, awaiting him silently (*P*, 57). It is "a hollow, / a woman waiting to be filled" (*P*, 206). The quietest inhabitation possible—silence as a suffused-encircling space—produces "a nothing, surrounded by / a surface" (*P*, 149). That phrase is a model of Williams's inhabited poetic space. It is also a model of his silence: an imageless act in the presence of an object.

Silence in the verbal space of *Paterson* fulfills the possibilities of Williams's early flower imagery. The poem's language releases pent-up motion, imitating the whirling spill of the falls. This linguistic replica of the falls, a relation of words to page, is set in motion when the reader enters the poem. Reading unravels the action and makes a thing, an inhabited space:

---

surrounded by spermatozoa, all trying to get in but only one successful. I myself improvised the idea, seeing, symbolically, a design using sperms of various breeds, various races let's say, and directed the artist to vary the shadings of the drawing from white to gray to black. The cell accepts one sperm—that is the beginning of life. I was feeling fresh and I thought it was a beautiful thing and I wanted the world to see it." *IWWP*, pp. 28–29.

The language cascades into the
invisible, beyond and above : the falls
of which it is the visible part

(*P*, 172)

Poet and reader deal with *Paterson* as an object; they encounter
the hard surface and density of the language and create a verbal
space on the page. Spatial form is not a loose construction of thematic abstractions but the texture and dimension of the poem before our eyes. Most of us admit that modern poetry is often different
heard and read. Attention to breathing can partly communicate
the configuration of the printed page, but cannot capture the
spatial relations among written words. Either we must take the
page space seriously—dealing with it as it confronts us—or we
develop for Williams a metaphysic of gratuitous rape. No other
alternatives even vaguely respond to his poetry, to the gentle violation Rilke calls "the space that ravishes." Though the spatial events
in *Paterson*'s whole structure are perhaps infinite, a few examples
reveal an entrance into the poem.

In Book One of *Paterson*, past the author's note, an initial colon
faces a blank page ("   : *a local pride* . . ."). Questions about the
colon's function typically arouse humorous speculation, and readers patiently thumb back, looking for mystical relations with the
publication date. Yet only Williams and *you* come before the ini-
tiating punctuation. The doctor invites us to resist pure internality
and devise an entrance into a new object, to continue perceiving.
In a very real sense, the structure of the poem awaits us; its hard
surface is bared to our approach.

Any number of other straightforward spatial devices are readily
apparent. Uses of space like this (*P*, 61)—

                                        a flame,
            spent.
                The file-sharp grass   .

—force abrupt new configurations of the page. Each time we read
this, the flame is lit and then extinguished by "spent." Neither "a

spent flame" nor "a flame, spent" would act in the same way, forc-
ing space into the verbal act. Moreover, only one process fills this
space—reading. And the newly created "thing" of reader-invested-
with-the-space sustained by "flame" and "spent" is then violated
by "The file-sharp grass," a visual model of a dead or motionless
flame. The phrase is a "thing" in the most concrete sense. Hard
and obdurate, it intrudes like a wedge.

The delayed period acts in a similar way, for we must bridge the
gap. We are forced not only to encounter an indifferent dot as an
object but even to maintain its existence in blank space and its
relation to the preceding passage, as here (*P*, 61):

> The crowd now numbered some ten thousand,
>
> "a great beast!"
>
> for many had come from the city to join the conflict.
> The case looked serious, for the Police were greatly outnumbered.
> The crowd then tried to burn the Ferguson house and Dalzell
> went to the house of John McGuckin. While in this house it was
> that Sergeant John McBride suggested that it might be well to send
> for William McNulty, Dean of Saint Joseph's Catholic Church.
>
> In a moment the Dean set on a plan. He proceeded to the scene
> in a hack. Taking Dalzell by the arm, in full view of the infuriated
> mob, he led the man to the hack and seating himself by his side,
> ordered the driver to proceed. The crowd hesitated, bewildered
> between the bravery of the Dean and   .

We complete the motion of the crowd in the place between "and"
and the period. It is not a literal image of what ten thousand people
might do, but a uniquely verbal act in a concrete situation. We
experience the event whole, joining in the crowd's hesitation
"combed into straight lines / from that rafter of a rock's / lip"
(*P*, 15). The geometric and representational tendencies of Williams's flowers have grown into a more intimate calculus—a "common language" shared by poet, poem, and reader in the act of
reading.

In this passage (*P*, 226)—

> Knower
> of tides, counter of hours, wanings and
> waxings, enumerator of snowflakes, starer
> through thin ice, whose corpuscles are
> minnows, whose drink, sand   .

—the rhetorical exuberance of the listing is completed by the infinite rhythmic progression between "sand" and the period. The printed word celebrates a succession of images, while we in reading fulfill the open-ended structure. The difference between ellipses and a leap across space to a still seed (or period) is clear here. Ellipses leave us with a series whose particulars are connected only by placing them consecutively on the page. The leap is a single movement filling a space with all possible additions to the series. Here (*P*, 79),

> started again wandering—foot pacing foot outward
> into emptiness   .   .

the two periods extend the statement. They force us to fall in with this spaceward pace. We commit a verbal act in blank space; indeed "   .   .   " can stand as a quotation from the poem, and a catalog of the poem's effects would include spatial clusters, faceless signs. *Paterson*'s blank space is often articulate:

> We leap awake and what we see
> fells us   .
>
> Let terror twist the world!
>
> (*P*, 79)

"We leap awake" signals our visual commitment to the printed line; "and what we see" brings the leap to the top of its arc—the line is poised like the water at the top of the falls. The verbal-visual field then shifts with "fells us," and we are propelled toward the period removed three spaces. That dot acts as a hole through which we fall toward the isolated "Let terror twist the world!" The leap and fall through blank space and the measured pacing into emptiness are both related and different. Space, words, and punctuation are dramatic events in the poem. They sustain the page as a field of force, making even a period a tangible function of the structure. A period is immense; yet it is the waste of absolute finitude .

This construction is a concentration of attention, a head-nodding rhythm, launched into nothing (called "this") to the still point where all attention began, "this" (*P*, 168):

> —of this, make it of *this*, this
> this, this, this, this   .

The same notion of "The World Narrowed to a Point" (*CLP*, 20) is translated into an action in this space (*P*, 96):

> a world unsuspected
>   beckons to new places
> and no whiteness (lost) is so white as the memory
> of whiteness   .

The line propels us through the period, a black doorway into the whiteness of the page within which the line acts. Speech becomes an enactment of silence.

> There was a time when
> they didn't want any whites
> to own anything—to
> hold anything—to say, This
> is mine   .
>
> I see things,   .   .
>
>   (*P*, 163)

In this quotation, we first take possession of so small a space that we are empty-handed, yet the almost frivolous act is forced by the whole passage. "I see things,   .   . " mimics the dialectics of inside and outside with a dot encounter: two eyes, or observant dots, both nowhere. Williams's definition of a poem—a "machine made of words" whose "movement is intrinsic, undulant, a physical more than a literary character" (*SE*, 256)—becomes relevant at every moment. Even when the intent is less serious, Williams still pulls us down to his page, his white field, where we *do* something together.

We speak through the poem's language; the poem speaks through us. It is a more open and universal model of *In the American Grain*, where dead men spoke through Williams (or he through them) in prose which mirrored the manner of their speech. One could argue that anyone might have spoken through *Paterson*, anything might have been included, but that once written the form is unalterable. Two things qualify this statement—the addition of "Book Five" (or Six), and the discovery that each act of reading violates and fulfills the form, sets it in motion.

If a poem is words on a field, it awaits our harvest. And who can say its form is the same once it is dispersed in us. There is no limit to what we may consume; the progression of *Paterson* is open-ended. But the verbal space it creates is not. Turned aside, felled, flung aloft, the reader is bound in the presence of the poem. The precise character of the space to be inhabited is unpredictable, but we come to expect its self-enclosure. Thrust forward, we curl with the whirling spill of the falls.

Anything—anywhere—can be given the motion of the falls and inhabited. All "the awkward names men give their emptiness" (*IAG*, 27) can achieve this fullness here. Inhabitation in *Paterson* formally embodies an earlier perception: "he looked into a white face, the face of a man convulsed with dread, saw the laughter back of its drawn alertness" (*KH*, 69). There is a sense in which all suffering in the poem (even the anguished prose passages) is mediated through the form we make on the page. Perhaps the closest Williams ever comes to playing Lear outside his poetry is in the incident Kenneth Burke relates—when Williams slaps the departing rump of a somber literary visitor.[4] Translated spatially: to have been ravaged by all this nonsense: I'd rather play the fool. Even

4. "William Carlos Williams, 1883–1963," *William Carlos Williams: A Collection of Critical Essays*, ed. Miller, p. 58.

then, as Williams tells us somewhat earlier in his perambulatory career, "Fools have big wombs" (*KH*, 33). Or a mad and empty playfulness takes place in inhabitable space. It is the poet who tells us "the birth of every baby . . . is a revelation" (*SE*, 270), who watches the doctor lean forward "and cut the baby from its stem" (*KH*, 69). It is the poet who, from any stem, can release a flowering human form.

Open the inward frame

Working in words I am an escapist; as if I could step
out of my clothes and move naked as the wind in a
world of words.
Robert Duncan, *Bending the Bow*, v

Art is ceasing to be a special object to be inserted in a
special kind of space.
Marshall McLuhan and Harley Parker,
Through the Vanishing Point, 29

the space of the writing is to be traversed, not penetrated.

a text consists of multiple writings . . . but there is one
place where this multiplicity is collected, united, and
this place is not the author . . . but the reader: the reader
is the very space in which are inscribed, without any
being lost, all the citations a writing consists of; the
unity of a text is not in its origin, it is in its destination.
Roland Barthes, "The Death of the Author"

Space wheels

The world wrenches up its roots
Our bodies
Stretched out
Weigh no more than dawn
Octavio Paz, in Strand, ed., *New Poetry
of Mexico*, 137

And the body . . . see, it can no longer contain
itself in space!—Where shall it bestow itself?—Where
shall it come into being?—This *One* wants to play at

being *All*. It wants to play at the soul's universality! It wants to remedy its identity by the number of its actions! Being a thing, it explodes in events!—It flies into transports!—And as thought, when excited, touches every substance, oscillates between pauses and instants, overleaps all differences; and as hypotheses are symmetrically formed in our mind, and as possibilities are arranged and numbered,—so this body exercises itself in all its parts, combines with itself, takes on shape after shape, and continuously leaves itself! ... Now at last it has reached that state which is comparable to flame, in the midst of the most active exchanges ... One can no longer speak of "*movement*" ... Its acts are no longer distinguishable from its limbs. ...

> Paul Valéry, *Selected Writings*, 198

I see an orphan, lawless and serene,
standing in a corner of the sky,
body something like bodies that have been,
but not the scar of naming in his eye.
Bred close to the ovens, he's burnt inside.
Light, wind, cold, dark—they use him like a bride.

> Leonard Cohen, *Flowers for Hitler*, 80

Phopho!! The meteor pulp of him, the seamless rainbow-peel. Aggala!!!! His bellyvoid of nebulose with his neverstop navel. Paloola!!!!!! And his veins shooting melanite phosphor, his creamtocustard cometshair and his asteroid knuckles, ribs and members. Ooridem-iny!!!!!!! His electrolatiginous twisted entrails belt.

> James Joyce, *Finnegans Wake*, 475

27. Hans Bellmer, "Woman on a Sofa."

NINE   The end of the body: radical space in Burroughs

> Language is a Trojan horse by which the universe gets into the mind.
>
> Hugh Kenner, *Dublin's Joyce*, 117

'Something on your
mind ,P.B.?'
'Well yes you might
say so. Thought some
of my words might
have strayed up here.'
'This is a free range
country feller say'
'Maybe a little too
free,Martin.'
'Don't know as I righ
tly understand you
XXXXXXXXXX P.B.'
(Cold distant point)
'Well you might put
it this way Martin.
Words have brands jus
t like cattle. You got
no call to be changin
g those brands,Martin
When you use my words
they carry my brand'
'Sorry,P.B. but I been
running brands for
years.. XXXXXXXXXXXXXXXX

(*APO*, 16)[1]

1. William S. Burroughs's works are abbreviated as follows and documented

"It is a long trip," Burroughs writes in *The Ticket That Exploded*.
"We are the only riders. . . . Not that we love or even like each
other. In fact murder is never out of my eyes when I look at him.
And murder is never out of his eyes when he looks at me" (*TX*, 1).
The force of critical invective directed at Burroughs's novels since
Naked Lunch suggests that the passage describes the reading ex-
perience as well. We may ignore both moral outrage and criticism
that refuses to deal with Burroughs on his own terms, but we can-
not ignore the genuine discomfort of readers trying to empathize.
This suggests that frustration is written into the novels deliberately.

Burroughs frequently warns that our enthusiasm for his writing
will be qualified, and our pleasure ambivalent: "I offer you nothing. I am not a politician" (*I*, 100). "I am a recording instrument....I do not presume to impose 'story' 'plot' 'continuity.'...In
sofaras I succeed in *Direct* recording of certain areas of psychic
process I may have limited function....I am not an entertainer..."
(*NL*, 221). While Burroughs's books do not always entertain, they
produce considerable affective response; although deliberately disjunctive and nonlinear, their stylistic presence is unmistakable.
Responding to moralistic criticism of his techniques, Burroughs
offers methodological and formal constructs that should be obvious
to any critic:

> People say to me, 'Oh, this is all very good, but you got it by cutting
> up.' I say that has nothing to do with it, how I got it. What is any
> writing but a cut-up? Somebody has to program the machine;

---

internally: *APO—APO-33 Bulletin: A Metabolic Regulator* (San Francisco, n.d.);
ART—"The Art of Fiction," *Paris Review* 9:35 (Fall 1965); *CEN*—"Censorship,"
Transatlantic Review 11 (Winter 1962); *E*—*The Exterminator* (San Francisco,
1960); *I*—"Introduction to *Naked Lunch*, *Soft Machine* and *Nova Express*," *Evergreen Review* (January 1962); *NE*—*Nova Express* (New York, 1964); *NL*—
Naked Lunch (New York, 1966); *SM*—*The Soft Machine* (New York, 1967);
T—*Time* (New York, 1965); *TX*—*The Ticket That Exploded* (New York, 1968).
Burroughs considers typographical errors to be fortuitous accidents and preserves them; all curiosities of syntax, spelling, and punctuation in the quotations
are his. Since his frequent use of quotations within quotations would make difficult reading here, I have eliminated initial quotation marks but retained internal
quotes. Three or four spaced periods indicate my omissions (ellipses); all others
are Burroughs's.

somebody has to *do* the cutting up. Remember that I first made selections. Out of hundreds of possible sentences that I might have used, I chose one. (*ART*, 30)

When the reader reads page ten he is flashing forward in time to page one hundred and back in time to page one. (*CEN*, 7)

Burroughs states his intentions clearly, and we are encouraged to recognize that our self-consciousness is generated by specific features of the text. Elevated to critical judgment, frustration and rage are repressive or pathetic; as responses to the reading experience, they may even be useful.

Both Burroughs's more outrageous passages and a variety of explicit devices alert us to our immediate perceptual situation: "I am reading a science fiction book called *The Ticket That Exploded*." To support this naked image—the book at the end of our perceptual fork—he suggests it is not the novel but our own situation which is fictional: "The story is close enough to what is going on here so now and again I make myself believe this . . . is just a scene in an old book far away and long ago" (*TX*, 5–6). Authorial intrusions physically interrupt the illusion of narrative: "Mr. Burroughs presence on earth is all a joke" (*NE*, 184). He teases the reader outraged by his sexual extravagances: "My page deals so many tasty ways on the bed" (*SM*, 54). These techniques effectively challenge our normally continuous sense of narrative time: "Shift tilt STOP the GOD film. Frame by frame take a good look boys" (*TX*, 4). In a recent pamphlet he proposes an alternative title, *"Right Where You Are Sitting Now"* (*APO*, 11), which echoes what he says in *Naked Lunch:* "There is only one thing a writer can write about: *what is in front of his senses at the moment of writing*" (*NL*, 221). He also borrows methods now traditional in "objective" verse, in which the page *does* what the text says:

```
     The grey smoke drifted        the grey that stops
 shift    cut    tangle     they    breathe      medium
      the   word    cut     shift   patterns      words
      cut   the   insect    tangle     cut        shift
```

that   coats   word   cut   breath   silence

shift   abdominal   cut   tangle   stop   word

holes. (*NE*, 69)

The passage short-circuits the perceptual processes we bring to the
novel. "The grey smoke drifted" taunts us with conventional narrative, but the printed page stops our forward motion. The word
"breathe" draws our attention to the altered breath with which we
read this disjunctive passage. We become aware of the unconscious
bodily rhythms which support and sustain the flow of conventional
language. Spread out, the words are eaten away by the "holes"
between them; we are drawn out of the temporal rhythms of speech
toward space.

Engaged in the exact moment of intersection with the text, the
reader quickly discovers assault, seduction, and mimicry in his
relation to the printed page: "he called them and read every word
it sometimes took him a full hour by a tidal river in Mexico slow
murder in his eyes maybe ten fifteen years later" (*TX*, 1). Who but
the determined critic, generating systems and fabricating historical
continuities, fulfills the image of a reader murderously peering at
a threatening text. The temptation to reassemble the novels in
linear form, evident in all our critical conventions, performs a
perfect inversion of Burroughs's writing. Burroughs tells us his
novels can be entered anywhere, and he invites us to cut up and
fold in our own material. Perhaps embarrassed by the prospect of
piously rearranging the novels into narratives susceptible to explication, the critic searches instead for "content" and declarative
statement: "One is constantly on the lookout for bits of shipwrecked meaning, searching for glimpses of significant images.
One scans the field of words for hints of purposive intent."[2] Even
his advocates fail to accept the novels as written: "Apart from the
frivolous distractions of cut-ups, Mr. Burroughs, we are reading
you loud and clear!"[3]

2. Tony Tanner, "The New Demonology," *Partisan Review* 33 (1966), 564.

3. Ibid., p. 565. Compare: "in the first part of this work, which is by far the most
effective, the cut-up method is used cannily and sparingly. . . . In his later trilogy

Such critical disengagement implies a decision to reject the reading experience, to disguise and obfuscate Burroughs's disruption of our humanitarian assumptions. The posture is familiar from critical response to Swift's work. Adverse reaction to the language and form of the novels, which occurs quite apart from an evaluation of their quality, is a defense against what they can *do* to us as human beings. Our uneasiness in confronting Burroughs's art has two sources. The first is an entirely justified suspicion that *Naked Lunch* may be read as a marriage manual, that Burroughs means to reveal the true violent content of our sexuality. The other, confirmed by his later novels, is a fear that Burroughs believes an act of murder is implicit in every human contact.[4]

Both dramas in the psychology of perception are literal rather than thematic—induced not by contact with Burroughs's ideas, but by the inescapable facts of the reading experience. His fantastic imagery of atomic sex and his revelations of unspeakable possession dismiss all questions of verisimilitude. It is the immediate, objective form of the novel—encountered moment by moment—which compresses the mushroom cloud into an emblem for the human head. Burroughs's radical style is designed "to *create* facts that will tend to open biologic potentials" (*NE*, 145), to move us beyond the body toward infinite space. To participate we must first understand Burroughs's unique mythology: "In *Naked Lunch, The Soft Machine* and *Novia Express* . . . i am mapping an imaginary universe. A dark universe of wounded galaxies and novia conspiracies" (*I*, 99). "A new mythology is possible in the space age

---

Burroughs worked more wildly." Ihab Hassan, "The Subtracting Machine: The Work of William Burroughs," *Critique* 6 (Spring 1963), 10. Similarly, "if Burroughs rejected his relentless obsession with literature-by-chance he could quite possibly produce some excellent, effectively original writing again." Richard Kostelanetz, "From Nightmare to Serendipity," *Twentieth Century Literature* 2 (October 1965), 130.

4. Hassan, "The Subtracting Machine," p. 22, rationalizes this fear as a failure of love: "he offers less than the major writers of our century . . . not because his scope and knowledge are less than theirs, which is indubitably true, but because his love is also smaller . . . and love is the energy of the soul, the will to life. . . ."

where we will again have heroes and villains with respect to intentions towards this planet" (*CEN*, 7).

Burroughs's mythology begins in mock-Christian fashion, with the primal word preceding the proliferations of human language. In its original unity, the word occurs at both the beginning and the end of history, for "the end is the beginning born knowing" (*TX*, 10). To his readers' discomfort, Burroughs does not take history on faith; he accepts it only as an antagonist, for "history is fiction" (*NE*, 13). "What we call history is the history of the word. In the beginning of *that* history was the word" (*TX*, 50).

The primary-terminal word is unknown and unspoken; it is antithetical to the circumlocutions of language. Bodiless and silent, the word exists at the opposite ends of history—beyond the limits of human perception: "You were not there for *The Beginning*. You will not be there for *The End*....Your knowledge of what is going on can only be superficial and relative" (*NL*, 220). Our ambivalent and terminal existence cannot enclose the whole of time. We are ignorant not only of history's ultimate form but also of the circumstances underlying the immediate moment. Knowing nothing of the larger theater of action, we cannot act freely in the present.

History—the naive perambulations of language—is bounded by a tautological word excluding all possibility of discourse. The theater of human action becomes the scene of endless talk. "Word is TWO that is the noxious human inter language recorded—And where you have TWO you have odor's and nationalism's word" (*NE*, 98). Human language is the invisible primal word that reproduces itself in time. The word is audible only as a repetitive series of contradictions:

So I am alone as always—You understand nova is where I am born in such pain no one else survives in one piece—Born again and again cross the wounded galaxies—I am alone but not what you call 'lonely'—Loneliness is a product of dual mammalian structure

> —'Loneliness,' 'love,' 'friendship,' all the rest of it—I am not two—
> I am *one*—But to maintain my state of oneness I need twoness in
> other life forms—Other must talk so that I can remain silent—If
> another becomes one then I am two—That makes two ones makes
> two and I am no longer one—Plenty of room in space you say?—
> But I am not one in space I am one in time—Metal time—Radio-
> active time—So of course I tried to keep you all out of space—That
> is the end of time— (*NE*, 85)

Desperate to feed on the escalating energies of language, the word
divided; forgetting their source, the two halves of the word began
to interact in the endless combinations of language: "The Word is
divided into units which be all in one piece and should be so taken,
but the pieces can be had in any order being tied up back and
forth, in and out fore and aft like an innaresting sex arrangement"
(*NL*, 229).

When the primal word divided in time, its interactions at once
achieved the density of matter: "What scared you all into time?
Into body? Into shit? I will tell you: '*the word.*' Alien Word '*the.*'
'*The*' *word* of Alien Enemy imprisons '*thee*' in Time. In Body"
(*NE*, 12). Human bodies are the accumulated residue of speech.
As it exists in time, "Word *is* flesh and word *is* two that is the
human body is compacted of two organisms and where you have
two you have word and word is flesh" (*NE*, 84). "Your bodies I
have written" (*NE*, 139). "When we came out of the mud we had
names" (*SM*, 178). Language for Burroughs *is* flesh: "These colorless sheets are what flesh is made from—Becomes flesh when it has
color and writing—That is Word And Image write the message
that is you on colorless sheets determine all flesh" (*NE*, 36). Language is an illusory dialectic which masks our essential and intolerable doubleness. It proliferates in the endless reproduction of male
and female bodies, for flesh is the speech of time: "The human
organism is literally consisting of two halves from the beginning
word and all human sex is this unsanitary arrangement whereby
two entities attempt to occupy the same three-dimensional coordi-
nate points" (*TX*, 52).

There are no mystical unions for Burroughs. Two organisms can occupy the same space only through an explosive fusion that is quite literally, not merely metaphysically, lethal. Like all human interaction, sex is a form of warfare—a series of outrageous violations which occur over and over again. History consequently proceeds in time through the sexual warfare of mutually dependent antagonisms. The word became flesh, permutating in hemispherical, double, warring dialectical forms. Conversing and intersecting, these forms now create history, which is the history of one word and its doubled fleshly variations. What we conceive as reality is merely "A God that failed, A God of conflict in two parts so created to keep a tired old show on the road" (*CEN*, 8).

This complex mythology, where language articulates "a planet based on 'the Word,' that is, on separate flesh engaged in endless sexual conflict" (*TX*, 52), informs every page of Burroughs's work. We know the word only in its double forms of sexual warfare. All identity is oppositional—a conversation, a polar antagonism. The antagonistic doubleness is reproduced on each level of perception. Whether talking, fighting, or making love, all relation merely disguises the narcotic metronome marking time in the human theater —"'I love you I hate you' at supersonic alternating speed" (*NE*, 180). In his pamphlet *Time*, a cut-up inflicted on "The Weekly Newsmagazine," Burroughs inserts into a story on China ("'Communism is not love!' cried Mao Tse-tung. 'Communism is a hammer we use to destroy our enemies!'" *T*, 4) a series of photographs illustrating proper Victorian etiquette for visiting a woman: "A man calls: The correct handshake, presenting cards, disposition of hat" (*T*, 4). Both the news story and the international relations it reports become as ritualistic and formalized as the photographs. For the "enemy must remain alive exterminated" (*T*, 9), thereby confirming "the necessity of a defense policy at once devious and unyielding firm and elastic so that . . . the free world is subject to burst out anywhere" (*T*, 7). The human theater is finally an explosive planet—a double planet or a sphere with cleavage: "The war between the sexes split the planet into armed camps right down the middle line divides one thing from the other" (*SM*, 157).

Rearranged in emotional terms, our tantalized flesh disguises our addiction to reversals of experience generated by verbal associations: "sex and pain words sir...vary the tape sir...switch the tape sir" (*NE*, 181). As another contemporary author writes, "You are locked into your suffering and your pleasures are the seal."[5] The human body is condemned to time by what Burroughs repeatedly calls the "Orgasm-Death gimmick," the obsessively repeated exposure to extremes of ecstasy and annihilation. Our dreams present torture chambers juxtaposed with the "Garden of Delights" (G-O-D). It is an image of consciousness as an organic form—the brain as the body's eruption into awareness—a two-halved, mushroom-shaped explosion: "Dual mammalian structure —Hiroshima People" (*NE*, 97–98). Our perceptions duplicate the male-female doubleness of our social and sexual roles, and our experience is a complementary alternation of pleasure and pain. Taut with desire and frustration, each single body is really a verbal illusion constructed over an amphibious-hermaphroditic form. If we stop listening to the flesh language of time, the body is revealed as "two halves stuck together like a mold—That is, it consists of *two* organisms" (*TX*, 159). "Watch what is covering the two halves with so-called human body—Flesh sheets on which is written: 'The spines rubbed and merged'" (*TX*, 160). Tension along the "divide line" keeps the two halves in an alternating state of absolute warfare—a war of sex and pain. Our minds and bodies are ignorant vessels of the primal word bisected into time. Each seeming variation, each apparently new form or illusory synthesis, is nothing more than a trivial variation on the essential conflict, an extension of deception and disguise. The program of complete control, the unvarying life script of the human theater, has been written on flesh sheets by the inflexible authority of word and image: "listen to your present time tapes and you will begin to see who you are and what you are doing here   mix yesterday in with today and hear tomorrow your future rising out of old recordings   you are

5. Leonard Cohen, *Songs of Leonard Cohen*, Columbia Records, 1967.

a programmed tape recorder set to record and play back" (*TX*, 213).

Speech in the biologic theater follows a flesh script of control words with their immediate and repetitive image track. All speech methodically reproduces its attendant images, from the most abstract discourse to the preverbal noises that affirm the physical presence of our bodies. To speak is to participate in and augment the biologic theater of control, to preserve the warring polar forms of slave consciousness. All language occurs in association blocks, lethal patterns of image that establish generalized conflict on global and cellular levels. Articulated over centuries, these association blocks force speech into preprogrammed birth-death cycles. They provide inflexible vessels for all illusory variation; they build biologic prisons for the double word incarnate.

"To speak," Burroughs warns us, "is to lie—To live is to collaborate" (*NE*, 15)."The word is spliced in with the sound of your intestines and breathing with the beating of your heart" (*TX*, 50). The word's control lines extend along the divide line of the body, hooked into erogenous zones maintained by sex words in the pleasure-pain syndrome. It simultaneously enforces association on stellar and molecular levels. "The word may once have been a healthy neural cell. It is now a parasitic organism that invades and damages the central nervous system" (*TX*, 49). We live on the "word dust planet"; we perceive objects as images linked to conflicting verbal association blocks: "Earth and water stones and trees poured into him and spurted out broken pictures" (*TX*, 93).

"All association tracks are obsessional" (*TX*, 213). Even sex—the traditionally sacred zone of nonverbal experience—is merely controlled rearrangement of image matrices, which are blocks of verbal association: "he came in spasms of light—Silver writing burst in his brain" (*NE*, 165). "The words dissolved—His body twisted in liquid fish spasms and emptied through his spurting penis" (*NE*, 163). "The sex charge is usually controlled by sex words forming an electro-magnetic pattern. . . . Flash from words to color on the association screen" (*NE*, 169). "Larval erogenous face spurting out through orgasm" (*TX*, 92). The word dust planet is the picture planet, the planet of "bring down word and image" (*NE*, 81). Image, we may economize, is speech. Burroughs, who is even more economical, brutally reproduces the archetype of human encounter: "Talk, Face" (*TX*, 92).

When character is frozen in such obsessive postures of addiction, Burroughs often unmasks an insect parasite hidden beneath the flesh script: "His smile was the most unattractive thing about him ... it split his face open and something quite alien like a predatory mollusk looked out" (*TX*, 2); "In his place of total darkness mouth and eyes are one organ that leaps forward to snap with transparent teeth" (*NL*, 9). Creating a mythological landscape to support this vision, Burroughs extends the metaphor of predatory control across the galaxy, terminating in implacable alien wills. In the Crab Nebula, at once light-years away and immediately beneath the tentative translucence of reality, the Insect Men of Minraud write the flesh history of Earth on their irrevocable tablets of stone. Black beetles, scorpion men with "faces of transparent pink cartilage burning inside—stinger dripping the oven poison" (*NE*, 79), and "red crustacean men with eyes like the white hot sky" (*NE*, 78) surround the ultimate "Controller of the Crab Nebula on a slag heap of smouldering metal" (*NE*, 79). The soulless planet of yellow plains and metal cities does not have "what they call 'emotion's oxygen' in the atmosphere" (*NE*, 77). Requiring Earth's hysteric theater to maintain (by opposition) their alien geometric existence, "The Insect People Of Minraud formed an alliance with the Virus Power Of The Vegetable People to occupy planet earth" (*NE*, 80). Addicted to our oxygen-fed flesh theater of alternating pain and pleasure, the Vegetable People absorb all human and animal experience. Meanwhile, the intractable thought patterns of Minraud control "whole galaxies thousand years ahead on the chess-board of virus screens and juxtaposition formulae" (*NE*, 80). Behind even these alien dramatists, planet junkies manipulating the myriad egg clusters of the galaxy, lurks a radically detached and sentient density: "the ancient white planet of frozen gasses—

a vast mineral consciousness near absolute zero thinking in slow formations of crystal" (*TX*, 129).

Against this cosmic background of metallic insect lust, the human body is nothing more than a "soft machine" programmed to satisfy the absolute needs of its controllers—"Paralyzed Orgasm Addicts eaten alive by crab men with white hot eyes or languidly tortured in charades by The Green Boys of young crystal cruelty" (*NE*, 159). *We* are the naked lunch that the universe feeds on; the "frozen moment" (*NL*, xxxvii) is when we see ourselves and our neighbors at the end of every fork. We are all unwitting but slavish "collaborators with Insect People with Vegetable People. With any people anywhere who offer you a body forever. To shit forever" (*NE*, 12). "Our entire image could be contained within a grain of sand" (*NE*, 57). Our lives are a flesh script written before birth on a soft typewriter. "Postulate a biologic film running from the beginning to the end, from zero to zero. . . . Nobody is permitted to leave the biologic theater which in this case is the human body" (*NE*, 16).

As Burroughs's mythology progresses, his tired and violent kaleidoscopic theater becomes a circus of demoniac possession, a virus, an incompatible combination of complete dependence and polar opposition: "There were at least two parasites one sexual the other cerebral working together the way parasites will—That is the cerebral parasite kept you from wising up to the sexual parasite" (*TX*, 144). With explicit social relevance, Burroughs describes the complementary dependence of "Rightness" and "Wrongness":

> The WhiteGodess pays her clean staff in 'Rightness' the 'White Junk'.And naturally the dirtier the work they are called to do the more 'Rightness' they need to stay clean. A burning down habit when you start feeding children to the screaming from Carthage to Hiroshima how much 'White Junk you need to cover *that*???????? . . . Now 'Rightness' is of course a derivative of 'wrongness' 'Somebody else to be 'wrong expected.After all burning slaves be 'wrong'. They need more and more slaves to be 'wrong' so they can wring 'White Junk' out of them: 'hospitals'

full of 'mental cases' stacked up like cord wood. .cells of sick
addicts yielding the white no smell of death clean decent 'White
Junk', millions of prisoners in the vast suburban concentration
camps of American and Europe all feeding White Junk to the
White Goddess. (*APO*, 4)

The White Goddess is a disguised version of the cerebral parasite,
a complex of abstract ideals dependent on mass suffering for her
existence. She articulates her idealized and bloodless values by
repressing alternative forms of consciousness.

"Rightness" and "Wrongness," identified with their human rep-
resentatives, develop a symbiotic antagonism. But the opposing
forms become continually more extreme. The power of the White
Goddess, maintained only by the snowballing warfare of incompatible symbiotic beings, becomes increasingly volatile. Our own
history provides an image of the apocalyptic resolution of oppo-
sites: "brains armed now with The Blazing Photo from Hiroshima
and Nagasaki" (*NE*, 79) commit lethal outrages on their own
consciousness. "Incredible forms of total survival emerged clashed
exploded ... Desperate flesh ... Transparent civilizations went out
talking" (*NE*, 71). "THIS IS WAR TO EXTERMINATION. FIGHT CELL BY
CELL THROUGH BODIES AND MIND SCREENS OF THE EARTH" (*NE,* 67).

As every consciousness attempts to supplant the universe, the
doubtful structure of reality is suffused with shadowy, improbable
life forms. In the human body, cell and planet are simultaneous,
superimposed images of microcosmic and macrocosmic violation.
Another version of the conflict also achieves its terminal identity in
every instant of time: the interstellar war of the sexes is fought in
cataclysmic intersections here and now and across the wounded
galaxies. Hiroshima screw—atomic sex—"and some of them are
consisting entirely of penis flesh and subject to blast jissom right
out of their skull" (*SM*, 25). "These bone wrenching spasms emptied me" (*SM*, 21); "sex words exploded to empty space" (*TX*,
88). "Shivering metal orgasms" "vaporized the words" (*TX*, 62,
83). "The dreamer with dirty flesh strung together on scar im-

pressions exploded" (*TX*, 67). "The neon sun sinks in this sharp smell of carrion" (*SM*, 41).

These violent confrontations have infinite variety, for the doubleness creates a self-perpetuating dialectic. But human history does not have time to catalog all the combinations. The doubled flesh of language exists in dependent relation to its progenitor. And the father will finally devour his children. The interacting forms of language escalate to the point of nova; the primal word is reborn in the apocalyptic death of speech. Outside history, the word maintains its unity by feeding on our agonized incarnation in time. Its bodiless and silent presence is addicted to our bodies' talk. But this parasitic word requires increasing doses of our history. The total theater of history is the planet, and the human body is its microcosm. As the level of violence increases, the difference between body and planet ("Globe is self you understand," *NE*, 177) becomes functionally irrelevant. Cellular and global conflict are merely rearranged verbal matrices.

These unexpected shifts in perspective contribute to the sense of violation in each encounter. As Burroughs writes, with typically literal irony, "Gentle reader, the ugliness of that spectacle buggers description" (*NL*, 39). Our shock is distinctly physical. Our most sacred biological illusions are threatened when we recognize the body as the residue of talk. The earth is a conglomerate of decaying bodies; talk is the true form of reproduction—reproduction that generates excrement. Speech, the rhythm of our addiction to time, is unveiled as a disguised form of defecation. But the discovery signals an end to talk. Matter, the verbal incarnation of space in time, explodes outward into the universe. Scatology becomes eschatology.

Outraged by the fusion of language and excrement, we purge ourselves of their common product, history—the history of a god of conflict. Writing of this satanic god of word and image, Burroughs describes its revelation in the inverted fusion of orgasm and death: "Gentle reader, we see God through our assholes in the flash bulb of orgasm" (*NL*, 229). "We Are All Shit Eaters . . We Worship A Nameless Asshole" (*E*, 25). In a famous incident in *Naked Lunch* a man is taken over by his asshole, which he has trained to talk: "the asshole said to him: 'It's you who will shut up in the end. Not me. Because we don't need you around here any more. I can talk and eat *and* shit' " (*NL*, 132–33).

In the end of time, in the moment of death, we shall know we have been supplanted by our assholes. "In the beginning was the word and the word was bullshit" (*TX*, 198). "Life on Earth originate and or implemented by garbage shit deposited by Space Travellers?. .The Shit wrote out the message that is you . . . 'SHIT' was Thee Beginning Word. .And the last word. .Rub out the Word" (*E*, 25). Burroughs's mythology of our present reality begins and ends with the word, but the end is the beginning born knowing.

The whole of this mythology is initiated and fulfilled on every page of Burroughs's work—in each moment of intersection between reader and text. His novels attempt to free us from our present reality. His mythology is the set of assumptions that leads him to write and that makes his writing possible.

Most modern apocalyptic writing moves toward scenes of extreme visionary intensity, and commonly involves the reader in this gradual process. But Burroughs believes linear narrative necessarily defeats the radical potential of a visionary posture. Conventional narrative is an act of domestication, one that enables us to integrate revelation into our established associative channels. It offers the "White Junk" fix for readers who cannot bear violence and outrage in discrete, total encounters. He pinpoints the lethal palliative of a continuous story: "Why all this waste paper getting The People from one place to another? Perhaps to spare The Reader stress of sudden space shifts and keep him Gentle? And so a ticket is bought, a taxi called, a plane boarded" (*NL*, 218). Burroughs has no interest in a journey he can plan in advance. He is committed to the end of the world he mythologizes.

This complex of beliefs, perception, and private mythology creates virtually insoluble problems for verbal communication. All language acts through control imagery and follows associative channels. Burroughs's own language is equally capable of taking over a novel and short-circuiting its radical possibilities: "I prefer not to use *my own words*, I dont like *my own words* because *my own words* are prerecorded *on my bare honestie and being dead doe stick and stinke in repetition*. . . . my words are prerecorded for me as yours are prerecoded for you" (*APO*, 16–17). Nevertheless, Burroughs says, there are degrees of complicity, and his experiments in literature attempt to break the birth-death cycle enforced by conventional language. Turning the enemy's own weapons against him leads to neither security nor complacency, but does offer a certain ironic satisfaction (a revolutionary fifth-column consciousness). Although Burroughs engages in a self-defeating paradox—using a defective instrument for redemptive purposes—he chooses the only conceivable solution. His assumptions deny us any satisfaction from minor changes in the flesh script. Language is encouraged to destroy itself: "So he sounded the words that end 'Word' " (*NE*, 69).

As all of us know, human beings often deal violently with insoluble paradoxes. Burroughs's cut-up methods extend this understanding to his own prose. As he writes in *The Exterminator*, a manifesto for his method, "The Word Lines keep Thee In Slots. . . . Cut the Word Lines with scissors or switch blade as preferred" (*E*, 5). The reader comes to realize the switchblade *is* preferred; Burroughs sees his writing as redemptive violence. But he never conceives his novels as vessels of revelation; they do not in any sense *contain* the texture of a new landscape. Nor does he wish us to read his books over and over again in a religious ritual of symbolic annihilation. The ideal reader would cease to exist in the same time continuum.

The mythology outlined above consequently may describe the universe in which Burroughs's fiction is written, but it will not provide a handbook for experiencing the novels as linear narratives.

The novels are not in themselves vehicles of revelation, and they do not, as *Leaves of Grass* and Norman O. Brown's *Love's Body* do, symbolically offer us the visionary body of their author. Burroughs instead continually rewrites the same book to perfect an instrument of aggression.

As he writes, in a telegraphic prose designed to make its content an event, "CUT UP AND SPRAY BACK of all minds is switch blade" (*E*, 12). Human consciousness is a primal act of aggression—the frustrated desire of the two halves of the word to recombine—and Burroughs tries to infuse the conflict with maximum energy. Describing his fold-in method, he invokes his mythology in its essential context: "The proportion of half one text half the other is important corresponding as it does to the two halves of the human organism" (*TX*, 65). There is only one landscape in which the event can occur: the reading (or writing) experience. All Burroughs's work tries to create a radical perceptual situation. When he invites us to fold in our own language, to enter the text at any point, he is not only proposing a specialized activity but also alerting us to what has been happening all the while. For we always randomize a novel's language, diffusing it in our own flesh. Though we carefully protect ourselves from the awareness, each sentence is truly a new entrance, a radical intersection of reader and text. Unlike other writers who share his assumptions, Burroughs does not wish us to reside or even to find temporary repose in a landscape of words.

The novels juxtapose the conflicting male-female human organisms, the double forms of the incarnate word. An absolute juxtaposition would create a miniature nova in the mind of the reader. The state of physical outrage—achieved by our intersection with the printed page—urges us to discover *now* the ultimate form of human history. If we can experience it now—in the conscious reading situation rather than in a self-righteous global war where we die in ignorance—the end of time need not be also the end of consciousness. The alternative apocalypse—already written on the flesh sheets of our bodies—will serve only the needs of our controllers.

Burroughs's fiction attempts to make *this* instant a spatial experience of all time, to make the present a radical implosion of the beginning and the end of time: "I was it will be it is? No. It was and it will be if you stand still for it. The point where the past touches the future is right where you are sitting now on your dead time ass hatching virus negatives into present time into the picture reality of a picture planet. Get off your ass, boys. Get off the point" (*TX*, 196). I spoke earlier of Burroughs's tendency to write as though every human contact were an act of murder. The intent of his style in *Nova Express, Soft Machine*, and *The Ticket That Exploded* is to make these murders a necessary and inevitable function of the reading experience. Each phrase in the later novels replaces and destroys all preceding phrases, arranging the novel in a new configuration. Each phrase, wholly possessing our attention, acts exclusively to occupy the whole of time in the space of the present.

Burroughs's novels occur in an instant bounded by the beginning and the end of time. The language progresses in an ontology of absolute juxtaposition, from zero to zero. Each communicating particle of language is equivalent to every other particle of language. Each phrase (or group of phrases) resonates in a cosmic vacuum and accumulates an exclusive mutuality of meaning. The form is repeatedly emptied, imploded, ravaged, or eclipsed by a slow fade. The biologic facts created are experiential facts of form and style—continual outrage, dismemberment, and violation. All perception, we discover, is a polar opposition in which perceiver and perceived are violently permutated through each other. What's folded in is you and me. "Everybody splice himself in with everybody else. Communication must be made total. only way to stop it" (*TX*, 166).

For Burroughs, total communication becomes either grotesquely funny or grotesquely hideous—the nightmare of an angel wounded in its loins. His humor, which many readers will not acknowledge, exists in the same context as the horror: "it's knowing at any second your buddy may be took by the alien virus it's happened cruel idiot smile over the corn flakes . . You gasp and reach for a side arm looking after your own soul like a good Catholic . . too late . . your nerve centers are paralyzed by the dreaded Bor-Bor he has slipped into your Nescafé . . He's going to eat you slow and nasty . ." (*TX*, 5). Burroughs's inescapable nightmare landscapes needn't be quoted. But amidst "screaming glass blizzards of enemy flak" (*NE*, 67), Burroughs suddenly inserts a tranquil poetic language, so original and unexpected that it hints at the existence of another universe:

> Two Lesbian Agents with glazed faces of grafted penis flesh sat sipping spinal fluid through alabaster straws (*NE*, 68)
>
> soft mendicant words falling like dead birds in the dark street (*T*, 15)
>
> From an enormous distance he heard the golden hunting horns of the Aeons and he was free of a body traveling in the echoing shell of sound as herds of mystic animals galloped through dripping primeval forests, pursued by the silver hunters in chariots of bone and vine. (*TX*, 86)

These passages of lyrical violence occur only in moments of ultimate confrontation. Duplicating the novel's juxtaposition of the two halves of the body, reader and text react at the limits of language. The cumulative effect, as "pieces of murder fall slow as opal chips through glycerine" (*NL*, 232), is to overload the flesh script. We can no longer process the novel through our association blocks. Its only relevance is to the naked moment of perception in which we read it. In this terminal landscape, where "one assumes that any one close to him or her is there precisely to kill" (*NE*, 104), where "every encounter quivers with electric suspicion" (*NE*, 104), the intersection between the reader and the printed page enacts the end of language.

"Globe is self you understand," Burroughs writes, "until I die" (*NE*, 109). His novels create a radical perceptual situation in which the reader can no longer maintain his sense of temporal continuity, in which the self we know does die. Internalizing Burroughs's language, the reader finds it incompatible with his own speech. Yet the novels have entered the reader's experience; their language now exists in his body. Attempting to exert his sense of personal continuity, the reader rejects this violated body in a primal act of self-assertion. But his own language now becomes inoperable, for the body controls the structure of his verbal identities.

As the word script is randomized, the body too dissolves: "no more word scripts, no more flesh scripts" (*NE*, 186); "Every part of your translucent burning fire head shut off" (*NE*, 173-74); "Legs and genitals lost outline careening through dream flesh" (*NE*, 170). "So?" asks Burroughs. "What is word?—Maya—Maya —Illusion—Rub out the word and the image track goes with it" (*TX*, 145). To stop the verbal processing of the environment, to annihilate language, is to witness our bodies dissolving into faded newsprint and randomized tape recordings. Reduced to its intolerably predatory archetype—"Talk, Face"—the flesh script unfolds, emptied of content: " 'You and I fading' he said"; "his voice muffled as if I were seeing his face through words fraying breaking focus" (*TX*, 191, 190). When we see through the crack in the double prison of control, the two biologic theaters, planet and body, come to an end: "All out of time and into space. Come out of the time-word 'the' forever. Come out of the body word 'thee' forever. There is nothing to fear. There is no thing in space. There is no word to fear. There is no word in space" (*SM*, 162).

The self for Burroughs, like the planet, maintains its sense of historical continuity through the body's influence. Our bodies keep us imprisoned in time. "All out of time," he writes, "and into space." Burroughs perhaps uses more images of body life and internal physical processes than any other author, but his violent imagery does not make us at home in our bodies. His radical space destroys the self as a structure continuous in time by ravaging and irreversibly transforming our biologic existence. "The hope lies in the development of non-body experience and eventually getting away from the body itself, away from three-dimensional coordinates and concomitant animal reactions of fear and flight, which lead inevitably to tribal feuds and dissension" (*ART*, 47). Burroughs rejoices in the end of the body. As inexplicable and intolerable as this statement will be to his readers, he literally intends the end of the human body as we know it.[6] He invokes a radical silence that follows the explosion of the body outward into space. Silence, for Burroughs, is unspeakable.

To his own vision of infinite space, Burroughs deliberately opposes the need to enclose radical experience in protective frames.[7] He himself prefers an image of the astronaut's vulnerable body about to explode into the universe. The "space-suits and masturbating rockets," traditional technological images of the human body, are for him overburdened containers of aggressive energy:

6. Burroughs believes the human organism can rapidly evolve beyond the need for its slavish fleshly structures; his vision is of consciousness freed from the flesh script, from the sound and image track we know as the human body. In addition to biologic changes induced by the reading situation, Burroughs dreams of rationally and scientifically planned human mutations: "Science eventually will be forced to establish courts of biologic mediation, because life forms are going to become more incompatible with the conditions of existence as man penetrates further into space. . . . We will simply have to use our intelligence to plan mutations, rather than letting them occur at random" (*ART*, 46).

7. Like many of Burroughs's contemporaries, Marshall McLuhan finds hope in the possibility that the body can provide an effective frame for an immensely widened perceptual field: "The totally designed environment necessary to life in the space capsule draws attention to the fact that the astronaut makes the spaces that he needs and encounters. Beyond the environment of this planet there is no space in our planetary or 'container' sense. . . . the astronaut must have his own environment with him. . . . Strong indications are given to the astronauts that objects, as well as people, create their own spaces. Outer space is not a frame any more than it is visualizable." Marshall McLuhan and Harley Parker, *Through the Vanishing Point* (New York, 1969), p. 25. McLuhan suggests elsewhere that Burroughs wants "to turn the human body itself into an environment that includes the universe." "Notes on Burroughs," *The Nation* (28 Dec. 1964), p. 517. McLuhan's phrase accurately describes Brown's *Love's Body* and perhaps Susan Sontag's novels, but Burroughs believes the body is already the vessel for a universe of birth and death. In his *Paris Review* interview, Burroughs answered McLuhan's description by suggesting an alternative to making the body an environment: "What I want to do is to learn to see more of what's out there, to look outside, to achieve as far as possible a complete awareness of surroundings. Beckett wants to go inward. First he was in a bottle and now he is in the mud. I am aimed in the other direction—outward" (*ART*, 23).

"All out of time and into space. . . . the naked astronaut. And the idiot irresponsibles rush in with space-suits and masturbating rockets spatter the city with jissom" (*SM*, 162).

The texture of Burroughs's vision, like the imagery that reaches toward it, suggests an infinite space in which any experience is immediately and wholly available. "*Nothing Is True—Everything Is Permitted*" (*NE*, 157), but each encounter achieves its total form in an instant, and there is no guarantee it will be successful. "We are still quite definite and vulnerable organisms—Certainly being without a body conveyed no release from fear" (*NE*, 103). The organism's experience is its total intersection with the present; it has no continuity in time. To achieve any possibility, we must be utterly open to it. "This means that the mediating life forms must simultaneously lay aside all defenses and all weapons" (*NE*, 136).

We are left with a tentative image of "the naked astronaut free in space," who found "that he could move on his projected image from point to point—He was already accustomed to life without a body" (*NE*, 103). The novels themselves do not contain that vision; they offer a violent encounter with a mock-Darwinian eschatology that Burroughs calls "the final ape of history." Simultaneously comical and demoniacal, the novels taunt us with an outrageous planetary self ecstatically exploding in space: "I still mushroom planet wide open for jolly" (*NE*, 55).

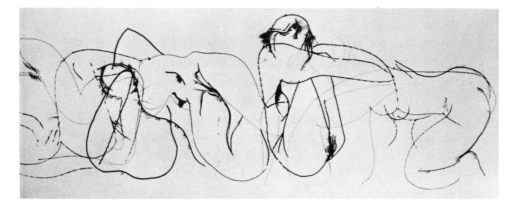

28. Avinash Chandra, untitled drawing.

TEN Fields: the body as a text

From the first, space is manifest in Rilke. "We live under the sign of the plain and the sky." The plain, the sky, are what is found everywhere and all around, what is beyond and immensely at a distance: ... A naked space, a virgin and flat territory. One goes across it endlessly, without an obstacle. One pours into it freely the objects of one's thought. From every object, from every thought, space extends. And every object of thought slides and plunges in space. . . . Space is therefore a sheet of still water, on which, in circles, is written the undulatory and excentric progress of things. All irradiates from it, all grows from it. It is the hollow which will overflow, the nothingness which will be filled, the absence which will become presence. . . . it is the field of becoming.

Space, then, is not any longer heterogeneous, not exterior to the mind. It is the field which the mind gives itself in order to proceed freely, through its own expansion, toward its glorification.

Georges Poulet, *Metamorphoses of the Circle*, 336, 301

1
Genesis
(a sensual nexus)

> a field of faery blithe as this flowing wild.
>> Joyce, *Finnegans Wake*, 281

> A fair feld, ful of folke
>> Langland, *Piers Plowman*

> For all the sloping pasture murmur'd, sown
> With happy faces and with holiday.
> There moved the multitude, a thousand heads.
>> Tennyson, *Poems and Plays*, 154

> The field where He has planted us
>> Hopkins, *P—Poems*, 17

Genesis: a beginning in which all endings are foreshadowed—Williams's "clean raked fields of hell" or Bly's "plains of heaven."

Genesis: a generating image to encompass both evacuated wastes and the farmer's intimate immensity, both "the blank field" (Snodgrass) and the "field of stiff weeds and thistles and tufted nettle-bunches" (Joyce, *Portrait of the Artist*, 137).

Genesis: imagine a sea swarm, seed pod, sperm-spawn, an egg cluster galactic or intimate. Conceive the first field coming into existence. Multiply. Magnify the nest. "The spirit finds the nest of immensity" (Bachelard, *PS—Poetics of Space*, 190).

> When he came wholly forth
> I took him up in my hands and bent

> over and smelled
> the black, glistening fur
> of his head, as empty space
> must have bent
> over the newborn planet
> and smelled the grasslands and the ferns.
>
> Galway Kinnell, *BN—Book of Nightmares*, 72

A field is an egg cluster hung with thought, a nest extended on eye-beams or lines of sight—ripe waiting speared by rays of light—consciousness—"and so she comes / To fields of light; millions of travelling rays / Pierce her" (Hopkins, *P*, 147).

As in the *Bhagavad Gita*, a field balances Field and Field-Knower. It is a dialectic or an implosion: knowledge and the object of all knowledge. "We are a meadow where the bees hum, / mind and body are almost one" (Denise Levertov, *Sorrow Dance*, 17). A field is a silent dream. We cannot sever the dreamer from his dream. Field and man.

> All those days we could keep
> Your mind a landscape of new snow
> Where the chilled tenant-farmer finds, below,
> His fields asleep
>
> W. D. Snodgrass, *Heart's Needle*, 47

Field and man are an emblem. Emblems are copulating (ant) agonists who exchange roles playfully forever. "Strawberry fields forever" (The Beatles). Or in another vein—"there's some corner of a foreign field / That is forever England" (Rupert Brooke).

> the priest and the doctor
> In their long coats

Running over the fields.
                    Philip Larkin, in Lucie-Smith, ed.,
                    BP—British Poetry since 1945, 132

Or in the snowy field of the insane asylum.
                    Robert Bly, *LB—Light around the Body*, 25

I watch the blue-veined snowfields bleed with sunrise
                    David Wevill, in Lucie-Smith, *BP*, 213

2
Animating an image—the point of departure

> When a master wanted to tell a monk what the mind of
> Buddha was, he said: "The white cow is lying by the cool
> stream in the open field."
> > quoted by D. T. Suzuki, *Zen Buddhism*, 251

> We think as wind skitters on a pond in a field
> > Wallace Stevens, *Collected Poems*, 518

> Man is therefore not only a living field, but also the son
> of the field, and not only the field and the seed . . .
> but also the king of the field, who plants good seed and
> hostile tares in the field: for what is a field without seed,
> and a prince without land and produce? These three in
> us are therefore one, namely God's field.
> > Ronald Gregor Smith, *J. G. Hamann*, 99

Field as nest
> web
> > wheel, each spoke a blade of wheat.
> surfacing in the circle
> > rising in its season

Man in his field—sower of wheat, breeder of corn, whose mind
can travel the spokes of the wheel and find the pattern of the web.
"The 'field' of action / with moving incalculable center" (A. R.
Ammons, in Hollander, ed., *PM—Poems of Our Moment*, 25).
"Plowed earth is not flat, but plays within the surface. It has no
center: instead, a continuous rhythm, broken and overturned and
always felt throughout" (Jean Hélion, in Kepes, ed., *Visual Arts
Today*, 104).

Man, who is the center of the field—nexus of the web—hub of the wheel. "A man's head is an eminence upon / A field of barley spread beneath the sun" (Roethke, *CP—Collected Poems*, 13).

> What is so strange about a tree alone in an open field?
> It is a willow tree. I walk around and around it.
> The body is strangely torn, and cannot leave it.
> > Bly, *S—Silence in the Snowy Fields*, 14

Man-play of vertical in a level field. A cross. A scarecrow crucifies the harvest.

> But when our heads are planted
> under the church, from those empty pods
> we rise in the fields of death
> > Louis Simpson, *At the End of the Open Road*, 61

The field is energy in transit. It mediates between the mind's grain (words) and their uncreated soil. Mind-hive, the cell-seed of grain.

3
Etymology

> touch, who lives on the naked plains of the skin
>   Malcolm de Chazal, *Plastic Sense*, 41

> I come to a field
> glittering with the thousand sloughed skins
>   Kinnell, *BN*, 65

A connection between field and flesh. All flesh is grass. "Our body's sod parabled with grain" (Bruce Cutler, in Stryk, ed., *H—Heartland*, 45). In Afrikaans, "veld" is both a wide grassland and an untanned hide or skin, as in "veldschoen," a shoe made of hide (Partridge, *Origins*, 210). Thus field is veld or pelt. Parchment is the pelt from the beasts of the field; papyrus is pressed grass: "Thou knew'st this paper when it was / Mere seed, and after that but grass" (Henry Vaughan). Or the cloth felt, a wool fabric often mixed with fur or hair, a pelt or flesh-cover that is good to feel, "the rich coverlet of the grass" (Whitman). Flesh, a field-pelt we have all felt.

To be clothed in the field is to lie in a grave dreaming. Or to be dreamed. "When I shall sleep with clover clad" (Housman). "Lying here among grass, am I dead am I sleeping / amazed among silences" (Muriel Rukeyser, *Speed of Darkness*, 17). To be dreamed by the flesh of an ancestor buried in the field. Whitman calls grass "the beautiful uncut hair of graves." The newborn soul—fishing in loose fields for a name. "White horses move through the fields / lifting men out of the darkness" (Sam Cornish, *Generations*, 50). "Passing the yellow-spear'd wheat, every grain from its shroud in / the dark-brown fields uprisen" (Whitman, *Leaves of Grass*, 330).

4
Farmer

> But now I straddle the field and break its back
> In the vise of my plow
>
> James Hearst, in Stryk, *H*, 76

> He plows the sand, and, at his hardest need,
> He sows himself for seed;
> He plows the furrow, and in this lies down
> Before the corn is grown
>
> Elinor Wylie, in Untermeyer, ed., *MAP—*
> *Modern American Poetry*, 308

To plant a field is to extend intimate space to the horizon, infinitely. A uniform and horizontal space, composed of inseparable clumps of handled earth. It never ends. Yet it is the waste of absolute finitude.

> I take a drop of sweat
> Onto my thumb,
> Watch the wind furrow its surface,
> Dream of a morning
> When my furrows will shape this field,
> When these rocks will form my house.
>
> Gene Fowler, *Field Studies*, 9

Planting a field is an act of domestication; it makes the world human, methodically creates an anthropocosmos. Who among us has escaped the furrows of the field? Culture is agriculture.

The formalized movements of farming generate immobility. The peculiar relation of man to earth is fulfilled by the first sowing, the first reaping. It is as though the solitary reaper moves ever more slowly, finally harvesting the crops merely standing with his tools, fulfilling the level repose of the land with the violent vertical thrust of his simple human presence.

All field wanderers are farmers. All motion or presence in the field tills the soil.

farmers sleepwalk without
Their women from houses   a walk like falling toward
the far waters
Of life   in moonlight   toward the dreamed eternal
meaning of
their farms
Toward the flowering of the harvest in their hands
James Dickey, *P—Poems*, 298

Like the farmer, with his hands on the earth before him and one wary eye on the horizon, we should not hesitate to handle the field entire: "the boy stared down at the river disappearing, the corn blowing back into the soil, the hundred house trees dwindling to a stalk, and the four corners of the yellow field meeting in a square that he could cover with his hand" (Dylan Thomas, *AS—Adventures in the Skin Trade*, 126). "Why do you walk through the fields in gloves, / Missing so much and so much?" (Frances Cornford, in Untermeyer, ed., *MBP—Modern British Poetry*, 306).

The furrows we stroke with our fingertips plow fields everywhere.

Hands—fingers—grass. To caress the field is to succumb to the field's caress: "far away, trailing his hand in the high waving meadow grasses" (Samuel Beckett), "whose fingers are fresh cut hay" (André Breton). "The feel of the neck of branches, of the mouth of the flower. . . . O leaves, your wet tongues" (de Chazal, *Plastic Sense*, 17).

> And, we loved to hear
> Spliced phrases of the wind, to hear
> Rasps in the field, where corn leaves
> Pierce like bamboo slivers.
>   Wole Soyinka, in Moore and Beier, eds., *A—*
>   *Modern Poetry from Africa*, 117

5
Meditative reaper

> Look at me from the depths of the earth,
> tiller of fields
> > Pablo Neruda, *MP—Macchu Picchu*, 67

> Bowed by the weight of centuries he leans
> Upon his hoe and gazes on the ground,
> The emptiness of ages in his face,
> And on his back the burden of the world.
> > Edwin Markham, in Untermeyer, *MAP*, 107

The farmer lingers. "At the edge of the field waiting for the pure moment" (Roethke, *CP*, 168). Germination takes time. Human intimacy nests in the wide furrows he cuts and is packed in the drift of seed about him. The drowsing musing farmer bent over his hoe, or Wordsworth's solitary reaper "o'er the sickle bending," assumes a meditative posture. And in that moment he becomes a vortex for all the ancient brooders buried in his land. For the role persists eternally. The man who puts on the body of a farmer, like the man who puts on the body of a king or a clown, becomes one with all his forebears.

To sit or dream (or pose as a dreamer) in a bare or ripe field is to inform a metaphor of absence with ceaseless change. "Who had openings within / as he walked in the fields" (Gael Turnbull, in Lucie-Smith, *BP*, 234).

> The stone lives on,
> commending itself to the hardness of air,
> to the long meadows of your looking.
> > Mark Strand, *Darker*, 31

All morning with dry instruments
The field repeats the sound
Of rain
From memory

W. S. Merwin, *L—Lice*, 55

Meditation is insemination—impregnation—extension along lines of thought. It celebrates the mind-seed at the end of its stalk. The meditative reaper incarnates the field dreams of a sacred posture. He is hunchback, saint, and fool—final crescents in the harvest moon.

From the hunchback we have his "aching stoop," his gnarled working body, and an affirmation of his solitary musing in the field. In his body, the field crouches. "The rack of ribs; the scooped flank; lank / Rope-over thigh; knee-nave; and barrelled shank" (Hopkins, *P*, 104). The saint or lunatic, moon-mad, gives us the ascetic half of the harvest. A fool, a clown, a clod—a country lout who has a sod or a clod of earth for his head (Greenough and Kittredge, *Words and Their Ways in English Speech*, 285). From that we have clod-hopper, or ploughman. Yet the posture is still not exhausted. Clod of earth for a head, mind or grain at the end of its spinal stalk, and the knobbed working tools of the farmer are emblematic of the meditative tension that gives the field its human resonance. Remembering the fool on the final card of the Tarot, carrying his mind-bag on the end of a staff, the archetype becomes a nexus for transformations: the scarecrow is merely an economical version of the farmer.

6
Fire dance

> Wake me, witch, we'll do the dance of rotten sticks.
>
> Roethke, *CP*, 64

> Coming down the mountain in the twilight—
> April it was and quiet in the air—
> I saw an old man and his little daughter
> Burning the meadows where the hayfields were.
>
> Forksful of flame he scattered in the meadows.
> Sparkles of fire in the quiet air
> Burned in their circles and the silver flowers
> Danced like candles where the hayfields were,—
>
> Danced as she did in enchanted circles,
> Curtseyed and danced along the quiet air:
> Slightly she danced in the stillness, in the twilight,
> Dancing in the meadows where the hayfields were.
>
> Archibald MacLeish, *Collected Poems*, 163

> Then in the distance across the dark fields I saw a
> flame.... The flame flickered ... and sometimes it glowed
> like a halo, as if it had sunk deep into water.
>
> Shohei Ooka, *Fires on the Plain*, 175

A dancer in the flaming field is a dreaming sower. A wet dream.

Dancing meditation. Burning the leaves. Burning the pages. A field of flame, as when the sun sets, or as lit by the mind's glances. "The high, green meadows are glowing, as if lit from within" (Sylvia Plath, in Lucie-Smith, *BP*, 164). The burning mountain meadows—the corners curl up to capture a bowl of flame.

> The stubble field catches the last growth of sun.
>
> Bly, *S*, 20

In a field of sunlight between two pines,
The droppings of last year's horses
Blaze up into golden stones.

James Wright, *CP—Collected Poems*, 114

A flame, intense visible,
Plays over the dry pods,
Runs fitfully along the stubble,
Moves over the field,
Without burning.

Roethke, *CP*, 160

The flame is wind, breath, or dream, a flight or dance of mind over field. A playful germination, seeding the field in miniature: "It used to be customary on the Eve of St. John to trundle a blazing wheel wrapt in straw over the fields to fertilize them"; "In this way the mock-sun itself, not merely its light and heat represented by torches, is made actually to pass over the ground" (Frazer, *Golden Bough*, vol. 10, 121, 190–91).

And he who had dreamed that a hundred orchards had broken into flame saw suddenly then in the windless afternoon tongues of fire shoot through the blossom. ... The trees were fireworks and torches, smouldered out of the furnace of the fields into a burning arc, cast down their branded fruit like cinders on the charred roads and fields.

Thomas, *AS*, 103

"Aloof in his field of fire / The hawk wheels pitiless" (Thomas McGrath, in Stryk, *H*, 122). I stand alone in the burning field. The burning field—the body known. I swim through meadow flame, and I sing, I do not burn.

7
Dream and sleep

> The haze of harvest drifts along the field
> Until clear eyes put on the look of sleep.
> Roethke, CP, 12

> we drowse as horses drowse afield,
> in accord
> Levertov, Sorrow Dance, 17

> these dreams that take my breath away?
> They come at evening with the home-flying rooks and
> the scent of hay,
> Over the fields.
> Charlotte Mew, in Untermeyer, MBP, 159

Breath. Sleep. Dreams. "The Winds come to me from the fields
of sleep" (Wordsworth). "My dreams are of a field afar" (Housman). To breathe the space of the fields is to sleep and dream. "On
a half-reap'd furrow sound asleep, / Drows'd with the fume of
poppies" (Keats). Dorothy in the deadly poppy field: "if the sleeper
is not carried away from the scent of the flowers he sleeps on and
on forever. But Dorothy did not know this" (Baum, *The Wizard
of Oz*, 73). Knowing we dream in the fields, we can approach the
Emerald City. But only flesh can dream: "The Scarecrow and the
Tin Woodman, not being made of flesh, were not troubled by
the scent of the flowers." So Dorothy is carried to where the fresh
breeze, the breath of the world's dream, can waken her from
her own.

Sleep brings dreams of "the unrevealed, treadable distances, the
trodden field" (Rilke). " 'On the plains I am always elsewhere, in

an elsewhere that is floating, fluid. Being for a long time absent from myself, and nowhere present, I am too inclined to attribute the inconsistency of my daydreams to the wide open spaces that induce them' " (Henri Bosco, in Bachelard, *PS*, 203).

> In the vast world of the non-I, the non-I of fields is not
> the same as the non-I of forests. The forest is a before-me,
> before-us, whereas for fields and meadows, my dreams
> and recollections accompany all the different phases
> of tilling and harvesting. When the dialectics of the I
> and the non-I grow more flexible, I feel that fields and
> meadows are with me. . . . But forests reign in the past.
>
> Bachelard, *PS*, 188

> To leave the open fields
> and enter the forest,
>
> that was the rite.
>
> Levertov, *O Taste and See*, 57

8
House

> At home, whispering of fields unsown.
> > Wilfred Owen, in Untermeyer, *MBP*, 358

> Her homes and fields that folded and fed me
> > Hopkins, *P*, 195

> By intermingled work of house and field
> Of the fireside or of the open field
> > Wordsworth

> A house for wisdom; a field for revelation.
> > Roethke, *CP*, 90

> > to the open fields I told
> A prophecy
> > Wordsworth

The ancient brotherhood, or balance, of house and field is not unlike the dreamer and his dream. The house is the meditating reaper crouched over his hearth, and the field is his meditation. House and field are two nests that, together, liberate a boundless nesting daydream. "I remember now. / We met in a nest. Before I lived" (Roethke, *CP*, 93). In a nest, or in a field. My house. Field present or field past—the inhabiting meditations of the race.

We remember Rilke's image of a distant hut, the hut that stands quite alone on the horizon before one comes to fields. And we know the intimacy of the distant hut is a door to the vacant fields. The house, hunched over its fire at the edge of a field, mimics the gestures of the man within. "It sees like a man. It is an eye open to the night" (Bachelard, *PS*, 35). To nest in a house in a field is to meditate on distance. A house or a body in a field is a focal point, a nexus, for absence. "Man's mounting spirit in his bone-house, mean house, dwells" (Hopkins, *P*, 70).

> What is the body covering? The corresponding Old English terms for the "body" suggest the answer: they call the "body" *flaesc-homa*, properly "flesh-cover"; *ban-cofa*, "bone-cave"; *ban-faet*, "bone-vessel"; or *ban-hus*, "bone-house." The "house," the "cave," the "vessel" made of flesh and bones are all "cover" for the invisible agency that has chosen the house, cave, vessel for its dwelling place.
>
> Thass-Thienemann, *Subconscious Language*, 277

> Arjuna said: Prakriti and Purusha, the Field and the Knower of the Field, knowledge and that which is to be known, all this I desire to learn.
>
> The Lord said: This body is called the Field, and he who knows it is called the Knower of the Field.
>
> *Bhagavad Gita*, xiii

> a man unrolled
> The scrolls of fire that burned in his heart and head,
> Torn and alone in a farm house in a fold
> Of fields.
>
> Dylan Thomas, *Collected Poems*, 131

House body cave. And field. And the Bible speaks of "the cave which he hath in the end of his field" (Genesis 23:9) as a house for the dead, as a burial urn for ancestral dreams. "A home in dark grass, / And nourishment in death" (Bly, *LB*, 44). "And the field, and the cave that is therein, were made sure unto Abraham for a possession of a burying place" (Genesis 23:20). "A silence before this one / Has left its broken huts facing the pastures" (Merwin, *L*, 45).

The house or cave is the body of the man who would dream. And the field is his dream, or his new body, the dream body. The dreaming body and its house and cave—this is the field folded. It is as wide as all distance, for the sun is its hearth and the tent of the sky over the field is its house. The living are the dreams of the dead. "They caress the roofs with their fingers . . . They yearn out over the fields" (John Gould Fletcher, in Untermeyer, *MAP*, 334).

9
Plow and woman

> turn me to a hot field
> ready for plowing
>> Adrienne Rich, in Hollander, *PM*, 242

> Royal wench!
> She made great Caesar lay his sword to bed.
> He plowed her and she cropped.
>> Shakespeare, *Antony and Cleopatra*

> We . . . left those fields spilled
> over sod with black
> soil. And full mooned nights
> we drove our wives there . . . they
> running like stark does
> down the naked land.
> And when they winded
> we buckled their knees
> and took them on top
> those furrows milky
> with their great moons full.
> Then the green corn came
> like mad
>> John Knoepfle, in Stryk, *H*, 94–95

"The farmer's wife undergoes, symbolically, all that is done to the wheat" (Mircea Eliade, *P—Patterns in Comparative Religion*, 341). Aeschylus writes that Oedipus had plow-sown in the holy mother's field, and a Greek vase shows a phallic plow mounted by the farmer. A Nez Percé Indian challenges the tradition: "You ask me to plow the ground. Shall I take a knife and tear my mother's breast? Then when I die she will not take me to her bosom to rest" (Rothenberg, ed., *Technicians of the Sacred*, 361). When her girls' school is opened to admit the wounded warriors, Tennyson's Prin-

cess Ida climbs to the roof and broods over the "swarms of men /
Darkening her female field." Whether affirmed or denied, plow-
penis and field-woman is a connection implicit in every propa-
gation. Even Mary was fertilized in her chastity by the dew of
heaven; she was "a field unfurrowed by any cultivation, which
gave a harvest when it was watered by the rain" (Yrjö Hirn, *Sacred
Shrine*, 305).

> "I am the earth," declares the beloved in an Egyptian
> love song. The *Videvdāt* compares fallow land to a
> woman with no children, and in fairy tales, the barren
> queen bewails herself: "I am like a field on which nothing
> grows." ... The Hindus identified the furrow with the
> vulva (*yoni*), seeds with *semen virile*. "This woman is
> come as a living soil: sow seed in her, ye men!" The
> Laws of Manu also teach that "woman may be looked
> upon as a field, and the male as the seed." Narada makes
> this comment: "Woman is the field, and man the
> dispenser of the seed." A Finnish proverb says that
> "maidens have their field in their own body."
>
> Eliade, *P*, 259

The relation persists both in miniature and in the entire landscape: "the warm woman / Your hands had imagined / Fondling
soil in the spring fields"—"We, who are men, how shall we know /
Earth's ecstasy, who feels the plough / Probing her womb" (R. S.
Thomas, in Walsh, ed., *Today's Poets*, 165, 159). "She is as in a
field a silken tent" (Robert Frost).

> I saw the midlands
>   Revolve through her hair;
> The fields of autumn
>   Stretching bare,
> And sheep on the pasture
>
> Lawrence, *Poems*, 120

A thousand golden sheaves were lying there,
Shining and still, but not for long to stay—
As if a thousand girls with golden hair
Might rise from where they slept and go away.
                    E. A. Robinson, in Untermeyer, *MAP*, 132

Valéry describes "a couple betrothed, alone, in the green night of the fields," and the image of the "bridal bed in the fields" is traditional. Dylan Thomas would have his barren brides listen "to the lewd, wooed field flow to the coming frost." "All kissed, yielded: in deep summer fields, tangled pressed grass" (Joyce, *Ulysses*, 166). "He saw her hands glisten among the spray of grain" (Lawrence, *Rainbow*, 119). We must invest plows and fields with our fantasies.

Musty with love, we are gathered up
By the wind and the wheat we lie in.
The sun drives the color of gold
Into our silent, white bodies.
                    R. R. Cuscaden, in Stryk, *H*, 35

The field is the cave unfolded. Darkness subject to light. Feminine space made vulnerable and waiting—open—which is why the Bible says no woman can protect her chastity in a field (Deuteronomy 22).

Through its fields, the world seduces us. Farming the field violates open space: penetration and dispersal, plowing and seeding. An introjection of feminine space, or an empty embrace. Plowing a field makes intercourse immense, a kaleidoscope of seasonal mutations; a farmer makes space participate in each sexual gesture.

We discover an identity between plow and play. Foreplay. Let us play. And we know that not all furrows are wounds. At play in the fields of the Lord. "Learn from the beasts the physic of the field" —"Some in the Fields of purest Aether play"—"And sport and flutter in the Fields of Air" (Pope).

Field day: "a period when full opportunity suddenly, unexpectedly, or finally appears to unleash and satisfy natural powers, thwarted ability, or restrained desire" (*Webster's Third International*).

All fields are playing fields.

10
Sea—air—nothing at all

> Some left green meadows for the greener ocean,
> Left the low rising, falling of that land
> For a more violent and reckless motion
> No landscaped brain and body could withstand.
>
> Paul Engle, in Stryk, *H*, 56–57

> On a wide plain, beyond
> The far stretch of a dream,
> A field breaks like the sea
>
> Roethke, *CP*, 124

> The flat fields run out to the sea there.
> There is no sand, no line. It is autumn.
> The bare fields, dark between fences, run
> Out to the idle gleam of the flat water.
>
> Merwin, *Green with Beasts*, 70

> in a dun
> and sumac-ridden surf of grass that rolls
> in slow insinuations
>
> Bruce Cutler, in Stryk, *H*, 44

Homer speaks of "the unharvested sea," Tennyson describes "the houseless ocean's heaving field," and Joyce writes of "fields of undersea." There are psychic fields without external surface, like the ocean's waveless depths, where water thickens to clot the lungs and fill the mind's field with terror:

> Fields where we slept
> Lie underwater now
> Clay meadows of nightmare
> Beneath the shallow wave.
>
> Muriel Rukeyser, *Body of Waking*, 93

Field as sea and sea as field are almost conventional transformations, but the moment of change is realized only in the human mediator—"she looked at the bay beneath her, making hillocks of the blue bars of the waves, and stony fields of the purpler spaces" (Virginia Woolf, *To the Lighthouse*, 270)—"I drown in the drumming ploughland" (Ted Hughes, *Hawk in the Rain*, 11).

> It was high summer, and the boy was lying in the
> corn. . . . He heard the corn sway from side to side above
> him. . . . Lying flat on his back, he stared up into the
> unbrokenly blue sky falling over the edge of the corn. . . .
> He stretched himself like a cat, and put his arms behind
> his head. Now he was riding on the sea, swimming
> through the golden corn waves, gliding along the heavens
> like a bird; in seven-league boots he was springing
> over the fields.
>
> Thomas, *AS*, 124–25

A psychiatrist relates the dream of a young girl who fears the depths of the sea: "I stand beside deep and limpid waters. About to plunge into the depths I notice that the water has changed into a green field" (Stekel, *Interpretation of Dreams*, 114). Though she may not know it, in her dream it is she the dreamer who compels the metamorphosis. The change is conscious, and it can go either way:

> She held her body steady in the wind;
> Our shadows met, and slowly swung around;
> She turned the field into a glittering sea
>
> Roethke, *CP*, 120

Lying motionless in an undulating field, the body becomes weightless: "I rise and fall in the slow sea of a grassy plain" (Roethke). A rippling field of corn will echo waves whose rhythm begins at sea. Yet if we run on a beach—beside fields of sawgrass and the sea—the waves of grass and water will crest in us and break together on the sand. Between the two we leap—like "birds in the fields of the bread of water" (Thomas). When we plunge into a field of grain, for a moment we hold our breath. "She moved in the swallowing, salty field" (Thomas). But the field is a sea made visible—it is water we can breathe in. For the unsheathed mind, the mind afield, can quicken the depths of the sea.

Field—sea—air—nothing at all. The field is a sensual axis—a nexus for change in a spectrum of densities:

> In the mice-sawed potato fields dusk waits.
> Philip Levine, *On the Edge*, 60

> The moon drops one or two feathers into the field.
> The dark wheat listens.
> Be still.
> Wright, *CP*, 127

> Cornfields breathed in the darkness.
> Norman MacCaig, in Lucie-Smith, *BP*, 313

> Scattering the glitter of the milky way over the bare fields.
> Mazisi Kunene, in Moore and Beier, *A*, 152

> The first dews tremble on the darkening field
> A. D. Hope, in Hollander, *PM*, 151

> At dawn, mist blows over the great meadow.
> Bly, *LB*, 22

> the hawk
> Resumes his yielding balance, his shadow
> Swims the field
> Alvin Feinman, in Hollander, *PM*, 77

Lies in the fields   in *this* field   on her broken back
                                                as though on
A cloud she cannot drop through

                                                Dickey, *P*, 298

There in an open field I lie down in a hole I once dug and
    I praise the sky.
I praise the clouds that are like lungs of light.

                                                Strand, *Darker*, 26

I brake to see the vacant field, the sky above the wall.
Between air and stone, I enter an unwalled field. I feel the
air's skin and yet we remain divided.

            André du Bouchet, in Aspel and Justice, eds.,
                        Contemporary French Poetry, 125

There are fields of hillocks and fields of snow, thick cornfields
weighted and ripe, and fields of wheat—swaying, bending, rooted
yet ruffling. Tawny fields and mottled fields, "meadows of benign /
Arcadian green" (Plath), "the green field where cows burn like
newsprint" (Strand), the "flooded, hoof-shattered / meadows of
spring" (Kinnell). In "Windsor Forest," Pope focuses the silence
of the field on a single creature feeding in solitude after the grass
has succumbed to the mower's scythe: "And in the new-shorn
Field the Partridge feeds." The stillness ends when a spaniel smells
his prey, while "secure they trust th'unfaithful Field."

*"For a Journey: House Field, Top Field, Oak Field, Third
Field"* (Alan Brownjohn). Throughout literature there are fields
of light, air, night, heaven, immortality, and Elysian fields where
the dead can play again. Milton has a spirit in *Comus* "suck the
liquid air" up "in the broad fields of the sky," and in *Paradise Regained* he makes the desert Christ's "Victorious Field." Blake
writes of "sweet fields of bliss." Wallace Stevens has a moment
when "children become the fields," and Dylan Thomas celebrates

"the twice told fields of infancy." Tennyson suggests we can "plow the Present like a field," but warns he has no affection for the "beast that takes His license in the field of time." In Shelley's *Prometheus Unbound*, the spirits proclaim they shall sing "in the void's loose field," and when Moses parts the Red Sea, there appears out of the great deep a springing field.

All and Nil—the sea and the void: from the field we know that each has its season. The "drear desolate whiteness of his fields" (Coleridge), the "waste of broad, muddy fields, brown with dried weeds standing and fallen" (Williams), "fields athirst" (Joyce), the "pitching drought-drugged field" (Wevill), or the "dance of rotten sticks" (Roethke)—all are implicit in the fullest harvest. When the crops are harvested, the fruitfulness of the land settles again into watery darkness. "Sloping, dank, winter-dark fields stretched away on the open sides" (Lawrence, "The Horse Dealer's Daughter"). Wide seas of barren land, the vacant fields evaporate in air.

> torn out of time: black leaves
> across the stubble-field
> acres where love summered,
>
> golden-ripe. The tall boys
> were that grain: lost now too
>
> Eckman, in Stryk, *H*, 50

Whereby the austerity of a field of grain, the leaning toward a formal, textural dry ripeness. In a field you can shiver in the summertime.

The ripeness of the harvest has no limit: "he saw the yellow fields upon the hillside and the smudge of heather on the meadow bor-

ders. The world was ripe" (Thomas, *AS*, 91). Field is a metaphor
for endless potentiality. Silent, evacuated, full. A field is an ear
listening to silence. A field of grain is a forest fallen to the ground
unheard.

> when I look out the window I see only flatlands
> And the slow vanishing of the windmills
> The centuries draining the deep fields
>
> Merwin, *L*, 19

Each year the field dies. Out of its winter absence grow the forms
of spring's later, more intimate nothingness.

> When the hounds of spring are on winter's traces,
>   The mother of months in meadow or plain
> Fills the shadows and windy places
>   With lisp of leaves and ripple of rain
>
> Swinburne

An empty-handed harvest: "the shroud of field and stone, / the
interstellar void" (Neruda, *MP*, 17). A watched seed is a tiny intense vacuum. Pregnant. Everything. Ripe. Zero. "The blood-
drenched breast of the new crops translated / into the radiant
weave of matter and adamantine hollows" (Neruda, *MP*, 59). In
Pearl, dead seeds prefigure a timeless dying germination. "Man-
in-seed, in seed-at-zero, / From the star-flanked fields of space"
(Thomas, *Collected Poems*, 51). Only nothingness can contain
what does not exist.

11
Page

the poem is made of things—on a field

Williams

How they ploughd the given field in rows,
                    prose and
versus . and brought landscape
                    into being

Duncan, *Roots and Branches*, 33

From the moment he ventures into FIELD COMPOSITION—
put himself in the open—he can go by no track other
than the one the poem under hand declares, for itself.
. . . And the line comes (I swear it) from the breath, from
the breathing of the man who writes, at the moment
that he writes.

Charles Olson, *Selected Writings*, 16–19

To write a poem is to breathe or dream in a field. The page is a
field on which a net of words or a sheaf of corn is stretched tight—
to catch birds. "The gust of birds / That spurts across the field"
(Thom Gunn, in Hollander, *PM*, 109)—"Out of the golden field
the black crows fly / to Van Gogh's black blood" (Duncan, *OF*—
Opening of the Field, 30)—"He flew like a bird over the fields, but
soon the bird's body vanished, and he was a flying voice" (Thomas,
AS, 114). "A number of children . . . were romping about in a
meadow. Suddenly they all grew wings, flew up, and were gone"
(Freud, *Interpretation of Dreams*, 301).

If a poem is words on a field, it awaits our harvest. And who
can say its form is the same once it is dispersed in us. "In the field
of the poem   the unexpected / must come" (Duncan, *OF*, 35). The

page is a white blankness, a feminine space or field, a female silence in which we sow words. The word is a seed at the end of its stalk. Farmer, poet, fool, body. He writes "over every square inch of the only foolscap available, his own body" (Joyce, *Finnegans Wake*, 185).

With the blank page or the empty plains before us, there are two alternative forms of the same metaphor—two field dreams—two inseminations of our generating image—two postures—two egg clusters hung with thought: love and war—battlefield and body.

12
Plains

> West of this wide plain,
> Animals wilder than ours
> Come down from the green mountains in the darkness.
> Now they can see you, they know
> The open meadows are safe.
>
> Wright, CP, 134

> I recognize the first hunger
> as the plains start
> under my feet
>
> Merwin, Carrier of Ladders, 80

In the gleaning of wheat and the binding of sheaves afield, in the shearing of sheep from the meadows, resides the dream of an inexorable final harvest—"like a rice field disintegrating" (Bly, *LB*, 54)—"peopling / The lashed plains of our minds with hollow voices" (Merwin, *Drunk in the Furnace*, 6)—a harvest of no season—harvesting the fullness of the world.

> Who are those hooded hordes swarming
> Over endless plains, stumbling in cracked earth
> Ringed by the flat horizon only
>
> Eliot, Complete Poems and Plays, 48

"Flat country denotes the apocalyptic end, the longing for power and for death. There is a Persian tradition that, when the end of the world has come . . . the mountains will be levelled and all the earth will become one great plain" (Circlot, *Dictionary of Symbols*, 170). "On the deserted plain the grass continues to sway round about me with that same eternal motion I saw when I was alive" (Ooka, *Fires on the Plain*, 245).

All open space invokes the otherness of absolution: "a burned-out tabernacle of a plain" (Cutler, in Stryk, *H*, 42). The plains seduce us with the human mask of an endlessness we can embrace: "houseless brown farmland plains rolling heavenward / in every direction" (Ginsberg, *Planet News*, 128). The deserts are indifferent to the verticality of a man, but the plains accept this last vestige of the harvester. "He began to dream of a flat land where he would never have to rise again and hold himself erect in equilibrium"—"the pure plateau" (Beckett, *Three Novels*, 246, 277).

> From the distant darkness
> The plain puts out its tongue
> The uncontainable plain
>
> Split happenings
> Scattered withered words
> Levelled faces
>
> Vasko Popa, "Forgetfulness"

The final metamorphosis is fusion. The dialectic of man and field assumes the presence of an undifferentiated union that can never be wholly rejected. Even the most incidental image of absolute separation is almost intolerable: "Snow ... rests ... on transformer boxes held from the ground forever in the / center of cornfields" (Bly, *LB*, 45).

The permutations of men in fields persist like foreplay preceding fusion. Alone on the unbounded plains, we rejoice in the emptiness of ravaged space. "Known love standing in deep grove / new love naked on plain" (Merwin, *Carrier of Ladders*, 113). The endless plains—an arena for staging two dramas of tranquillity—bleached bones or the body resolved to no house.

13
Battlefield

And we are here as on a darkling plain
Swept with confused alarms of struggle and flight,
Where ignorant armies clash by night.

Matthew Arnold

Over wastes grey-green crashing, among horses unbroken
From bellowing fields, past bone-wreck of vessels,
Tide-ruin, wash of lost bodies bobbing

Merwin, *Green with Beasts*, 11

Creatures were in the field; one, three, six: creatures
were moving in the field, hither and thither. Goatish
creatures with human faces, hornybrowed, lightly
bearded and grey as india-rubber. The malice of evil
glittered in their hard eyes, as they moved hither and
thither, trailing their long tails behind them.

Joyce, *Portrait of the Artist*, 137

"The myth of creation includes the ritual (that is, violent) death
of a primeval giant, from whose body the worlds were made, and
plants grew. ... This, we may say, is the pattern drama from which
originated every human or animal sacrifice intended to strengthen
and increase the harvest" (Eliade, *P*, 346). In certain tribes the human sacrifice "was taken to the fields where he was attacked and
killed amongst the wheat. After his blood had coagulated in the
heat of the sun, it was burnt, together with the frontal bone and the
brain and some of the flesh, and the ashes scattered over the land
to fertilize it. The remainder of the body was eaten" (Radford,
Encyclopedia of Superstitions, 22).

Battlefield. To reap the field with swords—the artillery had a
field day with the retreating infantry. "All migrants from green

fields, intent on mire" (Wilfred Owen). Brothers warring out on the field. As in the myth of Cadmus and the field of dragon seed. Cadmus kills a dragon that bars his way to a spring. On Athene's advice, he sows the dragon's teeth in a nearby furrow in a field, and the teeth of the slaughtered dragon seed the field with war. A harvest of warriors springs up—Spartoi, or "sown men"—and they fight among themselves until all but five are killed. We have already slain the giant, killed the brother, but to reap the final harvest—what unimaginable sacrifice? What vast battlefield, what field of blood.

Battlefield. "The shot-slashed furrows" (Ted Hughes). "Show me your blood and your furrow; / say to me: here was I scourged" (Neruda, MP, 67). "Sheaved in cruel bands, bruised sore, / Scourged upon the threshing-floor" (Hopkins, P, 17). Brothers warring out on the field. "And Cain talked with Abel his brother: ["Come, let us go out into the field"] and it came to pass, when they were in the field, that Cain rose up against Abel his brother, and slew him" (Genesis 4:8). "And thy handmaid had two sons, and they two strove together in the field, and there was none to part them, but the one smote the other and slew him" (II Samuel 14:6).

Battlefield. "Deliver him that smote his brother, that we may kill him" (II Samuel 14:7)—"and how on the fields of skin / he struts" (Levine, NTP—Not This Pig, 59). To initiate what Roethke calls the "ancient fellowship of rotten stems." Brotherhood as fratricide: "Field of the Forty Footsteps. The tradition is that at the time of the Duke of Monmouth's rebellion two brothers fought each other here till both were killed, and for many years forth impressions of their feet remained on the field, and no grass would grow there" (Benet, Reader's Encyclopedia, 378).

> Then Yahweh asked Cain, "Where is your brother
> Abel?" He replied, "I don't know. Am I my brother's
> keeper?" And he said, "What have you done! Listen!
> Your brother's blood cries out to me from the soil. Hence
> you are banned from the soil which forced open its mouth
> to take your brother's blood from your hand. When you
> till the soil, it shall not again give up its strength to you.
> A restless wanderer shall you be on earth!"
>
> Genesis 4:9-12, in Speiser, trans., *The Anchor Bible*

"Tree, hill and rock stood out resigned, severe, / Beside the strangled field, the stream run dry" (Adrienne Rich, *Diamond Cutters*, 32). The barren field—an open boundless sepulcher—mad neon stalks of irradiated weeds—dance of rotten sticks. "The weeds hiss at the edge of the field" (Roethke). "A land of grass without memory" (Burroughs) is an emblem for the dead end of civilization. A tortured sea with its empty-handed human harvest—a field of "human faces tentative flicker in and out of focus" (Burroughs) —this field is the cave painstakingly and obsessively unraveled, the darkness woven into a frustrated human fabric. "In the windy cave of a cornfield / your blood has dried on the bones of husks" (Dave Etter, in Stryk, *H*, 60).

> Our eyes are turned to you.
> Our lives entombed
> in fields of death
>
> Aldo do Espirito Santo, in Moore
> and Beier, *A*, 139-40
>
> On the bloody fields near the secret pass—
> There the dead sleep in jars
>
> Bly, *LB*, 56
>
> The blood vanishes into the poisoned farmlands
> Rain falls into the open eyes of the dead
>
> Merwin, *L*, 63

In Kon Ichikawa's "Harp of Burma," a Japanese soldier wanders the silent fields of Burma, burying the anguished dead. Battlefield, bleached bones or a field of corpses swelling with corruption: "robin breast / dragged through the mud of battlefields" (Kinnell, *BN*, 67), "fields, where now only wounds take root" (Saint Geraud, *The Naomi Poems*, 54). "A piece of flesh gives off / smoke in the field" (Kinnell, *BN*, 41). "I can remember a pair of hands (nationality unknown) which protruded from the soaked ashen soil like the roots of a tree turned upside down" (Siegfried Sassoon, *Memoirs of an Infantry Officer*, 170). "In March these fields of nettles / will bear a white scum" (Levine, *NTP*, 69). Or the frozen battlefields about Stalingrad, armies a whitened tableau, a mimicry or celebration of the fields of war. Bly's "the silence of snowy fields." No one disturbs the silence of the fields for long. "The peasant plods back and reclaims / His fields that strangers burned"—"we have won costly fields to sow / in salt, our only seed" (Snodgrass, *Heart's Needle*, 49, 62). Judas's field—Aceldama, the field of blood.

To die alone and in the body—death by drowning in a field of blood.

Fields for fighting, playing, plowing—all preserve a meditative silence. And we have not moved from our generating image—mind-hive, the cell-seed of grain. Nor will we ever leave the first field, though we witness the metamorphoses of an archetype through incarnations tragic and comic, sacred and profane.

> True, a new mistress now I chase,
> The first foe in the field
>
> Richard Lovelace

I walk out from myself,
among the stones of the field,
each sending up its ghost-bloom
into the starlight, to float out
over the trees, seeking to be one
with the unearthly fires kindling and dying

in space—and falling back, knowing
the sadness of the wish
to alight
back among the glitter of bruised ground,
the stones holding between pasture and field,
the great, granite nuclei,
glimmering, even they, with ancient inklings of
                madness and war.
                    Kinnell, *BN*, 66–67

14
Body

> This is only the body burdened down with leaves,
> The opaque flesh, heavy as November grass
>
> And not breaking into the pastures that lie in the sunlight.
> This is the sloth of the man inside the body
>
> Bly, *LB*, 47; *S*, 59

> All flesh is grass, and all the goodliness thereof is as the
> flower of the field.
>
> Isaiah 40:6

> The Lord said: This body is called the Field, and he
> who knows it is called the Knower of the Field.
>
> *Bhagavad Gita*, xiii

> Let us draw near to Thee, and let us exult and be glad
> in Thee, remembering Thy Heart that we have found
> in the dug field of Thy body.
>
> Anonymous, 12th century, in Williams,
> intro., *Pearl-Poet*, 97

> God, I can push the grass apart
> And lay my finger on Thy heart!
>
> Edna St. Vincent Millay, in
> Untermeyer, *MAP*, 461

> I thought of my body to come;
> My mind burst into that green.
>
> The heart in my breast turned green
>
> Dickey, *P*, 35, 19

The final choice is always an image of all choices at once, an
opening of the inward frame: "the far / Fields melt my heart"
(Plath, *Ariel*, 3), but the far fields are here. They reveal an open-

ended posture, a nexus of change between all field-bodies. In contemplating the field, our bodies are permeated with distance, made resonant with space: "a sparkling field of rhythmic flashing points with trains of travelling sparks hurrying hither and thither"— "enchanted loom where millions of flashing shuttles weave a dissolving pattern" (Sir Charles Sherrington). "A vast field of golden jewels, studded with red and green stones, ever changing" (Havelock Ellis). The stones of our bodies dreaming. Yet stones still: "The unsinging fields where no lungs breathe, / Where light is stone" (Roethke, *CP*, 196).

Body. Egg cluster and consciousness. "I am wrapped in my joyful flesh, / And the grass is wrapped in its clouds of green," or "My body hung about me like an old grain elevator, / Useless, clogged, full of blackened wheat" (Bly, *S*, 21, 37). "Suspended in my blood, caught in my mesh" (Valéry). "My taste was me; / Bones built in me, flesh filled, blood brimmed the curse" (Hopkins, *P*, 101). As in *The Tempest*, where Prospero's island seems alive, an organism with lungs, where breathing is walking in the body's field.

> Why, hear him, hear him babble and drop down to his
> nest,
> But his own nest, wild nest, no prison.
>
> Man's spirit will be flesh-bound when found at best,
> But uncumberèd: meadow-down is not distressed
> For a rainbow footing it nor he for his bónes rísen.
>
> Hopkins, *P*, 71

Field-body: to run in that field like the wind. Field-body: a thing that was opaque, suddenly it has an immense secular distance— places to go. The body becomes, like the mind, infinite.

Often I Am Permitted To Return To A Meadow
as if it were a scene made-up by the mind,
that is not mine, but is a made place,

that is mine, it is so near to the heart,
an eternal pasture folded in all thought. . . .

whose hosts are a disturbance of words within words
that is a field folded.

                                            Duncan, *OF*, 7

The opening of the field. The pastures outside us are already open, but opening the body's folds reveals a harvest of words in dark fields of flesh. Wordsworth's "subterranean fields." The silence of the human body celebrating a plenitude of words. At the empty center is a host of words—to be eaten. "Your bodies I have written" (Burroughs). "This is the Book of the Earth, the field of grass / flourishing" (Duncan, *OF*, 43). As in *Paradise Regained*, where Christ reads the meaning of his incarnation while wandering in the wilderness of his flesh. For the word becomes flesh in us; its meditative density is no bodiless fiction. The taste of speech roots language to the tongue.

The body is the archetype of form, and all form is a field folded. "They stood there folded, suspended in the night. . . . they stood there in the open, moonlit field" (Lawrence, *Rainbow*, 120). Field-body, which cannot help but be here and there at the same time; the body is always figural, the only prototype for beginnings and endings. The field-body generates immobility; it has been on the face of the earth forever. "At the field's end . . . One learned of the eternal" (Roethke, *CP*, 199). In *Pearl* the poet's body is the secret landscape for his dream of heaven.

some field, maybe, of flaked stone
scattered in starlight

where the flesh
swaddles its skeleton a last time
before the bones go their way without us

Kinnell, *BN*, 61

Great
fields of stone
stretching away under
a slate sky, their single
flower the flower
of my right hand.

Levine, "Breath"

Any object invested with daydream becomes a field. Or any
thing made resonant with consciousness. Wordsworth crouches
over the cave of his body, brooding on dark fields of flesh. Field-
body, hung with distance, infinite permutations without over-
crowding. "For me now fields are whirling in a wheel / And the
spokes are many paths in all directions" (Hearst, in Stryk, *H*, 77).
Field-bodies—a wheel of bodies bodying from a word:

in a teeming richness, move

the ripe-thighed temple dancers
in a field of force, a coiling honeycomb
of forms, the golden wheel of love.

John Montague, in Matthias, ed.,
23 Modern British Poets, 270

In the long fields, I leave my father's eye;
And shake the secrets from my deepest bones;
My spirit rises with the rising wind

Running through high grasses,
My thighs brushing against flower-crowns

Roethke, *CP*, 173, 161

I have fled, have
jogged
over fields of goldenrod,
terrified, seeking home,
and among flowers
I have come to myself empty

Kinnell, *Body Rags*, 59

a horse bows

under the fine whippings of rain.
The fields float in his eyes

Levine, *NTP*, 69

Running in a wheatfield, the dancing stalks a splintered field of motion, it seems no gesture can begin or end in us. Yet we are the field; our arms bend like the wheat, and we harvest their motion in our minds. "In every bosom a Universe expands" (Blake). Inside ourselves, we are everywhere.

their field opened and opened,
level, and more, then forever,
never crossed. Their world went everywhere.

William Stafford, in Stryk, *H*, 216

A calculus in motion, multi-limbed and transient, the body known is water and fire.

Field-body. To run blind and naked in that field is to fling the mind into a void of space.

The fields stretch out in long, unbroken rows.
We walk aware of what is far and close.

Here distance is familiar as a friend.
The feud we kept with space comes to an end.

A field recedes in sleep.
Where are the dead? Before me
Floats a single star.
A tree glides with the moon.
The field is mine! Is mine!

Roethke, *CP*, 13, 122

Bibliography

Abel, Lionel. *Metatheatre: A New View of Dramatic Form.* New York: Hill and Wang, 1963.

Adams, Robert M. *Strains of Discord: Studies in Literary Openness.* Ithaca: Cornell University Press, 1958.

Altizer, Thomas J. J. *The New Apocalypse: The Radical Christian Vision of William Blake.* East Lansing, Mich.: Michigan State University Press, 1967.

Aspel, Alexander, and Donald Justice, eds. *Contemporary French Poetry: Fourteen Witnesses of Man's Fate.* Ann Arbor: University of Michigan Press, 1965.

Auerbach, Erich. *Scenes from the Drama of European Literature.* New York: Meridian Books, 1959.

Bachelard, Gaston. *On Poetic Imagination and Reverie,* ed. Colette Gaudin. New York: Bobbs-Merrill, 1971.

————. *The Poetics of Space,* trans. Maria Jolas. New York: Orion Press, 1964 (1958).

Ballard, J. G. "The Atrocity Exhibition," *Encounter* 28 (March 1967), 3-9.

Barker, Arthur E., ed. *Milton: Modern Essays in Criticism.* New York: Oxford University Press, 1965

Barthes, Roland. "The Death of the Author," trans. Richard Howard, *Aspen Magazine* 5 and 6 (Fall and Winter 1967), sec. 3, n.p.

————. *Writing Degree Zero,* trans. Annette Lavers and Colin Smith. London: Jonathan Cape, 1967 (1953).

Baum, L. Frank. *The Wizard of Oz.* New York: Fawcett, 1960.

Beckett, Samuel. *Three Novels: Molloy, Malone Dies, The Unnamable.* New York: Grove Press, 1965.

Benet, William Rose. *The Reader's Encyclopedia.* New York: Thomas Y. Crowell, 1955.

Blake, Nicholas, pseud. *Head of a Traveler.* New York: Harper & Brothers, 1949.

Blake, William. *Blake's Job: William Blake's Illustrations of the Book of Job*, ed. S. Foster Damon. Providence, R.I.: Brown University Press, 1966.

————. *The Engraved Designs of William Blake*, ed. Laurence Binyon. New York: Da Capo Press, 1967 (1926).

————. *Jerusalem: The Emanation of the Giant Albion*, color facsimile edition. London: Trianon Press, 1951 (1804–20).

————. *Pencil Drawings by William Blake*, ed. Geoffrey Keynes. London: Nonesuch Press, 1927.

————. *The Poetry and Prose of William Blake*, ed. David V. Erdman. Garden City, N.Y.: Doubleday, 1970.

————. *Wiliam Blake: Poet, Printer, Prophet*, ed. Geoffrey Keynes. New York: Orion Press, 1964.

————. *William Blake's Engravings*, ed. Geoffrey Keynes. London: Faber and Faber, 1957 (1950).

————. *William Blake's Illustrations to the Bible*, ed. Geoffrey Keynes. London: Trianon Press, 1957.

————. *The Works of William Blake in the Tate Gallery*, ed. Martin Butlin. London: William Heinemann, 1957.

Blanch, Robert J., ed. *Sir Gawain and Pearl: Critical Essays*. Bloomington, Ind.: Indiana University Press, 1966.

Bly, Robert. *The Light around the Body*. New York: Harper & Row, 1967.

————. *Silence in the Snowy Fields*. Middletown, Conn.: Wesleyan University Press, 1962.

Borges, Jorge Luis. *The Aleph and Other Stories*, ed. and trans. Norman Thomas di Giovanni. New York: E. P. Dutton, 1970.

————. *Labyrinths*, ed. Donald A. Yates and James E. Irby. New York: New Directions, 1964.

Brown, Norman O. *Life against Death: The Psychoanalytic Meaning of History*. New York: Vintage Books, 1959.

————. *Love's Body*. New York: Random House, 1966.

Browne, Sir Thomas. *The Works of Sir Thomas Browne*, vol. I: *Religio Medici*, ed. Geoffrey Keynes. Chicago: University of Chicago Press, 1964.

Burgin, Richard. *Conversations with Jorge Luis Borges*. New York: Avon Books, 1969.

Burke, Kenneth. *The Philosophy of Literary Form: Studies in Symbolic Action*. New York: Vintage Books, 1957.

Burroughs, William S. *APO–33 Bulletin: A Metabolic Regulator*. San Francisco: City Lights Books, n.d.

————. "The Art of Fiction" and "St. Louis Return," *Paris Review* 9:35 (Fall 1965), 13–62.

————. "Censorship," *Transatlantic Review* 11 (Winter 1962), 5–10.

————. "Introduction to *Naked Lunch, Soft Machine* and *Nova Express*," *Evergreen Review* (January 1962), pp. 99–105.

————. *Junkie*. New York: Ace Books, 1953.

————. *Naked Lunch*. New York: Grove Press, 1966 (1959).

————. *Nova Express*. New York: Grove Press, 1964.

————. *The Soft Machine*. New York: Grove Press, 1967 (1961).

————. *The Ticket That Exploded*. New York: Grove Press, 1968 (1962).

————. *Time*. New York: "C" Press, 1965.

————, and Allen Ginsberg. *The Yage Letters*. San Francisco: City Lights Books, 1963.

————, and Brion Gysin. *The Exterminator*. San Francisco: Auerhahn Press, 1960.

Campbell, Joseph, ed. *Papers from the Eranos Yearbooks,* vol. 3: *Man and Time*. New York: Pantheon, 1957.

Circlot, J. E. *A Dictionary of Symbols*. New York: Philosophical Library, 1962.

Cocteau, Jean. *The Infernal Machine and Other Plays*. New York: New Directions, 1963.

Cohen, Leonard. *Flowers for Hitler*. Toronto: McClelland and Stewart, 1964.

Conley, John, ed. *The Middle English "Pearl."* Notre Dame, Ind.: University of Notre Dame Press, 1970.

Cope, Jackson I. *The Metaphoric Structure of "Paradise Lost."* Baltimore: Johns Hopkins Press, 1962.

Cornish, Sam. *Generations*. Boston: Beacon Press, 1971.

Crawford, John F., intro. *The Pearl*. San Francisco: Grabborn-Hoyem, 1967.

de Chazal, Malcolm. *Plastic Sense*. New York: Herder and Herder, 1971.

Dickey, James. *Poems 1957–1967*. Middletown, Conn.: Wesleyan University Press, 1967.

Duncan, Robert. *Bending the Bow*. New York: New Directions, 1968.

—————. *The Opening of the Field*. New York: Grove Press, 1960.

—————. *Roots and Branches*. New York: New Directions, 1969.

Ehrenpreis, Irvin. *Swift: The Man, His Works, and the Age*, vol. I: *Mr. Swift and His Contemporaries*. Cambridge, Mass.: Harvard University Press, 1962.

Ehrenzweig, Anton. *The Hidden Order of Art*. Berkeley: University of California Press, 1967.

Eliade, Mircea. *Patterns in Comparative Religion*. Cleveland: World, 1963.

Eliot, T. S. *The Complete Poems and Plays 1909–1950*. New York: Harcourt, Brace & World, 1952.

Evans, Joan. *English Medieval Lapidaries*. London: Oxford University Press, 1933.

Foucault, Michel. *Madness and Civilization: A History of Insanity in the Age of Reason*, trans. Richard Howard. New York: Pantheon, 1965.

Fowler, Gene. *Field Studies*. El Cerrito, Calif.: Dustbooks, 1965.

Frank, Joseph. *The Widening Gyre: Crisis and Mastery in Modern Literature*. New Brunswick, N.J.: Rutgers University Press, 1963.

Frazer, Sir James G. *The Golden Bough: A Study in Magic and Religion*, 3rd ed. London: Macmillan, 1911–15.

Freud, Sigmund. *The Basic Writings of Sigmund Freud*, ed. A. A. Brill. New York: Random House, 1938.

Frye, Northrop. *Anatomy of Criticism*. New York: Atheneum, 1966.

—————. *Fearful Symmetry: A Study of William Blake*. Boston: Beacon Press, 1965.

—————, ed. *Blake: A Collection of Critical Essays*. Englewood Cliffs, N.J.: Prentice-Hall, 1966.

Garrett, Robert Max. *The Pearl: An Interpretation*. Seattle: University of Washington Press, 1918.

Gérard, Max, ed. *Dali*. New York: Harry N. Abrams, 1968.

Geraud, Saint, pseud. *The Naomi Poems*. Chicago: Follett, 1968.

Ginsberg, Allen. *Planet News*. San Francisco: City Lights Books, 1968.

Godard, Jean-Luc. *Alphaville*. New York: Simon and Schuster, 1966.

Gordon, E. V., ed. *Pearl*. London: Oxford University Press, 1966 (1953).

Greenough, James Bradstreet, and George Lyman Kittredge. *Words and Their Ways in English Speech*. Boston: Beacon Press, 1962.

Greenwood, Ormerod, intro. *Sir Gawain and the Green Knight*. N.p., 1956.

Gropius, Walter, ed. *The Theater of the Bauhaus*. Middletown, Conn.: Wesleyan University Press, 1961.

Güntherová, Alžběta, and Ján Mišianik. *Illuminierte Handschriften aus der Slowakei*. Prague: Artia, 1962.

Hagstrum, Jean. *William Blake: Poet and Painter: An Introduction to the Illuminated Verse*. Chicago: University of Chicago Press, 1964.

Hartman, Geoffrey H. *The Unmediated Vision: An Interpretation of Wordsworth, Hopkins, Rilke, and Valéry*. New York: Harcourt, Brace & World, 1966.

————. *Wordsworth's Poetry 1787–1814*. New Haven: Yale University Press, 1964.

Hassan, Ihab. "The Subtracting Machine: The Work of William Burroughs," *Critique* 6 (Spring 1963), 4–23.

Hilles, Frederick W., and Harold Bloom, eds. *From Sensibility to Romanticism: Essays Presented to Frederick A. Pottle*. New York: Oxford University Press, 1965.

Hirn, Yrjö. *The Sacred Shrine: A Study of the Poetry and Art of the Catholic Church*. London: Macmillan, 1912.

Hollander, John, ed. *Poems of Our Moment*. New York: Pegasus, 1968.

Hopkins, Gerard Manley. *The Poems of Gerard Manley Hopkins*, 4th ed., ed. W. H. Gardner and N. H. MacKenzie. New York: Oxford University Press, 1967.

Horovitz, Michael, ed. *Children of Albion: Poetry of the Underground in Britain*. Baltimore: Penguin Books, 1969.

Hughes, Ted. *The Hawk in the Rain*. London: Faber and Faber, 1957.

James, D. G. *The Dream of Prospero*. Oxford: Clarendon Press, 1967.

Joyce, James. *Finnegans Wake*. New York: Viking, 1962.

————. *A Portrait of the Artist as a Young Man*. New York: Viking, 1964.

————. *Ulysses*. New York: Random House, 1946.

Kean, P. M. *The Pearl: An Interpretation*. London: Routledge and Kegan Paul, 1967.

Kenner, Hugh. *Dublin's Joyce*. Boston: Beacon Press, 1962.

Kepes, Gyorgy. *Language of Vision*. Chicago: Paul Theobald, 1964.

————, ed. *The Visual Arts Today*. Middletown, Conn.: Wesleyan University Press, 1960.

Keynes, Geoffrey, and Edwin Wolf, eds. *William Blake's Illuminated Books: A Census*. New York: Grolier Club, 1953.

Kinnell, Galway. *Body Rags*. Boston: Houghton Mifflin, 1968.

————. *The Book of Nightmares*. Boston: Houghton Mifflin, 1971.

Klee, Paul. *The Thinking Eye*, ed. Jurg Spiller. New York: George Wittenborn, 1964.

Kostelanetz, Richard. "From Nightmare to Serendipity: A Retrospective Look at William Burroughs," *Twentieth Century Literature* 2 (October 1965), 123–30.

Kott, Jan. *Shakespeare Our Contemporary*. Garden City, N.Y.: Doubleday, 1966.

Kronhausen, Phyllis and Eberhard. *Erotic Art 2*. New York: Grove Press, 1970.

Lawrence, D. H. *The Complete Poems of D. H. Lawrence*, ed. Vivian de Sola Pinto and Warren Roberts. New York: Viking, 1964.

————. *The Complete Short Stories*, vols. I–III. New York: Viking, 1961.

————. *The Rainbow*. New York: Viking, 1969.

Levertov, Denise. *O Taste and See*. New York: New Directions, 1964.

————. *The Sorrow Dance*. New York: New Directions, 1967.

Levine, Jay. "The Design of *A Tale of a Tub* (With a Digression on a Mad Modern Critic)," *English Literary History* 33 (1966), 198–227.

Levine, Philip. "Breath," *The New Yorker* (11 Sept. 1971), p. 40.

————. *Not This Pig*. Middletown, Conn.: Wesleyan University Press, 1968.

————. *On the Edge*. Iowa City: Second Press, 1964.

Levy, Mervyn, ed. *The Artist and the Nude*. New York: Clarkson N. Potter, 1965.

Löwith, Karl. *Meaning in History*. Chicago: University of Chicago Press, 1949.

Lucie-Smith, Edward, ed. *British Poetry since 1945*. Baltimore: Penguin Books, 1970.

McCarthy, Mary. "William S. Burroughs," *The Olympia Reader*, ed. Maurice Girodias. New York: Ballantine Books, 1967.

MacLeish, Archibald. *The Collected Poems of Archibald MacLeish*. Boston: Houghton Mifflin, 1962.

McLuhan, Marshall. "Notes on Burroughs," *The Nation* (28 Dec. 1964), pp. 517–19.

————, ed. *Verbi-Voco-Visual Explorations*. New York: Something Else Press, 1967.

————, and Harley Parker. *Through the Vanishing Point: Space in Poetry and Painting*. New York: Harper & Row, 1969.

Martz, Louis L. "*Paradise Regained:* The Meditative Combat," *English Literary History* 27 (1960), 223–47.

Matthias, John, ed. *23 Modern British Poets*. Chicago: Swallow Press, 1971.

Merwin, W. S. *The Carrier of Ladders*. New York: Atheneum, 1971.

————. *The Drunk in the Furnace*. New York: Macmillan, 1960.

————. *Green with Beasts*. New York: Alfred A. Knopf, 1956.

————. *Lice*. New York: Atheneum, 1967.

Miller, J. Hillis. "The Geneva School," *The Critical Quarterly* 8 (1966), 305–21.

————. *Poets of Reality: Six Twentieth-Century Writers*. Cambridge, Mass.: Harvard University Press, 1965.

————, ed. *William Carlos Williams: A Collection of Critical Essays*. Englewood Cliffs, N.J.: Prentice-Hall, 1966.

Milton, John. *John Milton: Complete Poems and Major Prose*, ed. Merritt Y. Hughes. New York: Odyssey Press, 1957.

————. *Poems*, ed. John Carey and Alastair Fowler. London: Longmans, Green, 1968.

Moore, Gerald, and Ulli Beier, eds. *Modern Poetry from Africa*. Baltimore: Penguin Books, 1963.

Moore, Henry. *Henry Moore on Sculpture*, ed. Philip James. London: Macdonald, 1966.

Neruda, Pablo. *The Heights of Macchu Picchu*, trans. Nathaniel Tarn. New York: Farrar, Straus & Giroux, 1966.

Neumann, Erich. *The Archetypal World of Henry Moore*. New York: Harper & Row, 1965.

Nin, Anais. *House of Incest*. Chicago: Swallow Press, 1958.

Oates, Joyce Carol. *Them*. Greenwich, Conn.: Fawcett, 1970.

Olson, Charles. *Call Me Ishmael*. San Francisco: City Lights Books, 1947.

————. *Selected Writings*, ed. Robert Creeley. New York: New Directions, 1951.

Ooka, Shohei. *Fires on the Plain*. Baltimore: Penguin Books, 1969.

Partridge, Eric. *Origins: A Short Etymological Dictionary of Modern English*. New York: Macmillan, 1959.

Paulson, Ronald. *Theme and Structure in Swift's "Tale of a Tub."* New Haven: Yale University Press, 1960.

Peake, Mervyn. *Gormenghast*. New York: Ballantine Books, 1968.

Pellegrini, Aldo. *New Tendencies in Art*. New York: Crown, 1966.

Pinto, Vivian de Sola, ed. *The Divine Vision: Studies in the Poetry and Art of William Blake*. London: Victor Gollancz, 1957.

Plath, Sylvia. *Ariel*. New York: Harper & Row, 1966.

Popa, Vasko. "Forgetfulness," *Triquarterly* 9 (Spring 1967), 203.

Poulet, Georges. *The Metamorphoses of the Circle*, trans. Carley Dawson and Elliot Coleman. Baltimore: Johns Hopkins Press, 1966.

Praz, Mario. "The Canticles of Hieronymus Bosch," *Art News Annual* 32 (October 1966), 55–69.

Price, Martin. *To the Palace of Wisdom*. Garden City, N.Y.: Doubleday, 1965.

Radford, Edwin and Mona A. *Encyclopedia of Superstitions*. New York: Philosophical Library, 1949.

Rahner, Hugo. *Greek Myths and Christian Mystery*. London: Burns & Oates, 1963.

Rich, Adrienne. *The Diamond Cutters*. New York: Harper & Row, 1963.

Richards, M. C. *Centering: In Pottery, Poetry, and the Person*. Middletown, Conn.: Wesleyan University Press, 1969.

Roe, Albert S. *Blake's Illustrations to the Divine Comedy*. Princeton, N.J.: Princeton University Press, 1953.

Roethke, Theodore. *The Collected Poems of Theodore Roethke*. Garden City, N.Y.: Doubleday, 1966.

Rolf, Ida P. *Structural Integration*. New York: Published by the author, 1962.

Rosenfeld, Alvin H., ed. *William Blake: Essays for S. Foster Damon*. Providence, R.I.: Brown University Press, 1969.

Rothenberg, Jerome, ed. *Technicians of the Sacred*. Garden City, N.Y.: Doubleday, 1969.

Rueckert, William H. "Kenneth Burke and Structuralism," *Shenandoah* no. 21 (Autumn 1969), 19–28.

Rukeyser, Muriel. *Body of Waking*. New York: Vintage Books, 1968.

————. *The Speed of Darkness*. New York: Vintage Books, 1971.

Salter, Elizabeth. *Piers Plowman: An Introduction*. Cambridge, Mass.: Harvard University Press, 1962.

Sartre, Jean-Paul. *Nausea*. New York: New Directions, 1969.

Sassoon, Siegfried. *Memoirs of an Infantry Officer*. New York: Collier Books, 1969.

Schilder, Paul. *Image and Appearance of the Human Body*. London: Kegan Paul, Trench, Trubner, 1935.

Shakespeare, William. *William Shakespeare: The Complete Works*, gen. ed. Alfred Harbage. Baltimore: Penguin Books, 1969.

Shapiro, Karl. *Poems 1940–1953*. New York: Random House, 1953.

Simpson, Louis. *At the End of the Open Road*. Middletown, Conn.: Wesleyan University Press, 1963.

Smith, Ronald Gregor. *J. G. Hamann: A Study in Christian Existence*. New York: Harper, 1960.

Snodgrass, W. D. *Heart's Needle*. New York: Alfred A. Knopf, 1959.

Sontag, Susan. *Death Kit*. New York: Farrar, Straus & Giroux, 1967.

Speiser, E. A., trans. *The Anchor Bible*, vol. I: *Genesis*. Garden City, N.Y.: Doubleday, 1964.

Stekel, Wilhelm. *The Interpretation of Dreams: New Developments in Technique*, trans. Eden and Cedar Paul. New York: Grosset & Dunlap, 1962.

Stevens, Wallace. *The Collected Poems of Wallace Stevens*. New York: Alfred A. Knopf, 1954.

Strand, Mark. *Darker*. New York: Atheneum, 1970.

————, ed. *New Poetry of Mexico*. New York: E. P. Dutton, 1970.

Stryk, Lucien, ed. *Heartland: Poets of the Midwest*. DeKalb, Ill.: Northern Illinois University Press, 1967.

Suzuki, D. T. *Zen Buddhism*, ed. William Barrett. Garden City, N.Y.: Doubleday, 1956.

Swift, Jonathan. *A Tale of a Tub*, ed. A. C. Guthkelch and D. Nichol Smith. Oxford: Oxford University Press, 1958.

Tanner, Tony. "The New Demonology," *Partisan Review* 33 (1966), 547–72.

Tennyson, Alfred, Lord. *Poems and Plays*. London: Oxford University Press, 1965.

Thass-Thienemann, Theodore. *The Subconscious Language*. New York: Washington Square Press, 1967.

Thomas, Dylan. *Adventures in the Skin Trade*. New York: Signet, 1960.

————. *The Collected Poems of Dylan Thomas*. New York: New Directions, 1957.

————. *Portrait of the Artist as a Young Dog*. New York: New Directions, 1955.

Untermeyer, Louis, ed. *Modern American Poetry, Modern British Poetry*, Combined Mid-Century Edition. New York: Harcourt, Brace, 1950.

Valéry, Paul. *Selected Writings of Paul Valéry*. New York: New Directions, 1964.

Walsh, Chad, ed. *Today's Poets*. New York: Charles Scribner's Sons, 1964.

Whitman, Walt. *Leaves of Grass*, Comprehensive Reader's Edition, ed. Harold W. Blodgett and Sculley Bradley. New York: W. W. Norton, 1968.

Wicksteed, Joseph. *William Blake's Jerusalem*. London: Trianon Press, 1954.

Williams, Margaret, intro. *The Pearl-Poet: His Complete Works*. New York: Random House, 1967.

Williams, William Carlos. *The Autobiography of William Carlos Williams*. New York: New Directions, 1967 (1951).

————. *The Collected Later Poems*. New York: New Directions, 1963 (1950).

————. *The Complete Collected Poems of William Carlos Williams: 1906–1938*. Norfolk, Conn.: New Directions, 1938.

————. *In the American Grain*. New York: New Directions, 1956 (1925).

————. *I Wanted to Write a Poem*. Boston: Beacon Press, 1958.

————. *Kora in Hell: Improvisations*. Boston: Four Seas, 1920.

————. *Paterson*. New York: New Directions, 1963 (1946–58).

————. *Selected Essays*. New York: Random House, 1954.

————. *Selected Letters*. New York: McDowell, Obolensky, 1957.

————. *Spring and All*. Dijon: Contact, 1923.

Woolf, Virginia. *To the Lighthouse*. New York: Harcourt, Brace & World, 1955.

Wordsworth, William. *The Poetical Works of William Wordsworth*, vols. I–V, ed. Ernest de Selincourt and Helen Darbishire. London: Oxford University Press, 1954.

————. *The Prelude*, ed. Ernest de Selincourt, rev. Helen Darbishire. Oxford: Oxford University Press, 1959.

Wright, James. *Collected Poems*. Middletown, Conn.: Wesleyan University Press, 1971.